Advance praise for *The International Family Guide to US University Admissions*

"The US university or 'college' application process is a period that affects not ~~only the applicant, but the whole~~ family as well as the high school. The process is complex with thousands of ~~universities~~ asking for different requirements—it is lengthy and often very stressful.

As Vice-Chairman of the Board of the largest IB School system in Turkey, I h~~ave witnessed this~~ every year and students, parents and school leaders try to find the best guide durin~~g this process. Even though our~~ college counselors know the process very well and try to help our students, it is i~~mperative that the whole process~~ is understood by everyone. As an international educator, administrator, and someone with extensive valuable international experience, Jennifer Ann Aquino truly becomes our Northern Light and our guide during this wearing process.

In her book, *The International Family Guide to US University Admissions*, Jennifer sets the tone and the path for all of the stakeholders. Her background and easy-to-follow instructions help each stakeholder understand the extensive and complex information regarding the whole process. The perfectly prepared timeline prepares everyone involved in the process to what each will face during the process: advice for parents helps them feel knowledgeable and prepared and the worksheets enable the students to prepare for what is expected of them in the application. The last, but in my opinion the most important part of this book, is the numerous case studies—real stories that we can learn from.

Having graduated thousands of students and closely experienced the US university application process with them, I strongly recommend this book to every parent, student, college counselor and school. This is an invaluable gem that everyone should read and every library should get ahold of."

—**Cenk Eyüboğlu, Vice-Chairman of the Board, Eyüboğlu Educational Institutions, İstanbul, Turkey; graduate of Harvard University Graduate School of Education, Tufts University and Bentley University**

"Our three boys went through the American university application system and I still find it daunting. Is it because we are foreigners? What are SAT's and ACT's? How do they differ and how do I prepare my kids for them? Do all universities ask for these standardized tests? Why do some universities ask for extra essays? What is Liberal Arts? What does it mean to apply as 'undeclared'? What documents do I have to provide to the universities? Where do I get all the paperwork for the visas done? Deadlines? The university of what? Where is that? Will my child 'fit in' being a foreigner? And most of all, what will our kids gain by attending an American university that other academic institutions around the world can't offer?

Jennifer answered all these questions while implementing the only approach that works, following the timeline. She got to know my boys and empowered them to find the right fit and she does the same for all the users of this book—parents and students alike. It is a must-have for any parent and student going through this process."

—**Brigitte Roulet, parent**

"I've had the good fortune of watching Jennifer Aquino work with students and families in person. I have observed, as she has enabled families to gain clarity, unpacking the necessary steps required to be successful in the increasingly complex process of university admissions. Within these pages, Jennifer has once again taken the complex and made it seem easy. The student advice and parent advice, case studies and words of wisdom contained in these pages, I know, will greatly assist students and families to shape their university admissions goals and understand what steps they need to take to achieve them. Quite simply, as an executive leader in schools for over 22 years, I've seen none better than Jennifer when it comes to university guidance and no text as comprehensive or beneficial as this."

—**Glen Radojkovich, Founding Head of School, Branksome Hall Asia, South Korea; former Head of Secondary School, Canadian International School, Singapore; Head of School/CEO GEMS Dubai; former National Chairman, Cambridge University International Examinations (NZ) and IB Heads Association (Korea)**

"In a landscape abound in myth and short on truth, Jennifer Aquino's book offers a step-by-step, comprehensive guide for international families as they begin the US university admissions process. It is no secret that college admissions should be about 'fit.' Rather than families manipulating their children's dossiers in the hope that select, name-brand universities will see the fit, Jennifer rightly challenges young people to first know themselves, embrace their interests, and then put their best selves forward in selecting from the dozens and dozens of excellent universities that would indeed be a good fit.

International students are uniquely poised to thrive in the university setting. In fact, they often carry the intangibles that US universities seeking a diverse student body crave: perspective. This book gives access to students, offering a clear path to an informed application and selection decision-making. I will use this book with my own children."

—Dr Paul Richards, Superintendent, American School of Dubai;
former Superintendent, International Schools Group, Saudi Arabia

"Throughout my career, I have felt enormous empathy for applicants and their families who just had no idea how competitive college admission is in the US. They simply did not have the experience to understand the importance of the 'fit' between the student and the school, and that a student who is self-aware and confident can help to make the case for admission.

Finally, Jennifer offers international families a guide that explains US college admissions and gives clear guidance through each step of the process. She identifies key milestones and provides clever worksheets and a writing handbook that will help the user to create a highly personalized and strong application for the student's best-fit universities. The case studies and strategic parent advice and student advice make this book a must for any US-bound student!"

—Ellen M. Sullivan, former Admissions Officer, Harvard College;
Executive Director of International Advancement, Boston College

"I have been helping students with their university planning and applications for more than 20 years, as a high school counselor in international high schools and as an independent university advisor. During each of those 20+ years, I have looked for a comprehensive, intelligent, and ethical guide to help families understand this process and how to approach it, and that I could feel comfortable recommending. This book is all of that. I will use it myself, and will ask each of the families I work with to purchase one for our work together."

—Mark Gathercole, Education Advisor and Consultant, Independent University Advising;
Certified Educational Professional (CEP); former Director of University Guidance
at international schools in Norway, the Czech Republic, and Indonesia;
Member, IACAC, NACAC & IECA

"Choosing the right university to attend is arguably one of life's greatest decisions. Jennifer Ann Aquino's book is an insider's guide, helping international students and their families find the right institution by navigating the complex and often overwhelming admissions process. As an internationally recognized expert in US university admissions, Jennifer shares critical information, insights, tips, tools and case studies that make the application process easier.

As a former international student myself, who applied to and graduated from a university in the US, and given my role as Dean of International Education, I understand well the value this book provides to international students. It is an important resource and reference for anyone interested in attending a college or university in the US."

—Warren Jaferian, Dean, International Education, Endicott College

The International Family Guide to US University Admissions

Jennifer Ann Aquino

WILEY

This edition first published 2017
© 2017 Jennifer Ann Aquino
The Author asserts her moral right to be identified as the author of this work.

Registered office
John Wiley & Sons Ltd, The Atrium, Southern Gate, Chichester, West Sussex, PO19 8SQ, United Kingdom

For details of our global editorial offices, for customer services and for information about how to apply for permission to reuse the copyright material in this book, please see our website at www.wiley.com.

Wiley publishes in a variety of print and electronic formats and by print-on-demand. Some material included with standard print versions of this book may not be included in e-books or in print-on-demand. If this book refers to media such as a CD or DVD that is not included in the version you purchased, you may download this material at http://booksupport.wiley.com. For more information about Wiley products, visit www.wiley.com.

Designations used by companies to distinguish their products are often claimed as trademarks. All brand names and product names used in this book are trade names, service marks, trademarks or registered trademarks of their respective owners. The publisher is not associated with any product or vendor mentioned in this book.

Limit of Liability/Disclaimer of Warranty: While the publisher and author have used their best efforts in preparing this book, they make no representations or warranties with respect to the accuracy or completeness of the contents of this book and specifically disclaim any implied warranties of merchantability or fitness for a particular purpose. It is sold on the understanding that the publisher is not engaged in rendering professional services and neither the publisher nor the author shall be liable for damages arising herefrom. If professional advice or other expert assistance is required, the services of a competent professional should be sought.

Library of Congress Cataloging-in-Publication Data

Names: Aquino, Jennifer Ann, author.
Title: The international family guide to US university admissions / Jennifer Ann Aquino.
Description: Chichester, UK ; Hoboken, NJ : John Wiley & Sons, 2017. | Includes bibliographical references and index. |
Identifiers: LCCN 2017011369 (print) | LCCN 2017019084 (ebook) | ISBN 9781119370963 (pdf) | ISBN 9781119370970 (epub) | ISBN 9781119370987 (pbk.)
Subjects: LCSH: Students, Foreign—United States. | Universities and colleges—Admission.
Classification: LCC LB2376.4 (ebook) | LCC LB2376.4 .A66 2017 (print) | DDC 378.1/982691—dc23
LC record available at https://lccn.loc.gov/2017011369

A catalogue record for this book is available from the British Library.

ISBN 978-1-119-37098-7 (paperback)   ISBN 978-1-119-37096-3 (ebk)
ISBN 978-1-119-37097-0 (ebk)   ISBN 978-1-119-37101-4 (ebk)

10 9 8 7 6 5 4 3 2 1

Cover design: Wiley
Cover image: © komkrit Preechachanwate/Shutterstock

Set in 11.5/14pt BemboStd by Thomson Digital, Noida, India
Printed in Great Britain by TJ International Ltd, Padstow, Cornwall, UK

To Mom and Dad, the most committed lifelong educators I know.

To my students, for teaching me and inspiring me.

To David, mi mellizo.

CONTENTS

If you grow up in the US, you are constantly surrounded by and influenced by "college" culture. Colleges are represented everywhere in American culture—the university that is located in everyone's home town, references made in the media, the sweatshirts Americans wear to sports events on the weekends, flags of alma maters displayed outside houses to support college sports teams. Yet for the hundreds of thousands of international applicants, they have experienced none of this. For as complex as the admissions process is to someone brought up in the US, this becomes one of the most complicated events at this stage of an international applicant's life.

However, there is no shortage of information out there. Often this information treats the international family and applicant as a less-than-sophisticated consumer, using platitudes, fear or outright incorrect information ("You must 'ace' the SAT to get into any good university!") to "guide" the very unique cohort of which you are a part. It is hard to find a trusted resource to guide you honestly and effectively through the process *based on how the process actually works*.

Daily experiences and encounters, both with my own private clients and also with friends and acquaintances living for years in Europe, Asia and Pacific regions, rather quickly convinced me that there was a critical need for this guide. Admissions in the US are based on fit: this means that the student/applicant *must* know who they are in order to determine which universities they will apply to. And it also means that the family of the applicant must also understand—and support—this. No one can bury their heads in the sand in this process ("My child is made for the Ivy League!") and it is too late to understand the day decisions are made by universities. Being enlightened, educated, and informed as an international family is critical to the applicant finding success in his or her applications and in the rest of his or her life.

When my first international homeschooled student, Matthew—you'll see his Case Study in Chapter 11—was rejected by all the Ivy League schools, it was the reaction by him and his family to these rejections that made me realize the need to educate the international family on US university admissions. Even as prepared as they were for the rejections, I realized society places an absurd amount of praise and worthiness on just two handfuls of universities. It bothered me greatly and I wondered how I might be able to help international families and students better understand how this process works, while trying to make sense of it in the greater whole. (Matthew is thriving and excelling right now, as you'll soon see.)

At every fair or event I attend I get asked the same questions. During a single event I attended in Southeast Asia, I had about 200 families come by and ask me questions, the most common one being: "What's the best college in the US for my son/daughter?" This is the absolute opposite way to approach it; you first need to start with the student. The question should be, "What's the right university for me and how do I best present myself in the application?"

As you'll see from the experiences and people that gave me the impetus to write this book, this is a process that has to be taken on actively by *both* the parents/guardian and the applicant. It is meant to be read and used by *both*. In the best of circumstances, each party has their own copy—there are things both parties need to do, sometimes together, sometimes separately. The idea here is that it is a process to go through together but also that each person has their own role.

HOW TO USE THIS BOOK

Read this book linearly. There is *no* jumping around—not in the book and not in the process. This is critical to understand if you're going to go through this process properly. It is critical for the applicant and the family to follow a very detailed timeline from start to finish, which maps onto the US application timeline. Each chapter consists of active Milestones for the student and parents, each one building on the next, to be accomplished in order.

There are 12 chapters with each chapter beginning with an overview of the period it covers in the timeline. This gives you an idea of what to expect and why you're doing what you have to do.

 The Milestones are those critical pieces in each chapter that you are expected to accomplish before moving on to the next chapter. Throughout the book Milestones will sometimes be accompanied by a Worksheet, indicated by this icon.

A great deal of work needs to be done in order to get the answer to the question, "What's the right university for me and how do I best present myself in the application?" Many students who attend university in the US will change their minds about what they want to study once at university. The system is set up to encourage exploration and the undecided applicant!

Worksheets are included at the end of each chapter unless otherwise indicated (in the case where a Worksheet will be utilized by more than one chapter). All are properly positioned and easy to find. *It is expected you will complete all Worksheets throughout the process.*

Some Milestones will have this icon located next to it. While I expect all Milestones will take you some time to accomplish, those with this icon will require an amount of time to accomplish, ranging from several hours to several days. These are not Milestones that can be accomplished quickly.

 As you get further into the process and you begin to write, you will be referred to the *Writing Handbook,* located at the end of the book. The Milestones associated with the *Writing Handbook* will have this icon. It will guide you through all of your writing requirements and options. I'm a stickler for writing as it will be one of the most important parts of your US application. Your essays will be given enormous weight and importance by the Admissions committee and will be your opportunity to show Admissions who you really are...and how you really *fit* into the institution. This will be the basis for your eventual acceptance.

Other features you'll see throughout the book include:

1. *Resources*: When a college guidebook or standardized test prep book is needed, I will tell you by name which I recommend based on my students' experiences and my own.

2. *Student Advice*! and *Parent Advice*! Found throughout the book and from my students and their parents. I think this advice will be extremely helpful to you.

3. *Case Studies*: In each of Chapters 2–12 I give you a case study of one of my dear students. This gives you an idea of the myriad types of applicants out there and just how arbitrary the selection process can be (results are found in the Conclusion) and focuses on the person, which is ultimately how this process works. Are you a fit for where you're applying? That's the key.

4. *Important*! These will be interspersed throughout and relevant to the Milestone at hand.

5. *Words of Wisdom*: Usually an incident related to the topic or Milestone at hand that is a first-hand account and will help you gain perspective and further understanding of the process and Milestone you are working on.

In this book, I will also use the words "college" and "school" and "university" interchangeably. "High school", "secondary school" and "junior college" may also be used interchangeably. I will at times reference the Northern Hemisphere calendar vs. the Southern Hemisphere calendar as I know users will be from both. At the end of the day, the timeline will stay the same for all users, however. While I will initially explain the application options, I may then use terms such as "EA" (Early Action) or "RD" (Regular

Decision) thereafter. Of course, there is also "ED" (Early Decision) 1 and 2 and "SCEA" (Single Choice Early Action) and "REA" (Restricted Early Action). Don't worry! I will cover all of these at the appropriate time.

If you trust and follow the advice given in this book, it will help you become a more enlightened, educated, thoughtful and therefore successful applicant through the US university admissions process.

Thank you for using this book and I look forward to hearing about your journey through the process!

ACKNOWLEDGMENTS

This happens to be the last page I write after finishing this book. For me it's the most difficult. One page to acknowledge all those who supported me, helped me, encouraged me, and inspired me to write this book? If only I could convince my editor to add another 20 pages...I have so many people to acknowledge and thank, and for so much.

Jeremy Chia at Wiley Singapore, my patient and adroit editor, helped me immensely to make this book read more fluidly and clearly. Thank you for your calmness and experience to make this book become what it has. Thank you, Syd Ganaden, for listening to my ideas for design and for offering your own. I am indebted to Thomas Hyrkiel, Publisher, for recognizing the potential this book had from the beginning and for signing me with such a world-renowned publisher. Thank you, Ben Hall, Marketing Manager at Wiley, for your support and ideas to get this book into the hands of users around the globe. It would have been impossible to have this book published by such a reputable and recognizable publishing house without the belief in my initial proposal, and subsequent work to get this book published globally by my hard-working, connected and outstandingly effective agents: Jay Vasudevan, Helen Mangham and Andrea Pasion-Flores, at Jacaranda Press.

Without my parents—truly the greatest (and smartest) educators I know on this planet—I would never have written this book. Mom and Dad, thank you for teaching me how to teach, to value the profession and vocation of teaching, and for never ceasing to teach me. You are the epitome of educators and I wish every student could have had the opportunity to be taught by you.

My students and my families! You've made me love my work and without you this book would not be able to show just how unpredictable, crazy, fun, and individual this process is, helping so many other families along the way. I would like to thank specifically those who contributed to this book and whose quotes and Case Studies you'll be reading about shortly: Veena McCoole, Mani Gupta, Pakhi Gupta, Caroline Liew, Matthew Liew, Adit Sharma, Shefali Agarwal, Mei Masuyama, Jacquie Weber, Sterling Gunn, Maya Schoucair, Michelle Layanto, Serene Layanto, Sacha Aymond, Asli Sagnak, Susanne Grimm, Asya Sagnak, Lori Gunn, Ariane Roulet Magides, Claire DePlanck, Zurah DePlanck, and Raj Raiyani. Thank you for inspiring me and for teaching me so much.

How I would love to name all of my incredible friends who have supported me throughout the writing of this book! I do believe without a doubt that I have the most amazing friends in the world and I love you dearly and thank you so much for always supporting me. Thank you to my colleagues at IECA who have taught me so much about this profession.

Finally, how could I have written this book, physically and mentally, without the unwavering support, humor, and dedication to me, my interests and my goals in life without you, Mellizo mío? You make life an incredible experience every day for me.

Jennifer Ann Aquino was born into a family of educators and started her own career after university teaching AP Biology as a dorm parent at a US boarding school, The Gunnery, in Connecticut. She moved on to educational publishing as an editor for secondary and university-level foreign language and science textbooks before working in management roles as an administrator in universities in the US and Europe.

Living in Singapore, Jennifer launched her own private educational consultancy, guiding secondary students and their families through the next stage of the student's life. Having followed her own interests and passions at university—majoring in Biology and Spanish Literature as a pre-medical student—she strives to show and encourage her students and readers to follow their own true interests, desires, and passions, guiding them to their best-fit university by putting forth a winning application that highlights their genuine and unique interests.

Jennifer double-majored in Biology and Spanish Literature with a Pre-Medical concentration from Boston College (US) and earned a Master of Arts degree in Spanish Literature from Middlebury College (US). She was accepted by and enrolled in Harvard University's Graduate School of Arts and Sciences, Department of Romance Languages and Literature.

Jennifer has worked as Director of Education Abroad (Bentley University, USA); Managing Director, International MBA Program (IE Business School, Spain); Director of International Advancement (Bentley University, USA); and Lead Recruiter, Undergraduate Admissions, Asia & India (Bentley University, USA). She has visited over 100 university campuses in a professional context and is a Professional Member of IECA and Member of International ACAC.

Her website is www.JenniferAnnAquino.com.

INTRODUCTION

"Where do I even start?!"
"What are the best engineering schools in the US?"
"We're very interested in Harvard."
"Will SAT scores matter most?"
"If I arrange my son's interviews with the universities will that be OK? He's got so much work on his plate."
"I will only pay for my daughter's education in the US if she goes to a university that is prestigious."
"Should my son pick up something less 'typical' as a hobby to make him stand out?"

I come from a family of educators: my mom, dad, aunt, uncle, cousins, and even my nieces! We are all educators. I started as a teacher—like my parents—and moved into educational publishing and then into various director roles in universities in the US and Europe. I've also worked and lived on four continents, and all whilst working in the field of international education. I believe I do have something to share.

Working exclusively with international families to guide them through the admissions process, my passion lies in imparting the truth in education and building the individual confidence of my students and families—and this comes from experience and knowledge. All too often, families come to me asking for black-and-white answers. What they do not know is that within this process are the answers to the questions they don't know yet, and will not know until they go through it correctly. There's no online-matchmaker equivalent to US university admissions. Why? Because there is no logarithm that allows applicants to find their fit and present themselves uniquely based on their educated understanding of why they are a fit for their chosen universities. Instead, this process requires every applicant to reach inside themselves and figure out what they need, want, or dream of, will be amazing at doing, and thus what they will succeed in, and then matching all of that to the specific universities that will offer that to them.

Most families come to me with a list of names of universities before we even begin. Early "researching" is great and I commend the student who's already begun. But this happens all too often, creating the situation we have now in society, where elitism in higher education causes students to learn in a one- or two-dimensional environment instead of a multi-dimensional melting pot of education.

THE RULES OF ENLIGHTENMENT

In this process, nothing is general: everything works on a case-by-case basis. You thought it would be easy? Consider this process as part of your last two years of high school curriculum. This process should challenge what you think you know about universities and where you want to attend, should challenge you to think about who you are and what you really want, and should challenge you to be bold and brave enough to take a risk at applying to and attending the university that is, deep down, truly the right fit for you— not for your mom, not for your friend, and certainly not for your pride. This is the first opportunity for you to begin to understand yourself, your needs, dreams, strengths, passions and true interests, and to pursue them by finding those universities that will support, challenge and be true to you as an individual.

So, I ask of you—family and student—to commit. Commit to taking months to dedicate to this process. Commit to being true to who you are. Commit to not succumbing to the draw of Ivy League schools, like the H-word.[1] Commit to understanding that when you find a fit, you are on the road to finding happiness and success in what you do throughout life. Commit to that freedom of choice. Commit to the awesome opportunity that you have before you.

If you want to do this correctly—and you should, it's a process that takes months of dedication and an open mind—follow these rules as you go through the process. As a rule of thumb, you should commit by reading through this together as a family and initialing each of the following points:

- Each Chapter, each Milestone, each university will be taken case-by-case. Do not generalize anything. (*And go ahead and initial here!*) ☐

- Don't believe the rankings at face value. If you are going to go by them, commit to understanding exactly how they are done. (Once you start doing this, you'll surely want to forget about them altogether.) ☐

- Question stats. All of them. 10% acceptance rate? Really? Do they take into account applications that were started but never finished/turned in? Average class size of 30?

---

[1]Of course, it's Harvard. An outstanding institution, but not the only outstanding institution and certainly not the best fit for many students.

Average of what? Freshman, sophomore, junior and senior classes or just one of these? Average ACT (American College Testing) of 32? Do they consider every single applicant's test scores or is there a special program in place for some accepted students whose scores are not accounted for (and thus improving the university's average)? □

- Remember: This process is subjective. You don't think that 20-minute "informal" meeting of the Admissions representative who visited your school didn't make an impression—positive or negative? What about at the height of "reading season" for the Admissions team when they are reading 100 applications per night and yours comes up last…on a Friday…when the Admissions officer is starting to get a cold and just broke up with his partner who…happens to be from your city/country. We're only human, and humans make up this process. So, that leads me to… □

- Control what you can control—your writing, your grades, your proactivity, your preparation—and let go of what you cannot—who will make the decision on your application, statistics, what your friend is doing, the results. □

- Be realistic. Be true to yourself and, if you're a parent, be true to your child. □

- Know that there are thousands of universities in the US. There are over 4,000 accredited degree-granting institutions in the US, over 3,000 of which are 4-year degree-granting institutions.[2] Each one has its own culture, character, strengths, weaknesses, student profile, professors, facilities, student life, and community. There *is* a fit for *every* student. (I remind you here to be realistic and to commit to the process. You won't end up disappointed.) □

- Be prepared to tell yourself that you're not ready, that you need a gap year of some kind—PG ("postgraduate") year, working, volunteering, finding yourself—before you enroll in university. While everyone at this age is going through the same process, not everyone should be. We're all human and go at different speeds. High school doesn't usually account for that. □

- Commit to research. This means committing to learning about—in depth and through my guidance—universities that you have never heard of. Most families come to me with about 10 universities they have heard of. There are over 3,000. Do you think those 2,990 other universities are not worthy or not very good? About 98% of the time, I have found, there are other much better fits. □

---

[2]National Center for Education Statistics (December 2012). "Table 5 Number of educational institutions, by level and control of institution: Selected years, 1980-81 through 2010-11". U.S. Department of Education.

- Parents, as best you can, set your child free in this process. The best way for them to find success—however you quantify success—will be through their happiness. They will be happy doing something they love. I had a father who refused to recognize his son's love of art. He believed that his son was going to be a doctor. Once he let go of this control over his son and let his son move forward through the process, he too realized just what a successful artist his son would be…and what a terrible doctor he would have made! Who wants to see a doctor who never wanted to be a doctor? You will not live your child's life after university and yet it's important to stop living it now, before university, giving your child the best opportunity to find their fit, to find true happiness—and success! ☐

- Once you apply, let go. This means you owe it to yourself to do your best up until you submit. It's called "no regrets" and doing your due diligence. ☐

- Be strategic. If you are looking for merit aid, you'll need to research and find those schools that are a fit and that may also be keenly interested in an applicant like you— whether you are an avid stamp-collector, hold passports from two nations that don't tend to have lots of students applying to that university, hold a very strong profile compared to those who generally apply to said institution, and/or have decided to apply to very different universities and thus have a very different "List" to those of your colleagues in your high school or country—merit aid could be in your future. It's a fairly gray process that is determined behind closed doors and is fully subjective, based on the individual university's needs and decisions that very year. You can be strategic about it and we'll discuss that, starting in Chapter 3 of this book and con- tinue throughout. ☐

- Commit to a well-rounded, realistic *List*. I'll refer to your list of universities as your "List", sometimes a "Long List" and sometimes a "Short List", depending on where you are in the process. A realistic List means that you've done your research and know your fit and can defend that. And, that you've created a list of around 10 institutions that range from those that you think you have a strong chance of getting into (always with the variable of not), those that seem like you are in-range with, to those that will be a real "reach" for you but you're aiming high for. ☐

- Finances, Part 1. I finished paying off my university loans when I was 39 years old. I've lived abroad for the past fifteen-plus years and so when I say this to someone out- side of the US they just about choke. In the US, this is a norm for many families. Yet, as US citizens, we are able to apply for subsidized loans and grants, something not available to international students. US higher education is outstandingly expensive.

This is the first conversation I have with my families: Is it realistic? Don't expect scholarships or merit aid from an institution. You cannot depend on it as it's a fairly gray area. That said, some institutions will offer need-based aid opportunities to international students. This is case-by-case and may vary from year to year. You must always check with the institution itself. ☐

- Finances, Part 2. You want to donate $100 million to get your son into a university? It's not as easy as writing a check. Universities are quite sophisticated in how this works, if it does work. I used to get offered large sums of money as Director of International Advancement for a university in the US to get a son or daughter into said university...and consistently turned the money down. Unless the family is strategically working with Development in a very sophisticated "you win, we win" approach, perhaps years prior, you can forget this approach. Yes, you may be a potential Development lead in the future and that can add to your appeal during the Admissions process if Admissions knows of you and you are truly and legitimately someone they would want to keep their pulse on, but this happens much less often than you think. The kid who told you that Antony got in because his father wrote a check probably doesn't know what he is talking about. Let it go. And, if you're up for donating the $100 million, start your discussions early and with the right people. That takes a lot of time. You'll need some strategic help. And, that's for another book; we won't get into that in this one. ☐

- Finally...enough about the Ivy League! Everyone—parents, teachers, journalists, the press: We have had enough of your pushing and judgment and biased-without-basis opinions—nothing makes these schools better than hundreds of others, and in fact sets everyone up for failure. Now, your best strategy? Let me put it this way: I will never recommend one of them for any of my students' Lists. If they put one on and it's determined it could be a fit after going through the process, I say go for it. However, with the odds against every student for acceptance and yet truly based on luck (as one of these school's Admissions officers told me, "I could replace this accepted class with four more equally-strong classes from this year's applicant pool alone"), why would you even want to try to play a game as arbitrary, based on luck, random and as cruel as this? As you work through this guide and the process, you will learn the value beyond just being able to say "I go to school X". ☐

Some of my students choose to apply to and are admitted to attend the Ivy League schools. They have found happiness and success—just like every one of my other students. However, my point is that their being accepted was like finding a needle in a haystack. If, as you go through this process, you realize that Yale is a fit for you, or Princeton is truly everything you want in a college—and you truly "fit"—go for it! I am the first to say follow your dreams. I am also the first to say one needs to be realistic, and by not attending one of these institutions you are no less, or setting yourself up for any less success. It's an absurdity to think otherwise.

Ready to begin? Let's start with *how* so that you can get a timeline in place and start to see progress and understanding in this process from day one.

CHAPTER 1

And You Are…?

Months: _____

(Fill in the months for your timeline for each of the first four chapters.)

The process to apply to US universities will involve working through all 12 of the chapters in this book in order. By completing the Milestones in each chapter, you will gain an understanding of why you need to do everything you need to do and how to do it successfully in order to apply to your targeted universities successfully.

A brief explanation of how this guide works: Every chapter will start with an overview of the time period—what this part of the process means for you and what your focus should be and why. This is followed by your *Milestones*, explaining the tasks that you will need to focus on along the way. Many Milestones will be accompanied by *Worksheets*, always found within the guide itself and usually at the end of each chapter. You'll always understand why you have to do something and what implications it will have on the process. I'll never ask you to do something that adds no value. If other *Resources* would help you with any Milestone, I mention that resource specifically by name and most of you will have it in your Library once you complete Milestone 5 on the next page.

This chapter is focused on you and who you are. Most of you would say you already know who you are. I'm not saying you don't. However, I would guess that few of you have ever sat down and really assessed who you are. Have you?

Half of this entire process is learning about yourself and who you are—a form of self-assessment. The other half is accomplishing goals and tasks for the applications such as getting strong grades, taking tests and writing stand-out essays. As you read from the Preface, the US university Admissions process is based on fit. That means understanding who you are, your strengths and weaknesses, likes and dislikes, goals and character, needs and interests. You'll then need to articulate how you—through this self-assessment—"fit" into the universities that you've identified that make your List and ultimately that you apply to. By following this process, you can confidently put your best self forward for this next stage in your life, and that will be reflected in your applications to universities.

Have you ever really sat down and worked on this? This is the first and most important step, and the essence of this chapter.

STUDENT ADVICE

"I would say it's difficult to understand now—it was for me, at least—just how much of an impact getting to know what I really wanted in a university had on me—on my not only finding my fit for universities, but then also being able to show that fit, write really strong applications, and then get in! I didn't realize this was the core of the process. I do want to tell you that you have to be open-minded and trust that this is the way to go!"

—*Marisa, Philippines*

Milestones will be your drivers. They will dictate everything you do throughout this process and must be followed in order and given due attention and respect. You'll see a list of Milestones at the start of each chapter as well as in your Timeline, which is the first Milestone you're about to complete. Each Milestone is then explained further throughout the chapter—giving you the reason for what you have to do. Your Milestones for Chapter 1 are as follows:

Milestone 1: Creating Your Personalized Timeline

Milestone 2: Signing the Agreement

Milestone 3: Thought Questions

Milestone 4: Creating Your CV

Milestone 5: Creating Your University Application Library

Following the list of Milestones at the start of each chapter, you'll have an ***Overview*** of this "period" in the process.

MILESTONES

Milestone 1: Creating Your Personalized Timeline

First, let's set up your timeline for the chapters so you know when you should be doing what throughout the process. There are 12 chapters you need to complete in order to complete the process. You can always refer to the Quick Reference Personalized Timeline Table 1.1 to see the Milestones you'll need to complete in order to get through the process. Your Milestones are addressed one by one in each chapter.

Table 1.1: Quick Reference Personalized Timeline

Chapter 1	Chapter 2	Chapter 3	Chapter 4
Months: September/October (junior year)	Months: September/October through January/February	Months: October through February	Months: February through April
Milestones:	Milestones:	Milestones:	Milestones:
1. Creating Your Personalized Timeline	1. Self-assessment, Student and Parents	1. Creating Your Long List	1. Factors (in a university that are most important to me)
2. Signing the Agreement	2. Reviewing the Components of Your Application That Will Be Assessed By Admissions	2. Researching Your Long List	2. Long List Research Stage 2
3. Thought Questions	3. Understanding How the US Admissions Process Works	3. Standardized Testing Plan	3. EGI: Efforts of Genuine Interest
4. Creating Your CV	4. Becoming a Strong Candidate	4. Meeting With Your Counselor	4. Look Who's Coming to Town
5. Creating Your University Application Library		5. Confirming Courses for Rest of High School	5. Confirming Break Plans
		6. Social Media Clean-up	6. Considering Recommenders and How
		7. Upcoming Break and Summer Plans	
		8. Adding to Your Long List	
		9. Updating Your CV	

(continued)

Table 1.1 (*continued*)

Chapter 5	Chapter 6	Chapter 7
Months and Dates: May—June	**Months: June—July**	**Months: August**
Milestones: 1. Moving From Your Long List to Your Short List 2. Mock Interview 3. Planning Campus Visits 4. EGI Progressing and Developing 5. Standardized Testing: IELTS/TOEFL, ACT/SAT, SAT Subject Tests 6. Requesting Recommendations From Your Recommenders 7. Writing Workshop 1	Milestones: 1. Confirming Your Short List (Again!) 2. Campus Visits and Interviews 3. Executing Summer Plans 4. Writing Workshop 2 5. Writing Workshop 3, Part 1 6. Standardized Testing	Milestones: 1. Registering With Application Portals 2. Other Universities and Their Applications 3. Confirming Recommenders 4. Finalizing Your Main College Essay 5. Confirming the Universities on Your Short List 6. Confirming All Requirements and Deadlines 7. (Re-)preparing for Standardized Testing 8. Requesting Interviews 9. Continuing EGI 10. Writing Workshop 3, Parts 2 and 3—Organizing and Brainstorming Supplement Essays

Table 1.1 (*continued*)

Chapter 8	Chapter 9	Chapter 10
Months: September	**Months: October**	**Months: November**
Milestones: 1. Re-confirming Your Short List 2. Confirming Requirements and Your Own Application Deadlines for Each University on Your Short List 3. Confirming Your Early Applications and Schedule 4. Completing Supplements for Your Early Applications 5. Filling in Your Applications 6. Reminding Your Recommenders 7. Completing Your Interviews for Early Applications 8. Sitting Standardized Tests	Milestones: 1. Meet With Your Guidance Counselor 2. Finalize Writing for Early Applications 3. Completing Your Common Application 4. Standardized Testing: Submitting and Reporting Scores, and Retaking 5. Submitting Your Early Application(s) 6. Regular Decision Applications 7. Checking Portals	Milestones: 1. Check Portals 2. Determine Internal Deadlines for Each Remaining Application to be Completed This Month 3. Retaking Standardized Tests 4. Sending Official Standardized Test Scores 5. Meeting With Your Guidance Counselor 6. Reviewing Common Application/Main Application Before Next Submissions 7. Finishing Interviews/Final Requests 8. Final Writing!

(*continued*)

Table 1.1 (*continued*)

Chapter 11	Chapter 12	Conclusion
Months: December	**Months: January to 1 May**	**Months: July, August & Moving In**
Milestones: 1. Managing "Early" Decisions 2. Reviewing Your Active "To-do's" 3. No Stopping Now	Milestones: 1. Tracking Your Applications 2. EGI for Deferrals 3. Regular Application (and ED2) Decisions Coming In and Your Deposit is Due 1 May 4. Being Wait-listed 5. Staying Engaged in the Classroom 6. Saying Thank You to Those Who Helped 7. Pros and Cons Lists 8. Double Depositing 9. Student Visa Process 10. Conscription 11. Gap Year	Milestones: 1. Thanking Others 2. Choosing Courses 3. Roommate Questionnaire 4. Orientation 5. Arrival on Campus and Departing Parents…

IMPORTANT!

Suggested timeline: I suggest starting this chapter in September of your penultimate year and working through October to complete it (Northern Hemisphere calendar).

As everyone who uses this book will be starting at different times in the process—a different month and week—it's important that you follow the steps below to determine

The International Family Guide to US University Admissions

how your own individual timeline will look. Again, this is the basis for the process, and critical: what I start off every family with before we do anything else.

Pacing is critical and by doing it properly you're setting yourself up for success. So, let's get your timeline figured out here to complete Milestone 1.

1. Please go to the Quick Reference Personalized Timeline in Table 1.1.

2. You'll notice that in Chapters 1 through 4 there is a preferred suggested date/s. Because everyone is different and will be starting this process at different points in the year, this still gives you the flexibility to go through the entire process but creating your own timeline.

3. Working backwards from Chapter 5—which will be the same for everyone regardless of when they start, meaning that everyone by May/June of their penultimate year of high school (Northern Hemisphere calendar) will be following a very similar timeline. It's getting there that will vary, with some people starting over a year prior, to some starting only a month prior.

IMPORTANT!

For those of you starting the process after May/June of your penultimate year of high school—and, while not ideal, this does happen for some—you'll need to work in overdrive in those months prior up until the month you begin **without missing a Milestone**. It is a lot of work but I've had students who have successfully completed it with hard work and dedication.

STUDENT ADVICE

"I had no idea coming from a French system that I should have started earlier! I started the entire process in September… just a couple of months before submitting my applications! I do not recommend it, but if you're in my situation, please be very organized and very determined. It worked out in the end but it was a rough couple of months!"

— *Vanessa, Ivory Coast*

For example, let's say you are just starting out in September of your junior year as you begin this process. Considering that you'll be working backwards looking at your timeline, which gives you a fixed month of May/June of your junior year, you could reasonably fill in Chapters 1–4 in the following way:

Chapter 1: Ideally you're starting and completing this chapter in September/October of your junior/penultimate year.

Chapter 2: Starting September/October and working through to January/February. (This chapter will take several months and many of you will finish in October/November and then be able to move on to Chapter 3. This depends on you and when I say "through to January/February" I mean that at the latest you should be finishing then, and moving on to Chapter 3 which, as you'll read below, should be finished by February, ideally.)

Chapter 3: Starting around October and working through to February. (Again, this chapter will take several months and can only be done after completing all the Milestones in Chapter 2.)

Chapter 4: Ideally you're starting in February and working through until April (depending on when you've completed Chapter 3).

That leads you to May/June for Chapter 5.

IMPORTANT!

Southern Hemisphere students: You should ideally be starting this in September/October of your penultimate year—usually year 12. You will finish the process at the same time as those in the Northern Hemisphere but it will be around the time you graduate as you're a semester "ahead" of your Northern Hemisphere counterparts. Keep the months the same as you're all moving along the same timeline with the same deadlines; it will just happen at a different time in your high school career.

4. Not all of you are in the situation described above, so pace yourselves for those chapters and commit to the process, with some leeway and some wiggle room. *Note: Chapters 2, 3 and 4 cannot be done in one sitting or in a week.* Now you'll understand this as you begin. Now you'll need to consider this and make a point of this as you create your timeline, giving yourself ample time to accomplish each chapter.

5. Please mark your dates in Table 1.1.

6. Now go through this book and at the start of each chapter (including this one, as you've seen earlier) put in the dates that the chapter corresponds to for you. Do this for Chapters 1–4 in the space available.

You should now have a US university Admissions timeline for yourself. Bravo! You'll constantly be referring to it throughout the process, so tab it so that you can easily access and modify it if you have any changes in your dates. Only you will know this and it's important for you to keep track.

IMPORTANT!

A quick note about Milestones: You will notice that there are specific Milestones referred to in the Quick Reference Personalized Timeline (Table 1.1) and at the start of each chapter. This is work you'll be required to do. Just as with your Biology class, you don't work on genetics prior to mitosis, so you'll only have success by following this sequentially and by doing the Milestones required of you at that stage before you can move on. Do not jump around!

You've just completed your first Milestone. Let's move on to the next four.

Milestone 2: Signing the Agreement

Before I meet with my new families I always ask that they, as the stakeholders in their child's future, and the student herself/himself, review and sign an agreement. The agreement is less a contract than setting the stage for how they will take on this process. It's a commitment by the student and the family to work honestly through this process with dedication and commitment, and to recognize the individuality of the student.

This agreement is also how the student shows commitment to listening to and understanding the advice given in this book, to working through it and completing every Milestone along the way and, finally, to being true to themselves. This is what it takes to achieve success.

STUDENT ADVICE

"I had no idea what being 'true to myself' really meant until I really started deciding where I would apply. I guess my advice to you is this: try to understand if what you want right now is coming from you or from somewhere else. I think this was the most important part of the process for me, not being fake with myself."

—Arun, Bombay

Please refer to the Agreement below.

Family and Student Agreement

The Student's Commitment

I, _____, declare that it is my ultimate responsibility to apply to and be accepted into the schools that I choose to apply to and should I not be accepted, it is the sole responsibility of me, the Student. I also understand that all work must be authentically done by me (e.g., essay-writing). Others (i.e., teacher, counselor, parent) are ethically permitted to guide me, provide feedback and offer insight and ideas; however, the work itself must be wholly mine and mine alone.

I understand and commit to being fully engaged, and to take initiative to complete Milestones as recommended, understanding that each Milestone leads to the next and must be done in the strategic order in which it is presented.

I also commit to being true to myself, my needs, my dreams and my own character strengths and weaknesses.

The Parent's/Stakeholder's Commitment

I, _____, commit to supporting my child for who she/he is and to helping her/him to find the best-fit university for her/him, regardless of "name brand". I commit to helping my child understand who she/he is and what she/he is passionate about, helping her/him to find the best-fit program for her/him—and perhaps not what *I* would necessarily like her/him to do or be, but rather what drives her/him.

Committing to the Agreement

This is an agreement between the following:

Student Name & Date: _____

Parent(s)/Stakeholder Name & Date: _____

Please also pay particular attention throughout the process to the standards of ethics that students and families are expected to abide by when applying to universities. Ethics play a huge part in this process. Students are expected to follow ethical standards from submitting what is their own work to not saying "yes" to more than one institution ("double-depositing") once they have been accepted. Following the ethical guidelines of this process will set you up for success—or failure—as it plays at the heart of this very complex system. Crossing ethical boundaries never pays off in the long run.

IMPORTANT!

A family/student who does not sign the Agreement, in my mind, lacks the intention to commit to this process in full and will manage, at best, a half-baked effort and an unsatisfying result. Don't bother using this book if you're not going to commit to the Agreement and follow through to the end as this is the basis of the process.

Milestone 3: Thought Questions

I ask my students to respond to the questions in Worksheet 1.1 before our first meeting together. While it's a great way for me to get to know them better and be able to ask them more poignant questions throughout the process, it's an even more fabulous way for them to remind themselves just how interesting they are.

About 80% of the time students will go back to a theme they wrote about in the Thought Questions to expound upon in one of their university essays. I've also yet to work with a student who had answered these types of questions about him/herself before. It's a great way to start to recognize your strengths and how you stand out.

Please take some time to answer the questions located in Worksheet 1.1. As mentioned earlier, almost all Worksheets will be located at the end of each chapter unless indicated otherwise.

Milestone 4: Creating Your CV

Some adults say that "kids" should not have a CV. I heartily disagree. You will spend a lifetime re-evaluating and reconstructing your CV and this is a great opportunity to start. Will you have to turn in your CV for university Admissions? It depends, as does most everything. We'll see on a case-by-case basis if the universities you decide to apply to would like a CV in the application process. But, that's a ways down the road. In short, every year more and more universities give students the opportunity to upload their CV. I'll advise you later and at the stage when it's appropriate—and perhaps when not—to do so.

Here are some other instances where you will be truly grateful to have your updated CV on hand:

- When a university representative comes to visit your high school and you perhaps are the only one meeting with them. This is a lovely opportunity to share your CV.

- When you go to a university fair and have some time to sit and speak with the university representative. You'll take along your CV.

- How about when you meet with your counselor for the first time—and those times afterwards—when you'll have the opportunity to share a lot in the perhaps short amount of time you are given in that one-on-one meeting. Keep it updated.

- When you go for an Admissions interview or have an online interview. I was always impressed when a student sent me a CV a day prior to our interview. Sometimes I would have a moment to read it before our interview and that was helpful and useful.

- When you get confirmation from your teachers who will write you a recommendation, it's nice to share this with them to give them more information about you, to help them help you. They will be writing loads of recommendations and every bit of help from the student helps. And, helps you.

- When you are inquiring about summer jobs or volunteer positions and want to introduce yourself. Here you have your CV!

- When you are applying to universities. I always have my students cross-reference their CV to the activities listed on their applications and also note if anything did not make it into their applications that they really feel strongly should. (And then how to do that.)

There are going to be many more other uses for your CV, so get on this!

While you are doing this Milestone, go ahead and add an additional Milestone to Table 1.1 for every chapter: "Update my CV". You're going to be doing new things that you'll want to add and adjust to make sure the CV is always up to date and ready to send out.

Please go to Worksheet 1.2, your CV template. You will want to convert this to an electronic format, of course. Not all sections are necessary and certainly do not pertain to everyone. Then there are times when someone with a unique experience will want to add a section. Niche candidates—actors, violinists, fine art students, athletes, photographers—will want to have a separate CV dedicated to their unique talent, so they will then have two.

Milestone 5: Creating Your University Application Library

If you've gone to the bookstore or online, you would have seen that there are a gazillion books dedicated to this process. How in the world do you determine which you need, if any?

I recommend a handful of books to my students and families and ask that they either purchase them or, if they don't want to spend the money, access them from a library, the counselor's office, or school. Here are the ones you should have and should be using/reading, some of which I will be referring to throughout the process:

- *The Fiske Guide to Colleges*: Excellent, non-biased guide on hundreds of universities in the US (with a handful from the UK and Canada). Take note of the cross-reference list, which shows how some universities overlap, to give you further ideas if you find a fit. There is an online version to this.

- *Colleges That Change Lives* by Loren Pope: A must-read and must-have reference. You should give some consideration to many of these colleges, both as a student and as a family. These universities are truly among some of the gems that are out there, and by "name brand" will not be on the international student's top-10 list before starting out this process. Even more reason to look at these top universities that will give an unprecedented education to the discerning and enlightened international family.

- *U.S. College and University Reference Map* (available on Amazon): A fabulous reference! Everyone should have this as it marks on the map of the US and Canada all of the universities—public and private—in each State, giving a real visual perspective to the international student and family of where these schools are and the clusters around them.

- *The Thinking Student's Guide to College* by Andrew Roberts: Truly an excellent book to have as a reference for the thoughtful student and family—you!

- *The Gatekeepers: Inside the Admissions Process of a Premier College* by Jacques Steinberg: This reads like a novel but is non-fiction. Former *New York Times* education reporter Steinberg follows an Admissions representative through his work, giving an inside look to the process.

- *There Is Life After College: What Parents and Students Should Know about Navigating School to Prepare for the Jobs of Tomorrow* by Jeffrey Selingo.

- *The College Finder* by Dr. Steven Antonoff.

- *K&W Guide to Colleges for Students with Learning Differences.*

For the niche candidates—with a listing of universities and templates for your specific talent CV—you can refer to:

- *Creative Colleges: A Guide for Student Actors, Artists, Dancers, Musicians, and Writers* by Elaina Loveland.

- *The Making of a Student Athlete* by Ray Lauenstein and Dave Galehouse.

Great job on completing your first chapter! Keep track of when you need to start Chapter 2. Remember that you've just determined when that will be in this chapter's Milestones, so set a reminder and start work when you said you would commit to it.

Please answer freely. Your answers will never be graded or judged.

Leadership   Give accurate descriptions of how you've been a leader. How have you influenced others, perhaps resolved disputes, or been an active group member? What initiatives have you taken inside and outside of school? These can be anything, big or small. The point is to get them on paper and think about them, talk about them.

Knowledge in a field and your own creativity   Describe your special interests and how you have developed knowledge in these areas. What are your experiences with creativity? How do you see alternatives, take diverse perspectives or come up with original ideas? Give examples.

Dealing with adversity   Describe the most significant challenge you have faced and the steps you have taken to address this challenge.

Did you turn to anyone in facing this challenge? What role did the person play?

What did you learn about yourself? Can you recount the incident, telling the story?

Community service   Explain what you have done to make your community a better place to live in. Give examples of specific projects in which you have been involved over time.

Handling systemic challenges   Describe your experience facing or witnessing discrimination. How did you respond and what did you learn from the experiences? How might they have prepared you to contribute to a new community? Again, recount the story.

Goals/task commitment   Articulate the goals you have established for yourself and your efforts to accomplish these. Give one specific example that demonstrates your work ethic/diligence.

Source: Oregon State University

NAME

ADDRESS | PHONE with country code | EMAIL | Date of Birth | High School Name

Academic Achievements and Awards:

• list your own here (include the following: achievement/award, dates, location, affiliation (school, community organization, etc.), with brief explanation)

Entrepreneurship/Publications:

• list your own here

Leadership:

• list your own here

Awards, Athletics:

• list your own here

Extracurricular Activities:

• list your own here

"Your" Activity:

• list your own here

Work Experience:

• list your own here

Community Service:

• list your own here

Interests/Passions:

• list your own here

CHAPTER 2

You've Got to Understand How It Works to Win

Months: _____

(Please fill in your dates. *Recommended timeframe: starting September/October of penultimate year and finishing by January/ February the year of application)*

This chapter should not be done in a day, or a week, or a month. It will take several months to complete if you're going to complete it thoroughly. It is OK if you are starting this chapter late in the game, but you will have a more intense time commitment to every Milestone before moving on to Chapter 3.

Milestones cannot be skipped. You've committed to doing this process correctly in order to guarantee your success with it.

First, you need to understand how the process works and how your application will be evaluated. As with any process in life, if you don't understand how it works or how you will be assessed, you're setting yourself up for failure and disappointment. I can't tell you how many students fail to take this into consideration with US university Admissions.

There are two components to any US application—and yours will have both of these:

1. The holistic and full application itself (i.e., The Common Application or other application portal, essays, recommendations, etc.); and

2. The self-evaluation of the candidate—that's you—to figure out what type of university and which specific universities will be a fit for you and why, and then to be able to make your List.

The second component must come before the first, but your self-evaluation never stops and will continue to run alongside the first component in a parallel process as you begin writing applications.

Everything—from your school choices to where you do campus visits, to how you approach each application, to the final product that is each application—will depend on the second component.

US university Admissions are based on fit. "Fit" describes your ability to show that you are an excellent profile for each university you apply to since you know those universities (you will have researched them in depth, been in contact with them, followed them on social media, etc.), reflect their student body and mission, and will be a positive contributor to that campus, both as a student and as a lifelong alumnus.

So, in this chapter we will be focusing on both of these components as we go through the Milestones you are required to complete. While this may seem "avant-garde" as it's not done in any other college guide, it's also basic stuff. Any seasoned, experienced and thoughtful counselor will bring you through this and we're doing the same here.

I always get a feeling of excitement at this stage with the students I work with. It's a luxury for you to be able to spend some time getting to know yourself and how you fit into this process and eventually each institution on your List.

PARENT ADVICE

"My advice to the other parents will be to build a relationship of trust with your counselor so that you are able to share with them who your child is, who you are, your expectations, your fears, everything. It's wonderful to have someone who understands you and who is there to help you through this tough process. As a parent it's our responsibility to let that happen. So be transparent and let your counselor know you. I am sure the result will be in the best interest of your child."

—*Mani, Singapore*

PARENT ADVICE

"I want to stress to parents how important this type of a discussion is—speaking openly with someone who is neutral about the student, expectations, fears and worries. The self-assessment meeting (Milestone 1 below) was almost immediately transformative, not only for my son as the student, but for me as the Asian parent where homeschooling is rare. The meeting wrapped up the occasional self-doubt, melted away uncertainties; most of all, it concluded with validations of having done our personal best—we moved towards discussion of my son's passions into the context of further education. With the discussion points and topics suggested, it sets the enthusiastic tone of the college application."

—*Caroline, Malaysia*

Let's begin with your Milestones for this chapter:

 Milestone 1: Self-assessment, Student and Parents

 Milestone 2: Reviewing the Components of Your Application That Will Be Assessed By Admissions

Milestone 3: Understanding How the US Admissions Process Works

Milestone 4: Becoming a Strong Candidate

Case Study

Name: Shefali

Gender: Female

Country: Singapore

Nationality: Indian

Started process: October, junior year

Program/Rigor: IBDP: Higher Level: Chemistry, Mathematics, Physics; Standard Level: French, Economics, English

Grades to date: Predicted 38

Standardized tests to date: SAT* 1430

Subject Tests: Chemistry 700; Mathematics II 760

TOEFL/IELTS: Required by one sticky school on her List, even though she had been in British/International systems her whole life in Indonesia and Singapore.

Challenges: Shefali was a typical Indian student from her high school. Call it un-PC, but here was the truth. She took the "Indian package" (she was the first to alert me to

(continued)

this phrase). As uncouth as it is and sounds, the classmates in her international high school literally gave unofficial names to who took what courses that more or less stood the test of time. She took a typically Indian international student package. She only had an Indian passport. She did typically Indian extracurriculars. Sounds ridiculous that we discuss university Admissions in these terms, right? This is how it's discussed and this is how frank we need to be. In fact, there is a counseling agency out of Boston that was quoted in 2015 as working with Chinese students to make them less Asian—if they were involved in badminton to have them take up bowling, etc. Now, that is a gross and disgusting reality. We are not here to tell anyone not to follow a passion because it won't be strategic for Admissions. Shefali loved her Indian dance and identified with it. So what if most Indians in her high school were also involved?

She was getting a bit lazy with French and was only able to commit a few weeks of her final summer to doing some serious lab work and engineering-related experience, something very critical considering she wanted to go for engineering.

Strengths: Very true to herself. When she learned to open up, her character showed brightly. She has a smart sense of humor. Her mother gave up trying to do everything for her by May of her junior year and Shefali finally got into the game. It was a great moment for everyone. She is very smart and her grades were getting better towards the end of junior year and into the start of her senior year. We call this an "upward trajectory". She found a very good internship opportunity at a lab in Jakarta for her summer between junior and senior year. This was found through contacts and not through a pay-to-play program. Even better. She discovered things she loved about chemical engineering and things she did not like. It made for excellent discussion points for her essays and interviews. She interviewed well. She was not a perfectionist. Her parents had a great sense of humor and at the end of the day were very realistic and supportive. Shefali was able to articulate her love for Indian dance not only into her extracurriculars but into how it was embedded into her daily life, helping her to cope, create and become.

Fit/Factors: Chemical engineering was her goal and her only choice, so this narrowed down the list quickly.

Interests: Loved chemistry and her beloved Indian dance.

Essay topic: A conversation she had with her parents when they explained to her having to accommodate the needs of her husband, once that time came. Shefali's essay was very genuine—she didn't fight the conversation the first time, but later realized it would resurface and was building her argument in the meantime. She knew she was at odds with her family's view of gender roles in society and at odds with her own country's view of women in society. She reflected on how she was willing to fight it but knowing that there would be costs. The tone of Shefali's essay was humble, strong and determined, yet not beyond her years, and realistic. There was uncertainty in her tone, and that's truly how she was feeling. It came across as well-written, thoughtful, true, genuine and very interesting, with not an ounce of cliché.

Short List: Cornell ED, Purdue, Minnesota, CMU, University of Michigan, University of Minnesota, University of Texas Austin, University of Illinois Urbana-Champaign.

Interviews: Everywhere that offered and in particular when they were in town in Singapore she took good advantage of this.

Visits: None. She had never even been to the US before.

EGI (Efforts of Genuine Interest—see Milestone 3): Fairly good but did not come naturally to Shefali. Clearly, there were several poignant questions she had relative to her major and the program that allowed for her initial connection to her Admissions officers. The interviews and follow up were excellent.

Dream school, if any: Cornell

Application strategy: Aside from Cornell, to get a list of schools that were not common to her classmates, that were not of the "Indian package".

---

*Note that all SAT scores have been converted to the "new" format to provide consistency throughout the guide. In 2016 the SAT changed their test and scoring system.

SHEFALI'S ADVICE

"I finally took control of the process when I realized my mother decided one day to leave everything to me. Thank goodness that happened as it pushed me to do everything on my own and, I think, to be totally genuine in what came across. I was really surprised she did that at first and then became so grateful to her!"

MILESTONES

Milestone 1: Self-assessment, Student and Parents

This Milestone marks the foundation for the entire process. If you don't know yourself, what you're looking for, what you need, you will not be able to figure out your fit university and make a compelling case for your fit and your admission. Skip this and it will be like making a pizza but trying to add the crust last. It won't work.

What you need:

a. At least an hour.

b. To decide if you are going to write out your responses—parents and student use the same Worksheet (see Worksheet 2.1) but have their own copies—or ask a neutral friend (preferably not a sibling or one parent—it's natural that they will tend to opine or judge and we want a forum without judgment here!) to ask you the questions that follow in a group discussion.

   If you are opting for the "neutral friend" option—the one I recommend!—ask a friend who knows you well to do this. This option is best—instead of sitting and writing down answers and then sharing them, student with parent and parents with student—as it allows for more discussion and, I've found, gets to more depth in the topics being discussed. Ask your interviewer to take notes.

c. Every stakeholder in this process is present for this Milestone. I have indicated both models and instructions in Worksheet 2.1.

d. Worksheet 2.1: Self-assessment, Student and Parents.

e. Honesty.

Assuming you have an interviewer, let's begin. (If not, the student will fill out Worksheet 2.1 and parents will fill out Worksheet 2.1 in their respective copies of the book. You will come together afterwards to discuss.)

The interviewer will begin by going to Worksheet 2.1. Please follow the instructions in the Worksheet. Once finished, please return to this page and continue.

★ ★ ★ ★ ★

Finishing this Milestone is a rite of passage for the families and students I work with. You're starting to gauge your fit by self-assessing and by sharing thoughts, ideas, worries and perhaps even opinions (in some cases that you know don't serve you—think of the father and how he responded in the incident I shared with you in Part 4 of Worksheet 2.1) that help to put stakeholder emotions and presumptions and wants and needs on the table, to set the stage for continued honest discussions as the process moves forward and becomes more challenging. You don't have to come to "conclusions" after this Milestone. This is truly a never-ending conversation and one I'm delighted you are starting.

Milestone 2: Reviewing the Components of Your Application That Will Be Assessed By Admissions

In order to submit an excellent application, you need to know *what* is going to be reviewed—and then *how* (Milestone 3)—by Admissions. You know from the Introduction of this book that US university Admissions is a holistic process, one in which various components are considered when assessing if an applicant will be granted admission or not. Of course, every application will be different in some way—from what a college requires you to submit, to what it may recommend, and then how much weight it will put on each component—but I'll go over what you should expect to become a component of your application and what will be assessed as a part of the process in determining if you are accepted or not. Although there are hundreds of factors that are assessed, there are 10 in particular that I want to go over with you, in order to focus on those that are the most important and relevant right now.

Worksheet 2.2 exposes you to other factors that may be considered—some of which you can control, some of which you cannot, many of which will not be a factor to your schools, many of which will. I share this with you to give you an idea of just how unscientific the process is and to reinforce our motto—control what we can, leave the rest. As a general rule, everything in this process varies on a case-by-case basis.

IMPORTANT!

Before I launch into the 10 factors mentioned above, it's important for you to understand that behind those closed doors of Admissions officers' offices they will determine what is most important that year. What I am going to give you is a standard overview, yet each university—and sometimes I can advise my students specifically when I have more "insider" information about a school—will put emphasis where it wants and not necessarily tell the applicant (let's read it as not telling the applicant) specifically what that is. Bottom line? There are two. Grades and rigor are the most important. That's a pretty solid rule and one of the only non-gray areas in this process. The second will be not to try and guess what else is important. Behind those locked doors I've heard of a school desperately needing a baton twirler for their marching band as their current one was going to graduate. That there were not enough females applying to the engineering program or interested in mathematics. Or that the school's orchestra was in need of violin players. All of that will get to the Admissions office's ears and will be taken into consideration, in particular when very similar applicants may be differentiated by one cutting edge (read: baton twirling). So, while we cannot control this, we should take this into consideration. I'll discuss more about this in Chapter 3 as we build your Long List.

Now, here are your top 10 factors:

1. **Grades and rigor**. There's not much dispute over this. Colleges first and foremost want to see your academic strength and that will be assessed through your grades as well as through what courses you have elected to take within the context of what was available to you to take. Remember that we are talking about grades and courses taken in high school. Most will evaluate your last four years of high school; few will evaluate only your last three years in high school. A few finer points on this topic:

    a. You should, where and when possible, be taking courses that will challenge you. Every Admissions office will evaluate you based on your high school's profile. This is particularly important as an international applicant. Your colleges will have or will request from your Guidance Counselor a high school profile sheet to better understand your high school when evaluating your application. What courses are on offer? Did you take advantage of those that would challenge you most in those subject areas? Or, did you try to obtain better grades by taking "easier" classes? I don't need to tell you that it's near impossible to fool an Admissions officer. At the same time, don't take all AP (Advanced Placement) classes because you think it will "get you in". I've had many students who are not AP students, have AP classes offered, but chose not to take them, or to take only one or two. Be true to yourself. (And, parents, be true to your child.)

    b. In general, colleges will look for the following courses taken throughout your high school career:

    4 years English

    4 years Mathematics

    3 years Science (laboratory)

    3 years Social Sciences

    3–4 years Foreign Language.

    In some cases, a student will not have taken all of these courses (in particular if your national curriculum does not allow for such options, as is the case with the NCEA in New Zealand, for instance). In some cases, a college won't require all of these.

It's case-by-case on both ends—it depends on the student and his whole story and profile, and can depend on the university. For the latter, when you start to investigate your Long List, you'll be instructed to become very familiar with the requirements on a case-by-case basis. And, in some cases (in particular for Engineering candidates or CS candidates) you'll have requirements that will vary by program within the institution. (The latter is not as extreme as, say, UK universities, where admission is built around program-specific applications; however, in some areas applicants will have different requirements than the rest applying to the same university.)

c. If you have a very keen interest in a subject, you'll want to show that to Admissions by taking higher level/advanced courses in that subject or, if not offered, taking an accredited online or local university course additionally on this subject. When none of those are presented as options, you can still show your keenness and aptitude in a subject…keep reading…

d. An upward trajectory in your grades is viewed positively by Admissions. Poor grades in 9th grade, but you managed to slowly build on them and perform better in 10th and even better in 11th grade? That's excellent. What will not be assessed positively is the reverse, a downward trajectory in your grades as you move through high school.

STUDENT ADVICE

"I had only taken one year of foreign language by the time I was in my last year of high school simply because of our curriculum. As soon as I started to figure out some of the universities on my Long List, I started to email them to tell them about my predicament. Some recommended I take an accredited foreign language course online (it wasn't available to me at a local "community college") and some said they would take my situation into consideration at the time of the application and to make sure I mention this, and to have my counselor do the same on his recommendation for me. I was really stressed about it but in the end I have to tell you just to start to ask your Admissions officers because it really is considered case-by-case."

—*Charles, New Zealand*

---

2. **GPA grading and/or Class Rank.** For many students coming from international schools, this is not a factor as your schools do not provide a class rank or a GPA. If you don't have one, it's neither positive nor negative. Not all schools do this.

If your school does give students a class rank and GPA, this will be asked of you on every application and will be considered.

3. **AP/IB/A-level/Maturité/Bac/Abitur/Other rigorous curricula scores.** This is a very simple way for Admissions to "level the playing field" if you've taken or are taking any of these exams; they will be evaluated and given great importance.

4. **Essays.** Honest, thoughtful, self-introspective, humble, sometimes funny, sometimes serious, visual, storytelling, relevant, exposing essays will be highly valued by your universities. Why ever would you be spending months on writing them if they were not? You'll begin these in earnest over the summer and be done before the year ends. In some cases you'll be writing just one essay—The Common Application/other application portal main essay—for a school. In other cases you'll be writing several additional essays along with some short answers for a university. Be prepared...to write.

5. **SAT/ACT/Subject Test scores.** This is another way for Admissions to be able to "level the playing field" by assessing applicants with very different curricula, programs and classroom pedagogy on the same test. Unfortunately, these tests are clearly not for everyone, so it totally does not level the playing field. I have students who graduate top of their class with the highest IB scores, Bac scores, AP grades...and who have terrible SAT or ACT scores. Unfortunately, these tests are considered by many institutions (and help the human being do a quick, yet incomplete, assessment of a university—"ah, their median ACT score is a 33—must be a great university!"). Please note, as I get this question often—there is no "cut-off" for standardized tests. There is a range—and that's the middle 50% of their accepted applicants—that is published. As I mentioned in the Introduction, some schools will have special programs set up to "manage" their test score range to "appear" more selective and work their way up in the rankings. They should just get rid of these non-conclusive tests. However, I have seen perfect test scores rejected and dismal test scores accepted. As I have said, acceptance of an applicant is not a science. This is why it is important that you understand how the process works.

IMPORTANT!

At the time of printing, Brown University publishes on their website the number of students who were accepted this past year by ACT score. You can see here that there were 21 who were accepted and who had below 26 for the Class of 2020. It happens.

6. **Activities.** This is very important. They show your interests and depth of interest. They'll help an Admissions officer gauge if you're committed, show intellectual

curiosity, and if you've done what you say is important or interesting to you. We're going for depth here, not breadth. On the Common App you can fill out a maximum of 10 activities. I've had students go over that number and mention additional activities relevant to their application, referring to them in a strategic way in Additional Information. (I'll discuss this in later chapters.) I've had students go far under 10 activities to show their commitment and depth of interest to just a few. Both can be very positive. It becomes negative when there are next to none or far too many activities to convince anyone you're really committed and instead just doing something for the sake of college applications.

7. **Recommendations.** This is also very important. Admissions will not just be looking for your recommender to speak to your intellectual "abilities". In most cases, Admissions will look for your recommenders to speak to your character, curiosity, how you deal with adversity or failure, your strengths and your challenges. These recommendations are best when they are holistic. You'll be guided by me to look for recommenders who know you well—not necessarily in whose class you've done the best—and who can speak to a holistic self who is growing and achieving.

8. **Awards, recognitions, and honors.** Again, many high schools and curricula internationally do not give awards or honors. Not to worry if that's the case with your high school. It will not be considered as part of the evaluation.

     If, on the other hand, these are a part of what you have achieved—and these can be awards or honors received inside or outside of your high school—they will be reviewed and assessed. A laundry list of awards from before high school will not be reviewed—or may even be reviewed negatively—by Admissions. Most of my students have none or one award or honor. It's not something that is expected, but if you have them, you'll want to share them.

9. **Special talents.** If you're a musician, artist or athlete, you'll want to make this clear in your application. This can range from the D-1 track star to the self-taught ukulele player who is committed to their talent and has made this a part of their life. Of course, if you have a talent that you're considering as a profession, the way you will showcase this and approach the Admissions process with that in hand will be different (i.e., connecting with coaches very early on in the process for D-1 schools, having a set of clips and videos) than if you have been playing tuba for most of your life, love it, are committed to it, want to play in a band in college, but don't want to make this a career or even a major. Regardless of the level of your talent, if you've got one, you want to showcase this. And there are many ways to do this, which we'll discuss.

10. **Interview.** While many colleges do not interview their candidates (they have far too many applicants to do so), many still do. Most colleges that do interview candidates

make this optional and leave the ball in the candidate's court, so to speak. You'll see on the Admissions page of these colleges that they offer the opportunity to interview with the college—whether through an alumnus or with an Admissions officer—but that opportunity is up to the candidate to pursue. How one pursues this depends on the university and, again, is on a case-by-case basis. (You'll go to your university's webpage for this and I will guide you through it in future chapters.)

If you have this opportunity with any of your universities, seize it. While alumni interviews really won't have much sway with Admissions (they do report back to Admissions on their conversation with you, anything particular, extraordinary or exceptional...or not), an interview with an Admissions officer may very well be significant to the Admissions process. Imagine that your job is to go through thousands of candidates' profiles. Then one pops up where you can put paper to a face to a conversation. It's a human process and even if Admissions says that interviews don't play a huge part in Admissions, they can certainly have an impact.

WORDS OF WISDOM: INTERVIEWS

I had a colleague who was interviewing candidates in South America. She had her list of requested interviews by candidates and was meeting with them one by one in her hotel lobby after she had visited high schools to meet with students interested in the university where we worked. One of her final interviews was with a candidate whose profile was quite below the standard profile of the university with regards to grades and test scores. (She had still not received his application and was going on what had been shared with her by his counselor at his high school.) He blew her away with their discussion, his interests, his candor and his personality. She phoned me that evening to say that she was going to "go to bat" for this candidate, and that while his grades and test scores may be an issue, she would love to see him on the university campus and thought he could make great contributions to the school. Long story short, he was one candidate who came up during the committee review—when Admissions officers go over candidates who may be borderline admit or reject and need to be voted upon by the entire committee. She made her case for this candidate. All officers voted. He was admitted.

The Case Studies presented in this chapter and in the following chapters throughout the book will show you just how arbitrary the process is *and* that you cannot be assessed at the surface level (i.e., just by grades and test scores). As you read through the Case Study of each chapter and then the results in the Conclusion, you'll realize it's safe to assume that there were components in each student's application that either had a positive or negative impact on colleges to help them determine if they were accepted or not.

Milestone 3: Understanding How the US Admissions Process Works

If humans functioned as machines, our decisions would not be laden with emotions or subjectivity and they would be much more black and white. Thank goodness we have not been replaced by machines—life's decisions would get really boring. But what that means is that there are a myriad of factors that come into play. Whether you're taking the decision to buy that new mobile phone, purchase a bubble tea, hire extra help for your summer start-up endeavor or whether an Admissions officer is deciding whether to admit you to their college or not, there's a huge element of subjectivity—and that also means luck when we talk about humans choosing humans. So, when your application is next up on the Admissions officer's desk, you want to make sure you've done your best up to that point to control what you could have controlled prior to submitting it, and adhering to an approach post-submission of not trying to control what you cannot. You'll never win that game.

Aside from the subjectivity involved in humans making decisions regarding other human beings (from the same home country, speak the same language, love the same food, have someone they know in common, etc.), we can and should take a look at what factors Admissions may or certainly will take into consideration when evaluating your application.

Keep in mind the following that may sway an Admissions officer:

- All of the components of your application—those we just reviewed in Milestone 2 earlier.

- What does the university need this year? In most cases you won't know this, but in some you may. Don't stress about trying to figure this out, but if you do get an indication—perhaps your counselor mentions something to you, the actual Admissions officer mentions something to you in the interview, or the college actually states blatantly on their website what qualities or qualifications they are looking for in candidates—this will be important to keep in mind. Knox College, for instance, clearly states on their Admissions webpage what they will consider for incoming applicants.

- When did you apply (EA, ED, REA, SCEA, ED2, RD…)? This can have an impact, but will depend on the university and whether the university clearly states this information. For instance, Grinnell College clearly encourages applicants on their website to apply ED if Grinnell is their first choice. Or, if you find out from reliable insider information (e.g., your counselor). We know that many colleges are accepting higher and higher percentages of their class through their ED application round. This helps a college with their enrollment management at the end of the day.

- Do you "fit"? Have you articulated and shown that? Think of why we just went through Milestone 1. Aside from having a thoughtful conversation with yourself and your family to recognize and reaffirm who you are and what your needs and wants may be in terms of university, so much of what you discussed in Milestone 1 will help you determine which universities are right for you, and that's called *fit*. US Admissions offices will accept candidates based on fit. What does that mean? Well, look at a college's profile, for instance on its website. It's obvious that one of the key values at Macalester College in Minnesota is building an ethically responsible community, among other things. You won't be a great fit if you don't share this value and show this specifically through your application. At Carleton College it's clear the values lie in breadth and depth of liberal arts studies. You won't be a fit if you're looking for a research university with a large business school. At Willamette in Oregon it's clear there's a huge focus on sustainability, and whether or not that's going to be directly related to what you study, it should show up relevantly in your application to show a fit of values.

Like anything that is based on fit, you're going to have to work to understand what each college community on your Long List is about and what its values are in order to assess if you would naturally and organically fit into that environment. And, once you figure that out and determine if that school will fall onto your Short List and will be one to which you are applying, you'll have to make that clear in your application—both in your essays in saying what you've done, do and value, and also in what you *do* and *have done* to prove that those values are aligned, yours with the school's.

- Niche applicant. A niche applicant can either be someone who has a very specific talent that draws them out of the application pool—published author, artist, athlete, actor, musician, etc.—or someone whose experience fits very neatly into what the Admissions committee would love to have on their campus—an experienced blogger on issues that mirror campus values, a unique life story that will add color to their class profile, a particularly young high school graduate, or someone who has done what the college feels are extraordinary accomplishments and this will set them apart from the applicant pool.

In some cases, an applicant will know if they are a niche applicant—the violinist who has been in touch with the college's strings director over the past year and who has been given a clear indication that they are interested, or the accomplished track star who has made the regional headlines and successfully approached coaches who have an explicit interest in getting him/her on their campus—and in other cases it will be something only discovered and discussed behind those Admissions office doors.

I do try to make each of my students a niche student in at least a few universities on their final Short List. No, most of my students don't have special talents and have not published books. They are hardworking, unique, curious and interesting people with opinions, values and experiences that they learn to match up with colleges that may be looking for their type of profile and—and this is the most important part—*will not fall on everyone's Short List in their high school, country or region.* I'll get to that in future chapters but it's important for you to keep in mind as this will be part of your work as you go through this process. In addition, in those cases where students have successfully identified a college where they could potentially be reviewed as niche candidates, they have more often than not received a merit scholarship to that college, which is an effort by that college to get a student to attend, saying "Hey, we really, really would love to have you on our campus this fall."

STUDENT ADVICE

"I really wouldn't consider myself a "niche student" because I'm pretty normal, but I guess I was able to make myself "niche" by exposing my totally unique, quirky, real self. Yes, that made me different. And, I tied that to the colleges that ultimately made my List. Of course, they all matched me and my quirkiness, my activism, my total respect for nature and animals, and for planning to be a very active member of the community in my areas of, well, uniqueness!"

—*Jessica, Mexico and Spain*

• EGI: "Efforts of Genuine Interest". Focus in on the word "genuine". This is also known as "Demonstrated Interest" but I like to call it EGI, as I think there is a clear differentiation between those who just "demonstrate interest" (sending an email to the Admissions officer to ask a non-specific question) to try to tick that box and those who show a truly genuine interest by making efforts to connect with the school and let them know they are interested and, perhaps, to get themselves on the school's radar.

EGI can and will vary and should not start too early. There are all sorts of forms of showing genuine interest from campus visits to requesting information, to request-ing an interview in order to, I believe, establish a relationship with your Admissions officer. The latter is something I will take you through and something that will take time, finesse and honesty and even then will not guarantee that you "establish" this relationship, particularly with larger schools or with schools that manage tens of thou-sands of applications. But, you'll see EGI on your Milestones throughout the process and it is something you must never skip. The fruits of that labor pay off dividends but you won't see that until you've done it—or have not, and by then it's too late.

- If they accept you, what are the chances you'll accept back? Going on my earlier comment regarding my students who receive merit aid as essentially a plea by that institution to get the candidate to say yes, colleges and Admissions staff most definitely will be looking at this factor as they review your application. Of course if you apply ED—a binding Early Admissions option for many schools—you have to accept back. So, in this sense, last year when one well-known institution accepted almost half their class in the ED round, they knew that they had already filled half the incoming class by December. In terms of enrollment management, that made things easier for themselves come the RD round.

  An Admissions officer will always be trying to gauge if you will accept them back, thereby making up their yield number—the higher the better for them—and may make a decision based on this. A college may ask you where else you are applying to see where they land on the totem pole. If they feel they are "just a safety school", they may not accept you for fear there is very little chance of you accepting them back. This is where applying "Early" comes into play as well; usually if a student is applying EA, SCEA or ED, the college knows they are at the top of this student's list.

IMPORTANT!

Of course there are exceptions—and most institutions want to get as many applications as they can and may modify their applications in order to do so (i.e., no required additional essays, questions or even SAT/ACT scores from international applicants). Remember that numbers play a big part in the ranking game and at the end of the day this is a giant business. Be enlightened…

Sometimes my students are asked in an interview what their top schools are in order for the Admissions officer to gauge. (Of course, you never want to leave that school off the list. Even if it's not at the top, make it near the top!) In some cases Admissions will be able to gauge this from the quality of the applicant versus the actual student profile and determine that the student is using it as a safety school and may therefore not accept the candidate. We see this happening more and more.

- Do you have an international or unique passport? Are you a full-pay candidate? If you're international, you would be unless you are:
  1. Applying for a very university-specific scholarship for need-based financial aid just for international applicants;

2. Holding a US passport and can and will apply for financial aid as a US citizen;

3. Applying in the US to strategic schools in an effort to see if you are awarded any merit awards, which is the only way you would be able to attend university in the US (and I hope you are also applying to other universities in other countries and not relying on the merit-aid piece).

The P&L ("profit and loss") at any university in the US—public or private—is enormous. While most institutions that you apply to will have an endowment, this does not mean they are not tuition dependent. Being full-pay is usually a very positive thing, but of course would never guarantee admission. There are many full-pay candidates applying everywhere.

Being international and perhaps even carrying a "unique" passport can also be factors in an Admissions decision. International students on campus make up a very important cohort and you'll get used to seeing the "% international students" numbers on every college's website. Diversity is key. Add to that a "unique" passport that could potentially add another country to the stats ("our students come from 50 states and 31 countries") and this could be a factor.

The flip side is the passports that are plentiful and there's no beating around this fact. For those countries that send the most students to the US, those passports can at times have a negative impact on the candidate. You can't control this, so there's nothing to do about it other than to know and understand how it fits in. Not fair? Nothing subjective is ever "fair" unless it turns out in your favor. That's life. Educate yourself on how this works and be an enlightened applicant.

- The human process means it's not perfect. There's no science behind it and there's really no way, ever, to find out why you were accepted or why you were rejected. Commit now to letting this go. And, to control what you can control and leave the rest...

Control what is in your control:

- Your fit.
- Grades, and the courses you take.
- Testing.
- Essay and supplements.
- Being proactive and showing EGI.
- Strategic planning: Building a proper and well-rounded List.

- Your recommendations (yes, you can control this—we'll discuss how).

- When you turn in your application (even for Regular Admissions—don't wait until the last day before the deadline…is that really the type of proactivity and planning nature you want to show to a college?).

- Developing your story—through your application and through this process.

- Extracurriculars: Leadership, depth and involvement.

- Being a niche applicant.

- Intellectual curiosity—and this doesn't have to be what you automatically think it should be. One of my students loves stamps and shows her depth of curiosity through this passion.

- Figuring out where you will be happy (which equals, plain and simply, success).

Don't try to control what is not in your control:

- The very nature of the process: it's arbitrary for the most selective universities.

- Needs of the institution during your application year.

- Subjectivity: The Admissions officer reading your file recruited in your country last year got pickpocketed, had food poisoning and had a very serious debate with his boss while there. He's not thinking fondly of your country, fair or not.

- Your competition.★

- Who reads your application, at what time of the day, and at what time during the process.★★

   ★   You can control this to an extent and that is by not coming up with the same final List as everyone else in your high school, country or region. I've talked about this before and will continue to stress the importance of this, oh, en-lightened family.

   ★★ Many universities and Admissions offices will not just take applications as they come in, but parse them out by country or region in terms of when they are read. You can't control if Taiwan ends up being the last country on that Admissions office's list—when everyone is tired of reading applica-tions, not fresh, in a rush to get to the deadline. At the same time, perhaps Taiwan is first on the docket to read. You just won't know and you just can't control it.

The Enlightened Insider: Trends and Realities

There are always changing trends and realities in this field that should be accounted for by any enlightened applicant. Here are a few and we'll continue to discuss more as we move through the process.

- The "Early" game: Played by universities who are keen to employ enrollment management tactics such as filling half the class with their ED applicant pool.

- Filter-reading: This is happening at more selective institutions that receive tens of thousands of applications and manage them by doing a quick filter read of most to gauge if they are worth reading thoroughly.

- Fit is more important than ever. And it's up to the applicant to articulate and demonstrate this.

- Essays are golden: More and more important, these are what will showcase your individuality...and fit.

- Yield game: There are new "programs" popping up at several universities to manipulate these numbers of yield by accepting students into special programs whose yield numbers do not need to be registered or recorded and thus are not taken into account when final yield numbers are published. It's a dirty game and many are playing it.

- Look beyond the name brand. You don't have a choice nowadays. With acceptance rates at an all-time low, you have to be wise and enlightened to look elsewhere, and usually elsewhere is both a better fit and a more successful choice.

- Colleges are looking more and more for diversity. And diversity comes in many forms.

- "We had 30K applications but could only read 20K," said by one famous Admissions dean at one of the country's most selective institutions a couple of years ago.

- Pressure for Admissions officers to read and decide on applicants, making deadlines. Your Admissions officer had a terrible week, has 50 more applications to read in one day and yours is next to last...

- "We had to send two Admissions officers out to get pizza...but we continued voting without their presence." The reality. And maybe your application was the one that came up...for better or for worse.

(continued)

Some Unhelpful Myths:

- The more colleges you apply to, the better your chances! No. Create a well-rounded list.
- Only test scores matter.
- Only one candidate from each high school will be admitted.
- You can pay your way in.

I realize this is a lot of information and that's why you have this guide to refer to whenever you need to. We'll continue to discuss many of these points in context as we go through the process.

Milestone 4: Becoming a Strong Candidate

I think it's appropriate to end this chapter's Milestones with a summary of how you can be a strong candidate—something that is in your control. Here are the most important ones that I will refer to actively again throughout this book:

- Intellectual curiosity;
- Showing the real you: Being true to yourself and being honest;
- Depth, both of character and in terms of interests and academics;
- Showing your fit and EGI;
- Doing your own work;
- Staying clear of sounding privileged;
- Strong essays and written components;
- Leadership; and,
- As a niche candidate, showing your depth of involvement. If you're going into engineering, for instance, discussing any true research that was done. If you're an artist, putting forth a well-thought-out and comprehensive portfolio.

My advice to parents or guardians: Step aside and let your son/daughter shine through and be who he/she really is.

"I feel the major ingredient to successfully make the 'strong candidate' broth is firstly, the university needs to be one that you are eager to attend, and you need to show it to the Admissions officer, not just tell them. Secondly, which I think is the most important, you need to research thoroughly and ensure that you will be a match to the specific university; that you would fit in well in the environment. For example, personally, I preferred universities with a smaller size class, meaning I would interact much better with the professors and students. Perhaps that is something which you are looking at as well."

—*Adit, Singapore*

Identify your uniqueness—who are you? What do you like and enjoy? Where are you a passionate learner? How do you learn? All of these things you either discussed directly or hit upon them indirectly in Milestone 1. Reflect on these as you round out this chapter and remember that in order to find your fit and to articulate that fit to ultimately find where you'll be happiest and have the most success, you'll have to continue to recall what you reflected on in Milestone 1 and build upon that as you move forward.

Worksheet 2.1: Self-Assessment for Student and Parents

How to use this Worksheet

Either:

a.   Self-lead (no interviewer): Student, please fill out your Worksheet (Parts 1 and 3). Separately, and without discussing, Parents/Family, fill out your Worksheet (Part 2). Get together and go through each response, Student, beginning with you and going through yours. When you have shared Parts 1 and 3 and Part 2, as a group, go through Part 4, always having the Student answer first.

Or:

b.   With an interviewer (preferred mode): All of you should be together in a comfortable space, with no distractions. I'd ask everyone to have paper and pen at the ready to take notes—I especially find that Parents like to do this at this point—and really this is a discussion, and it should always begin with the Student.

Interviewer, please go through Part 1, asking the Student the following questions. Please take notes. When you have completed this, turn to the Parents and go through Part 2. Part 3, in this case with an interviewer, should also be done at this time, but after Parts 1 and 2. Please continue below.

Part 1: For Student

1.   Describe yourself.

   a. Academically

   b. Your character

2.   Transitions in your life: What have they been? Describe them.

3. Interests and passions: What are they—within and beyond academia?

4. Family influence/other influencers: Who influences you in life and how?

5. Goals/dreams: University, career, life (specific university criteria?).

Part 2: For Family

1. Describe the student—academically and his/her character:

2. How was the student raised (parenting style)?

3. Impact of transitions on the student throughout life?

4. Strengths and challenges—both inside and outside of the classroom.

5. How does the student learn best? (Knowing the teachers? By debating in class? Taking notes?)

6. Goals and expectations/dreams: University, career, life (specific university criteria?).

   Note to family interviewer at this point: Please move on to Part 3 below and don't let anyone leave the room! Continue the "interview" here asking the Student the following questions.

   Families: if you are taking this "alone" and without an interviewer, the Student should continue to write down his/her answers here to share them together with his/her family after Parts 1–3 are completed.

   Move on to Part 4 to finish up.

Part 3: For Student

1. Describe yourself in three words.

2. Where do you feel most comfortable?

3. What motivates/demotivates you?

4. Relationships—what are they like with:
   a. Parents/Family

   b. Friends

c. Teachers

5. Your strengths

    a. Academically

    b. Personally

6. Your challenges
    a. Academically

    b. Personally

7. Describe your ideal university.

8. Describe your ideal life/career/future.

Part 4: For Everyone—Moving on to Factors

At this stage you've gone through a lot of discussion about the Student. Insightful but exhausting at the same time! It's so important to go through these steps at this stage in the process. Now, with a bit less need for self-introspection and to get you thinking about factors that may or may not be important to you as you start to discover universities, go through the following list of factors (see below), always starting with the student, and mark your ratings of 1 to 5. If your interviewer is still with you, even better! Please ask him/her to go through each factor, asking for a ranking from each participant, beginning with the Student.

You'll see there is room at the end of this factors chart to add your own factors. You're encouraged to do so now and in the future.

Important note! As you go through each factor, feel free to discuss it. Often I get not just a rating response from a student or parent but also a qualification of their response. That's great as it allows for everyone in the group to get a better feel of where she/he is coming from.

What I would ask you not to do is to over-assess the factors. The intention here is not to get you to stick with your rating for the whole process. Instead, it's to get you thinking about what might or might not be important to you in order to find your fit, and to get a discussion going with the family/stakeholders. Here's one such discussion that just recently happened with me as the interviewer:

Interviewer/Me: "Prestige".

Student: I don't know what that means.

Me: You know what the word means. Now, what does it mean to you vis-à-vis university?

Student: I think a 3.

Me: OK, Dad?

Father: For me it's a 5.

Me: Tell us why.

Father: If I am to be honest, I come from a culture where name is important. I know a few names of universities as do my colleagues and they are talked about in my country. We think those are the best universities and I am being honest by saying, yes, if my son were to go to one of those and I could say he did, that would bring pride.

Me: What about the other hundreds of universities you are going to look at that you don't know the name of that are probably a better fit for your son and will give him a better education and a stronger chance to be successful and happy?

Father: I was just being honest. At the end of the day, I want my son to be happy. I know that by telling someone he goes to a brand name institution only brings pride for a moment, and then it's fleeting.

Mother: I give it a 3.

We all laugh (because we knew Mom would follow her son) and move on.

Rate the following factors from 1–5, with 5 being highest.

Factor Type	My Rating
Location	
Academic Offerings	
Prestige	
Social Life	
Size	
Diversity	
Job Prospects	
Exploring Courses	
Cost	
International Student Population	
Professors	
Leadership of Institution	
Housing	
Study Abroad	
Internships	
Class Size	
Rigor	
Retention Rate	
Male–Female Ratio	
Urban/Rural/Suburban	
What Friends Say	
Happiness	
Advising System	
Types of Majors	
Graduation Rate	
Facilities	
Independence	
Socially Aware/Active Campus	
Weather	
Close to "Home"	
(Add your own factors…)	

Not all of the factors below will be taken into consideration; at best, only a few will. However, this list gives you an idea of how many factors there can be and how unscientific the process is. That's why you should stick with the 10 factors I advised you on in this chapter.

- Relative who is an alumnus

- Profile of the applicant's high school

- Family's ability to pay

- "Additional Information" essay

- Extenuating circumstances (illness, etc.)

- Member of an underrepresented group

- Choice of major

- Socioeconomic background/level of parents' education

- Character (suspensions, criminal history, etc.)

- Volunteerism

- Portfolio (for art, architecture, interior design, etc.)

- After-school/summer employment

- Audition (music, performing arts, etc.)

- Comes from a "famous" family, or the student him/herself is famous

- Development case: Family is able to make/has made a very significant financial contribution to the college

- Geographic/regional desirability

- Number of students applying to that institution from a given high school in that particular year

- Applicant comes from a high school that has historically been a "feeder" high school for that college

- Gap year experience

- Intellectual curiosity/enthusiasm for learning

- Has taken the initiative to seek out outside courses, in cases where the student's high school might not offer "high-level" courses such as APs

- Participation in a rigorous academic summer program

- Demonstrated leadership

- How early/late the application was submitted (in particular in rolling Admissions but not necessarily)

- Independent research

- Had something (written work, etc.) published

- Documented Learning Difference

- Essay in response to question: "Have you ever been suspended or dismissed from a school?"

- Child of that college's administration, faculty, staff

CHAPTER 3

Being Your Nerdiest Self…
and Taking Time to Do It

Months: _____

(Please fill in your dates. *Recommended timeframe: starting in October and working through February of your penultimate/Junior year (Northern Hemisphere)*)

If you're a junior reading this, you're in your penultimate year of high school, or perhaps if you're a Southern Hemisphere student you're finishing up your penultimate year in December. Regardless, *this is your moment.* Universities will be dissecting your grades, the comments that accompany those grades for each term, and the classes you've chosen to take as a scientist dissects his data in order to draw conclusions. Your effort should be put at one hundred percent, no less.

If you're taking a gap year or finishing conscription,[1] this is also a critical period for you. What have you accomplished and done during your gap year up until now and how will you build on what you worked on in Chapter 2? These will be critical components of your application in terms of you and Admissions articulating your genuine fit.

Before we hit this period's Milestones, there are some very important bits of advice to consider alongside those you should be heeding during this period.

Number one is your commitment to your academics. This is your most important year overall in terms of Admissions for university.

---

[1] Conscription: This is compulsory military service to your country.

You should also be making a genuine effort to get involved outside of the classroom. Again, this should be a pleasure for you to do as "getting involved" means doing what you love—and not doing what you think Admissions wants to see. The latter is not genuine and won't fit into your "story" in the end. Remember what we discussed in Chapter 2. Now's your time to build the depth of your interests and passions—by *doing*. Choose clubs, volunteer programs, sports, hobbies and work that will show your depth of involvement, leadership, interest and more about who you are and what you value as a person.

IMPORTANT!

Community service is something that is a huge part of US society and thus also a very large part of most universities' offerings to its students. Admissions will expect you to have given back to your community through service and volunteer work and in meaningful ways (read: not just that required class trip to Ladakh with your school to build irrigation systems for a local community—while outstanding, they will look for ways in which you've individually sought out opportunities to engage in community service). And, as is often the case, some of the most profound community service experiences are those that are not "organized" projects or programs, but rather those opportunities that you've sought out and perhaps even suggested to organizations/causes that you love and care about and became involved in. I always encourage my students to step back and look at what their interests are—both inside the classroom and outside—and brainstorm organizations, charities, communities they could approach to ask if they can become involved. This takes extra time and a bit of creativity. Many organizations will say "we would love your help but we don't have an internship program". No problem—suggest ways of helping! One of my students is a science freak, self-admitted. She approached an organization she knows from her community to see if she could create a weekly class for the youth to teach them about science. It worked. Another one of my students loves animals. She approached a local animal shelter to see if she could help out during her two-week break and in doing so she helped to create a special program to build awareness in the community for street dogs and cats. You can imagine how powerful these stories then come across in an application, not to mention the most important lesson—the impact these experiences had on my students.

STUDENT ADVICE

"For me, community service means to share my experiences with the community, being the people or the environment. For me, community of course stands for my immediate surrounding society, but as a global citizen I consider the whole globe to be my community. I believe that community service should not be something that you do because it is required or because it makes you look good. I think that it should be something that you truly enjoy from the heart. I know that it can sound egoistic by saying 'do something that makes you feel good', but you won't give your best and get something out of the experience unless you are passionate about it, and the community deserves your passion."

—*Mei, Japan*

I also want you to make an effort to meet with your teachers during this time. In particular, if you've just started a new program (i.e. IBDP) or school year and are getting used to your new teachers, make a point of meeting with them one-on-one to discuss any concerns or questions you might have about the class, topics, how you are doing and also explaining to your teacher how you learn best. (If you don't know the latter, help your teacher help you in understanding how you learn best.) In many cases, your teacher may not teach to your needs or to your style, but this is a learning experience and one that will help you get to know yourself better. Remember Milestone 1 of Chapter 2, where you were asked to describe how you learn best? Don't forget that that question is ongoing. So, start to become your own best advocate. This will go a long way through the rest of your high school career and certainly in college where you'll be expected to be an advocate for yourself.

There's a lot to cover in this chapter and over this time period in order to progress. We'll begin with the most important aspects first and cover all those that need to be completed before moving on to Chapter 4.

These are the Milestones for this chapter:

 Milestone 1: Creating Your Long List

 Milestone 2: Researching Your Long List

Milestone 3: Standardized Testing Plan

 Milestone 4: Meeting With Your Guidance Counselor

Milestone 5: Confirming Courses for Rest of High School

Milestone 6: Social Media Clean-up

 Milestone 7: Upcoming Break and Summer Plans

Milestone 8: Adding to Your Long List

Milestone 9: Updating Your CV

You'll remember from the Introduction that I will suggest resources in this book that I believe will be helpful to you throughout the process—and many of which you already have from Milestone 5 in Chapter 1: Building Your Library. These resources can be found outside of this guide and are highly recommended for you to use as reference. Their details are listed in the References section on page 287 of this guide.

- *The Fiske Guide to Colleges*
- *Colleges That Change Lives*
- *The College Finder*
- *U.S. College & University Reference Map*
- *Creative Colleges*
- *The Making of a Student Athlete*
- *K&W Guide to Colleges for Students with Learning Differences*

Case Study

Name: Mei

Gender: Female

Country: Japan and Singapore

Nationality: Japanese

Started process: Approximately 2 years prior to graduating high school

Program/Rigor: IBDP–HL: Psychology, Biology, Japanese Literature; SL: History, English Language and Literature, Mathematics

Grades to date: Predicted 39–40

Standardized tests to date: ACT: 29

Subject Tests: No

TOEFL: Reading: 28, Listening: 30, Speaking: 28, Writing: 30, Total: 116

Challenges going into the process: Mei will say her challenges were narrowing down the colleges, researching and time management once it came to writing and submitting. I found Mei to be unbelievably organized. I think her challenge was her low ACT

---

score relative to her intellect and grades. It just did not reflect her potential and she was looking at colleges that required those scores.

Strengths going into the process: Mei's strengths were that she definitely knew the type of college she wanted to attend, and was able to go and visit the colleges. Mei was also very organized and very level-headed about the entire process. She was able to manage her stress quite well and also not get too out of touch with the reality of the process. Mei was also very true to who she is throughout, and was also a published author at a young age.

Fit/Factors: Small liberal arts college in sunny California (ideally no cold!) and a campus where she can always stand a chance of passing by someone she knows walking from class to class.

Interests: Sports, reading, traveling, hiking, community service.

Common App essay topic: Her experience volunteering in the AIDS ward in Singapore and the adversity she encountered.

Short List: Claremont McKenna College, Pitzer College, Scripps College, Pomona College, Boston College, Tufts, University of Rochester, University of British Columbia, Middlebury College, Brown University.

Visits: Claremont McKenna College, Pitzer College, Scripps College, Pomona College, University of British Columbia, Occidental College, Pepperdine University.

EGI: Mei sent poignant emails to Admissions officers and visited schools over the summer. She also interviewed with every university that offered the opportunity.

Dream School: Claremont McKenna College

Application strategy: Mei had a balance of reach, fit and safe schools and also ED-ed to her top choice. And, it was very, very clear to her what her top choice was.

MEI'S ADVICE

"Summer before senior year is arguably the most important summer when it comes to narrowing down your college/university options. Living in Singapore, this was the only time where I was able to physically go and see my potential schools in the United States. This experience was extremely valuable for me because, despite reading about all the amazing colleges and listening to stories about them from current students, I didn't really "feel" what the college was like until I actually saw it. Walking around the campus and participating in tours provides you with another perspective of the college that you can't gain from reading. Saying all this, summer is the time for relaxation. So my recommendation would be to not stress out too much about college and its admission process but to definitely keep it in mind. I know that it could be difficult to visit schools and do an internship and relax, but find a good balance."

MILESTONES

Milestone 1: Creating Your Long List

You are fully capable of developing your own Long List and I'm here to guide you through that with guidelines, ideas, examples and cases. By the end of this Milestone, you will have your Long List created and can start to really get into the nitty gritty process of finding the universities that are going to be the best fit.

Your ultimate college List—sometimes referred to here as your Short List (includes those colleges you will ultimately apply to) will reflect your character and personality. It will reflect what you answered in Milestone 1 of Chapter 2, the factors you continue to rate highly as you go through the process. If done correctly, your Short List will be composed of those universities that reflect you as an individual (think "fit") and will therefore give you the best chances of being accepted. But, before you get to a Short List, you have to start somewhere and with over 3,000 four-year universities in the US, it can be a tough place to start (thus the reason why so many will start with names they've heard of). Let's break that mold and start afresh.

I draft a Long List for my clients, of course based on the self-assessment in Chapter 2, along with my own knowledge and experience of *which* colleges *could* have aspects to them that are a fit. Please note the word "aspects" here when I am talking about a Long List. The point of your Long List is not to create a list of schools you will definitely apply to; instead, it is to create a list of schools that may have aspects that could potentially be a fit for you and to look into those aspects and others of each of these schools to see which you like and which you don't, and record, reflect and discover.

As a reminder, what about the aspects you will uncover in your Long List, which are important with regards to eventually developing your Short and final List? The fit. And that includes the following aspects of the institution:

- Academics
- Character and student profile
- Interests aligning
- Value system
- That it makes sense [for you★]
- That it fulfills what you want and need
- And ultimately what you will give back to the school

    ★A note about it "making sense". I had a student this year trying to push that two competitive colleges in the Chicago area were both a strong fit for her. They could not be more different in terms of types of institutions, student body, profile and environment. Her ultimate defense was that they both had the same major (every school has this major) that she was considering and were in the same geographic region. I told her she wasn't doing her work. Finally she realized, after going through the criteria I will make you go through for each university on your Long List, that one was really not going to be a fit for her at all.

How is developing the Long List and eventually your Short List accomplished? Clearly by following this guide step by step. But, along with that, you must commit to the following if you're dedicated to drafting an appropriate List for yourself:

- Time. That it takes a lot of time to develop your Lists before you come to an "ah-ha!" moment of understanding as to which are a fit and which are not.

- Preparation. Again, why you bought this guide and why you are taking the time to do this well. Preparation is embedded in the philosophy of being an enlightened family through this process.

- Research. It will be up to you to do your appropriate research. I'll guide you through it, what you'll need to do and how to do it, but it will be you who captures the data and feedback to ultimately lead to...

- Understanding. You'll come to this by going through the above. Understanding what schools are right for you, where you'll find a fit, where you'll find happiness and success.

- Lots of self-reflection. You may find, as many of my students do, that some of your answers for Milestone 1 in Chapter 2 will change through this process, in particular in understanding what you need and want in terms of a university and those factors you evaluated. This comes from self-reflection coupled with knowledge. The more you know, the more educated and enlightened you become, the more you can take that information and draw conclusions from it based on your own self-reflection. This leads to a solid List.

IMPORTANT!

I always send this letter (or a version of it) to parents before I send out the Long List to my families. It gives you an idea of what the purpose of the Long List is—that the "whole" schools on it are not as important as the parts. Once the student can start to identify parts—aspects and specifics that are of interest—the easier and more fruitful a Short List becomes.

Dear Parent,

I often get this question as I deliver the Long List to my clients: "How do you come up with a Long List and what does it mean for my child/for us?" Great question—and I want to share my answer with you. The more you and your child can know and become knowledgeable about this process and how "Admissions" works, the better. There is so much information to impart, absorb and learn throughout this process (I find I am still teaching my students up until application submission and beyond) that it's impossible to get it all out in just a few emails or meetings.

First, the start of a Long List is a real mix of schools with at least a few factors that I think could pertain to the student. *I want my students to start learning how to research universities and to start forming opinions, thinking about things they have never consid-ered before, and sharing thoughts and questions—with you, with their teachers, with me. Like anything that is abstract at the start, this begins to put more concrete thoughts and ideas to the end goal. The typical response of "I think it's a good school" or "I like the cam-pus" won't help students find and get into the school that is the best fit for them. So, for you, I did what I do with all of my students: We have our initial conversation/s and meeting/s and I take lots of notes, including reviewing various factors involved in university (for exam-ple, class size, weather, location, etc.) and getting to understand the student better. I then dig into my trove of knowledge and experience and come up with a selection of schools that might appeal to the student. In some cases it's based on student life and campus cul-ture. In other cases it's based on type of curriculum and academics. It can also be based on programs, attention to specific needs and/or specific interests the student has. The idea is to get a good mix of institutions to begin with so you have lots of factors to evaluate and dissect.*

Second, this is just a starting point. *The list will start to grow and then with time it will start to narrow itself down. It's possible that not one of the universities that started on the List remains. That's one hundred percent acceptable and possible. The idea is to get the student (and parents) thinking, exploring, opening up their minds to all the possibilities out there, so they can then begin to formulate opinions and questions, as their understanding increases, as to what might be a better fit for them over another.*

It's critical that this "List" starts to become populated with the student's own ideas as he/she does more research and learns more about what will be a fit for him/her, individually.

Third, there are so many outstanding universities out there! *And they are all so unique and have their own strengths and personalities. Don't limit yourself to the 10 that everyone talks about. This sets up the student and family for disappointment and, frankly speaking, those 10 that everyone talks about are not the 10 best universities. Commit to developing a List that is true to the student and is not the same as everyone else's.*

Finally, it's important to understand how college Admissions work in various countries, *why we only hear of a handful of universities, what rankings are all about (and how numbers are manipulated in myriad ways to affect the rankings—it's shameful in many cases) and sharing through the process some "cases" I have had in years past to show you just how arbitrary (and without reason) the process can be, and therefore why we must be thoughtful in how we develop the List.*

Sincerely, Jennifer

So, while I will not be making your Long List for you, the secret is out: you can and will do it for yourself just as well. Here's how it works:

1. First, you'll need resources.

Books and Guides

    a. *The Fiske Guide to Colleges*

    b. *Colleges That Change Lives*

    c. *The College Finder*

    d. *US College & University Reference Map*

    e. *Creative Colleges*

    f. *The Making of a Student Athlete*

    g. *K&W Guide to Colleges for Students with Learning Differences*

Websites

    a. https://www.unigo.com

    b. https://campustours.com

    c. https://collegesupports.com (for finding colleges specific to learning differences)

    d. The College Navigator: https://nces.ed.gov/collegenavigator

People

    a. College counselor

    b. College representatives that visit your high school

    c. Professional associate websites, social media and affiliated campus charters (for example, for interior design, look at https://www.ASID.org and their affiliated campus charters)

    d. Admissions officers: EGI when done properly will help you to draw up your List

e. Alumni from your high school who attend schools you might be interested in

f. Teachers

2. Second, I'll ask you to work on Worksheet 3.2 now. You will need at least an hour to complete this and may want to do so together as a family. Please complete this fully before moving on.

★ ★ ★ ★ ★

3. Third, each Case Study in the book has a corresponding Long List found in the Conclusion. You get the Short List in each Case Study. But what did the student start out with on their Long List? Please see the Conclusion for these examples to give you an idea of the very different types of students, needs, wants, personalities, interests correspond to a very wide range of Long Lists.

4. Finally, it's time to create your own Long List on Worksheet 3.1. Commit to these criteria as you draft your Long List...and refer back to the letter I send to families if you're tempted to skip one of my criteria below. It's critical you follow each point.

Critical Guidelines for Developing your Long List

• Start with 20–30 universities. You will use the guides to get you started with options.

• Have at least 15 different US states represented on your Long List.

• Have at least three regions represented on your Long List: East Coast US, West Coast US, Middle America. Use the suggested map from your Library to gauge.

• At least 50% of your Long List should consist of names of colleges you have never heard of. Critical!

• Use Worksheet 3.2 to help you determine initial colleges that might make your Long List. This is not scientific and need not be overly precise. Remember my letter above and remember that you have yet to be guided on how to research each college!

• Have at least five universities with over 10,000 students (undergraduates), five with 5,000–9,000 undergraduates and five with fewer than 5,000 undergraduate students.

• Have at least 10 research universities and at least 10 liberal arts colleges.

• If you specified a geographic area (remember your factors exercise from Chapter 2), make sure you have at least five institutions *outside* of this area.

Please draft your Long List of approximately 25 universities in Column 1 in Worksheet 3.1. This will take days or weeks to complete, amounting to several accumulated hours.

★ ★ ★ ★ ★

Once you have this completed, you may move on to Milestone 2.

IMPORTANT!

I sent out a Long List to a new client of mine. He is Korean, lives in Southeast Asia and is smart, funny, creative and just a lovely human being. His parents, too, are warm, reasonable, realistic and grateful. So, when they came back to me after Joe reviewed his initial Long List, as you have done in this chapter, with their own Long List theirs included every brand-name you've heard of and they asked that these, too, be added. Joe will not get into those schools and in fact they are not a good fit for him. It was because we had the long discussion already about creating a balanced list and the "chances" of getting into one of the most highly selective universities in the country that prompted my surprise at receiving their list. Luck plays such a huge part and that's for those who generally have near perfect grades, test scores and national awards. Joe does not have any of those. But I was not totally surprised because it often happens at this stage. Even if a family and a student understand intellectually how the process works, understand that some above average grades and very average test scores, some involvement in school and outside of it, will not make their son or daughter a candidate for those brand name, always-talked-about institutions, they still make it on to the List. Months from now they will come off the List but right now they are on there and they are not realistic. This is where I reiterate how the process works with families and where I also start to ask them to define for themselves where every school on their List falls in terms of creating a rounded, realistic List. That means this: Which would be a "reach" for you as an individual candidate? Where do you stand less than 10% chance in your mind, after assessing requirements, profile and statistics, of being admitted? Ultimately, when you come down to your Short List, you should have one or two of these on your List. At the other end of the spectrum is the "likely" school, where you expect to have a more than 80% chance of being admitted, looking at the same aspects and considering your fit. When the time comes to prepare the Short List, I like my students to have two or three of these. And these are schools that my students would be delighted to attend; they are not schools that get added on at the end of the day to fill the quota of having a "likely" school on the List. Then there is that sweet spot center—the "in range" schools where you would stand a strong chance of being admitted and where you really fit. By the time you get to your Short List, you'll know what these schools are and they should make up the bulk of your List. For now, however, take a look at your Long List and do an initial gauge—an honest one as you're only fooling yourself if you don't—of where each lies in the spectrum: "likely" to "in-range" to "reach".

Milestone 2: Researching Your Long List

So, you've developed a Long List of over 20 universities by now. It took a while but is the basis for your research and developing an ultimately well-rounded list of universities to which you will apply.

Researching is critical. Not only is this Milestone not accomplished in one day or one week, it is ongoing…until you commit to your final, final Short List in several chapters to come. I don't need to tell you, then, how important it is to learn how to research a university and record your feedback.

There are two main parts to researching universities:

1. Knowing how to research, which you will do by referring to Worksheet 3.3.

2. Keeping record of your research, which you will do now and continue to do in Worksheet 3.4, following the explicit instructions on what to research now and what to research later. You will use your Long List as reference, of course.

With this approach you can plan to confirm your Short List anywhere from June to September. It's a process and will take time. And, the beauty of keeping your notes here in this book is that you have your how-to and your ongoing research work in the same place.

- Please go to Worksheet 3.3 and review it thoroughly now. It explains why and how you are going to research. When finished, please return here and go on.

IMPORTANT!

You've read about the importance of creating a balanced List. One factor will be identifying adroitly which schools on your Short List are "likely", which are "in-range" and which are "reach". The other important dimension to creating a viable, realistic and ultimately successful Short List will be to make it unique and based on strategy. A unique List means that your List is not the same as everyone else's in your school or region. Not only should you not be following or applying to all of the same schools—which shows you have not really done your work on this hugely important process in your life—but you should be finding schools that don't make it onto others' lists. This leads to a strategy. Your strategy should be to identify schools that are not only a fit for you based on what we've discussed and will continue to discuss but that will also give you the opportunity to be a very unique candidate to this school. I make sure this is the case with all of my students' Lists—fit comes first and from those that could be a fit determining which (these are usually the ones that my clients have never heard of but that we are well aware of in the US by name) could present a very strategic win-win for my students: that the student sees this college as being a fit for them and that the college sees my student as someone they would love to have on campus. This year one of my students in Manila found Kalamazoo to be a great fit for herself; she was the only applicant from her school as it turns out. She also was awarded a USD$26K four-year scholarship to the college. Win-win.

★ ★ ★ ★ ★

- Please go to Worksheet 3.1. You'll start with one university and work your way through. For now, choose one to tackle today.

- Now turn to Worksheet 3.4, and:

  - understand what you are looking for in each university you research;

  - pay attention to how to record your feedback;

  - keep a record of everything you review! You'll be amazed at the need for this; believe me when I tell you that without recording you're wasting your time. You simply will not recall everything you reviewed, what you felt, at which college it was, etc., as you move forward.

Now you will spend some serious time going through Worksheet 3.1 My Long List and filling out a Research Page for every university. Please note that this will take several hours/days to complete.

It is critical to keep up with the timeline! You will be coming back to this Milestone throughout this period, working on this while continuing to move through the Milestones that follow. Please make sure that you have them all completed by the end of this time period as per your Individual Timeline.

IMPORTANT!

The questions you're posing in your Research Pages may very well turn into EGI—something you may pointedly and directly ask an Admissions officer via email in the near future. By the way, I do not have my students—except those who have issues with their general requirements and as I noted earlier in Chapter 2—begin their EGI writing to Admissions officers until Chapter 4. Admissions officers at this stage are still knee-deep in Admissions decisions and enrollment management for the class ahead of you. Get them while they are fresh, not while they're tired and could potentially be annoyed by your too-eager (?) requests.

Milestone 3: Standardized Testing Plan

Even if you end up applying to many universities that do not require standardized tests or have a test-optional plan (you can submit something else or nothing else in lieu of standardized test scores), you *do* need to have a standardized testing plan.

- Do not plan to take both tests—the ACT and SAT. Choose one and choose strategically in order to prepare for one test.

- Do try to get all of your testing done by your junior/penultimate year where and when possible. This allows for a lot more freedom, flexibility and "one thing less to do" in your senior year.

- Try to take a diagnostic that will help you gauge the best test for you. A diagnostic can be helpful both in giving you the opportunity to try out both tests and see which one you prefer, while also giving you an idea of which one you could perform more strongly in. Don't prepare before taking the diagnostic.

- Take a full practice test in each and have it evaluated. This is an alternative to taking a diagnostic, although it's more time consuming and should be properly assessed/evaluated. Remember, though, at this stage you're taking a diagnostic or practice test to determine which test you really prefer, not for the score.

  Sample tests to take:

  SAT: https://collegereadiness.collegeboard.org/sat/practice/full-length-practice-tests

  ACT: http://www.actstudent.org/testprep/

- Plan on taking the test you have chosen *twice* as you set up your schedule. Few of my students take it once—meaning that they are satisfied with their first score (and are fairly strong test-takers)—and few of my students take it more than twice. Statistically speaking, improvement from the second to the third time of taking a standardized test is minimal at best and many times a student will dip; it's also expensive. Ideally, you plan this out so that you can take the test without a huge gap between the two sittings. For instance, the ACT is offered in April and June internationally in most countries and I often—depending on students and what they have in terms of schoolwork (always a priority) and life—recommend this as they can prepare for the April test starting in February and then do some brush-up work (no need to take another course here if you've done one already and worked hard throughout) on your own for the June test.

- Plan on either paying for a very good, ethical, experienced test prep tutor/class that will prepare you about 6–8 weeks out leading right up to the test (this could be face-to-face, one-on-one or through Skype in many cases) or committing to self-preparation if you feel you are capable. When in doubt, ask around. No one can guarantee an increase in scores or even guarantee a certain score. If a test prep center is doing so, move on.

IMPORTANT!

I have a few of my own favorites for test prep and they took me a long time to suss out and find. There are way too many prep centers who "do it all" and who make false promises, have inexperienced tutors and doctor their results. No one is monitoring these prep centers for their validity and so parents and students can often be prey to the fearmongering, "we guarantee a certain score", in-your-face, expensive and often shameful test prep organizations. There are some out there that are fantastic. Like anything in life, dig deep. Ask questions. Talk to parents and students who have used them. Find out the background and experience of the teacher who will teach you. All of this information should be very readily available to you. If it's not, it's a red flag and move on.

- Avoid taking a test officially too soon "as practice" without studying for it. I've had students come to me who had already done this—"I wanted to give it a shot to see how I did"—and it turns out to be a waste of time, money, and it can affect your applications. Remember that some schools that end up on your Short List will require you to submit all scores for all tests taken. Go in with that mentality.

- Once you have gone through the steps to determine which test is right for you, **set up your standardized testing plan now on your Personalized Timeline Table 1.1**. Please insert that in your personalized Timeline at the front of the book.

- Set reminders by visiting either ACT or SAT for when registration opens for each test. This is critical. I cannot tell you how many students have been shut out of testing for their preferred dates due to trying to sign up later and the seats being full. This can happen unexpectedly, in particular in Asia. **Set up reminders** now.

- Policies on the possibility of canceling or deleting your scores on either test change and that's why I will direct you to their respective websites to see what the current policy is and to also encourage you to understand your rights as a student vis-à-vis your scores.

PARENT ADVICE

"Setting up your child with accommodations [for Learning Differences] for the SAT or ACT internationally: If we were doing it again, I would start this process much, much earlier. Luckily our children scored well the first time around as we did not leave enough time between applying for accommodations and the date when applications were due. Give yourself plenty of time as the accommodation process can be quite lengthy and varies by ACT and SAT and in terms of where you live and what school your child attends (e.g., if there is a formal testing center for accommodations in your country; if your school has a person dedicated to this and recognized by ACT or SAT)."

—Jacquie, Singapore

IMPORTANT!

Learning Differences? This is the part of the process when you want to be educating yourself on LD accommodations for students offered at universities throughout the US. The website: https://www.collegewebld.org is a fantastic resource for this. Unfortunately, there is a stigma associated with Learning Differences in some countries, making it very difficult to seek the appropriate resources for your specific Learning Difference. Worse, a student may not get an LD diagnosed for fear of social stigma. Horrific. I believe this is changing, but too slowly. In the US, an LD is not a stigma. Depending on the student, some will self-report an LD during the application process and some will not. For now, it's important that your diagnosis is up-to-date and that you know, as the student, what accommodations you need now and will need in the future at your university. Accommodations range very widely and just stating that "we accommodate students with LD" won't be enough. You need to find out the level of accommodation and how it's granted and in what forms vis-à-vis your LD. The key here is knowing your own LD and what you need and then getting versed on the myriad levels of accommodation at universities throughout the US and which will be right for you. It's an added layer of work but one that, for my LD kids, goes with the territory and is a part of their lives.

 IELTS/TOEFL. If you're in a non-English educational system, you can pretty much bet on the fact that you'll have to take one of these tests for admission to all of your universities. That's not to say it's a guarantee. Like anything in this process, take everything on a case-by-case basis. If English is not your first language, I'd like you to *put IELTS/TOEFL into your Timeline as part of the process,*

something you're likely to have to take. Indeed, I have many students who are in international schools or local schools in a country where English is an official language of that country, but in order to know for certain if a university will require you to take the TOEFL/IELTS or not, you must check in with the university. And, since at this point you don't know where you'll be applying, you don't know the answer to this yet. Following my ideal of finishing testing where and when possible before senior year, plug this into your timeline at a time that will work for you. This will be a requirement I'll ask you to review for certain once we move into your Short List.

Milestone 4: Meeting With Your Guidance Counselor

Some students tell me at this stage that they "are not allowed" to meet with their Guidance Counselor yet. I find that troubling but also understand that many counselors are overwhelmed with the numbers of students they have to manage and, in their defense, are very much overworked in this area. For those students who "are allowed" to meet with their counselor at this point, make an appointment. I like to have my students make an appointment or stop in and introduce themselves, share with their counselor where they are in the process and what they are thinking at this stage ("Yes, I'll be applying to the US."), and to ask how to stay informed of upcoming campus visits by Admissions officers if it's not posted on the school's website.

In fact, some schools ask that juniors not attend visits by university Admissions officers until they are seniors. I find this difficult to understand and have told many students to go and sit in on an information session, take notes and ask any relevant questions—and take the visiting Admissions officer's business card to write a thank you—in their junior year. Sometimes they are hesitant as some international school cultures, in particular the more competitive ones, dissuade juniors who try to attend these meetings. This is foolish and you should not be swayed by others.

IMPORTANT!

Along the lines of what you've just read, I said to a student recently who told me that he would not go to a university rep's visit for fear of social repercussions, "And so that will prevent you from understanding a university that sits on your Long List and whose Admissions officer will be in town next week, from whom you can learn a load more than just off the website and not wait until senior year to do so?" He sheepishly agreed and although he was nervous to attend the meeting, he finally did.

Milestone 5: Confirming Courses for Rest of High School

If you're not in the IB program or taking A-levels where you have by now most likely determined your courses for the final two years of your high school career, now is the time to review and confirm with your GC and family what courses you're going to take up until you graduate and why. Keep in mind the factors, discussed in Chapter 2, that are critical to take into account as you determine final year courses.

I have advised students from all over the world and, as you would expect, there are very different systems from one country to the next. With New Zealand's national curriculum, for instance, I have found that many of my students are lacking social sciences or lab sciences and foreign language courses that will be required or highly recommended by US universities. In cases like these, sometimes students are able to adjust their courses to align with the general requirements reviewed in the previous chapter, and which I aim for all of my students to have by graduation:

4 years English

4 years Math

3 years Science (laboratory)

3 years Social Sciences

3–4 years Foreign Language

In some cases this is not possible. In these cases, I will have students get in touch with Admissions at schools early—the schools on their Long List that they may not even be applying to eventually—to get a sense of how Admissions handles cases like theirs. I also have them look at appropriate online courses from accredited online high schools if they are lacking in any of the general requirements. Sometimes by taking an online course—if you cannot take it with your school or at a local community college—can also show initiative, maturity and direction on the part of the student. It goes without saying that taking a course additional to the general requirements or the student's program would go above and beyond. I'm not saying this is necessary but in the case of some of my students—I have one now who is a math whiz and wants to study mathematics—he chose to pursue an online, accredited math course as part-hobby, part-passion, and partly to show his intention.

Milestone 6: Social Media Clean-up

I don't need to tell you that you should be cleaning up social media...regardless of your university applications or not...as you move into adulthood. But I will.

Please make a list of all of the social media you use or have used (the latter may still be active and accessible by the public) here:

———————————— , ———————————— , ———————————— ,

———————————— , ————————————

Now go ahead and start to clean up your social media presence. Change privacy settings where necessary, and where comments by friends or by you can be seen by the public, erase all photos, words, symbols, and so on, that could be offensive to someone or show the less thoughtful side of you. You don't need to—and certainly shouldn't— create a new site of perfect selfies or you surrounded by volumes of books. But do go in and clean up. I'm often amazed at the comments my students' friends put on their accounts—rude, offensive, stupid, even racist…I could go on. Aside from reconsidering that friendship, block that friend from opining or make a regular effort of deleting their comments.

Will a university really look at your social media accounts? Yes. And, of course, it depends on the situation. Maybe one evening after a visiting Admissions officer meets with you and your classmates they go and check you all out to see your accounts. Maybe during the Admissions committee meeting one of the members is charged with reviewing each candidate that comes up. Perhaps before interviews—in particular Skype ones—the Admissions officer will see what your social media says about you. So, don't ignore this. Clean up your online presence. This is something that *you should put in your Personalized Timeline Table 1.1 to revisit in the months ahead.*

Milestone 7: Upcoming Break and Summer Plans

This is a time when I ask all of my students and their families to start to think about their ideas, options, and considerations for break and summer plans. There are some very important aspects to determining what you will do over your breaks, some of which we've already discussed and some we will cover now, but all are critical as you determine what is right for you:

- Don't do something over the break if it's solely for the purpose of "looking good" on a college application. It won't.

- Do make sure you are doing something both productive and relevant over your breaks, this year in particular. Sitting around or sleeping in all day will not fare well, either for your development or for your college applications.

- Do something that speaks to you—this means something that you're genuinely interested in doing, reflects your passions or interests, and will teach you something relevant to you. Too many students end up doing college courses on a "known" university campus, thinking this is the way to get into that college or its homologue. Not the case. In fact...

- Think outside of the box. Some of the best plans students have made they've created on their own. Following on from the discussion in Chapter 2, look at your passions and interests—something I'll ask you to do in this Milestone and Worksheet 3.5. Break Plans: Ideas and Opportunities, Survey—and think about how you can build on them. It does not have to be related to your major (unless you are considering engineering or already know of a very specific major you want to pursue, such as journalism or veterinary/medical studies, as graduate work) but it should be related to you, building on what you know and related to what you want to learn more about.

- While it may be easy to do for some of you, don't go for the internship your parents can get for you in one of their offices because it's easier and "gives you office experience". I've never met anyone who came out strong in an application or interview because they had great office experience. Yes, maybe they did "have great office experience", but there was something else that impacted me.

- Make it last. Don't go for the quick one-week internship. If you can, do something that has more meaning and that can give you more depth.

- Your break plans should have the following components:

  - It should provide you with meaningful experiences.

  - It does not have to be "organized" or "paid for" (let's make that "should not be 'paid for'", except in very unique circumstances).

  - The more you can create and help design what you want to get out of it, the better for all and for your outcome.

  - There should be an outcome—whether it's a project, an experiment, a written piece or an experience—the outcome should be something you can talk about clearly.

  - It should be something you can really get involved in and perhaps has opportunities beyond once you're there. One-dimensional plans won't give you much depth and breadth and are usually quite boring. Which brings me to...

  - It should be fun.

- Plan ahead. Please take this time now to complete Worksheet 3.5: Break Plans: Ideas and Opportunities, Survey.

Once you've successfully gone through this Milestone and its related Worksheet, you will have some solid ideas to pursue for your upcoming break/summer plans. Nice work! I'll ask you to get moving on them so that by the next chapter you can confirm what you're going to do.

Milestone 8: Adding to Your Long List

Indeed, by the end of this chapter you've finished researching your original Long List. Now's the time to make sure that there's been an organic development of the universities on that List since you created it from Milestone 1. Go ahead and adjust that, add to it, keep it dynamic and do the appropriate research for those universities that you've added since. Add at least 10 more to Worksheet 3.1: Your Long List, and research as you did the initial 20–30 universities. Do not cross any off your list yet. We will get to that in the next chapter.

However, please do keep this in mind: your ultimate Short List should reflect who you really are, your character, personality and interests. You should be able to "argue" why you are a fit for each university on your List. Do you fit into the college profile? Can you figure out your niche at these schools? What will the schools give you and what will you give back to them and their community? All of this and more will need to be answered in the upcoming months...by you.

IMPORTANT!

Don't fight who you are. It's also at this stage in the process when I find many students are thinking or hoping or pretending they are someone that they are not. I think this happens to all human beings at different phases of our lives and it's only normal. One student says he's smart, intellectual, wants rigor and a competitive drive on campus. He says he will flourish in a Stanford environment. I know, frankly speaking, that he will not. I'll let the student come to this conclusion, but it can take a long time. I'll ask you to try to be true to yourself from the get-go here. Fighting who you are usually stems from social pressures and expectations. You will eventually come to a head with this dilemma and when you realize the college you wanted to be a fit for you turns out most certainly not to be.

Being niche and adopting a merit-aid strategy: This ties in to strategy and creating a unique list. The more strategic you are—knowing yourself, your strengths and needs, where and how you will fit into each school by knowing the profile and school as best you can and by creating and developing an ultimate Short List that is unique to you and not to your neighbor—the more you are setting yourself up to be a niche candidate, showing the college that you are someone who they will want to have on their campus and as a life-long alumnus. And, in doing so, you're also adopting a merit aid strategy, setting yourself up for the possibility of receiving one. Merit aid, as we've discussed, is something that is determined by an individual Admissions office behind closed doors and based on that college's needs and wants for incoming students that year. You won't know what your colleges are looking out for to grant merit aid to the lucky ones. You'll only know if you receive it. Yet, that said, every year the majority of my students receive merit aid. They are full-pay students whom the college knows would be full-pay (let's face it, this is good for a college) yet the college is giving them scholarship money to attend because the college wants that student on their campus. The college has recognized that the student will bring something unique to their campus and they want that student so badly that they are offering scholarship money to get them to attend. More often these students of mine who receive merit aid are positioned in the top 25% of the applicant pool; this means these are usually schools that fall within their "likely" qualification or "in-range" but the school is nary on another student's list from that high school, region or country. This all comes down to what we've discussed and what I've highlighted: don't fight against who you are, know yourself; be realistic and create a balanced list; choose schools that are not on everyone's list; and know and articulate how you'll be a fit with that school and what you'll bring to the community. Creating a unique list means you will probably also be a unique candidate to that school and unique—or niche—candidates can really stand out and be wanted, to the point of being offered thousands of dollars to attend, and having the prestige of being a scholarship recipient.

Another resource to check out here is bigfuture.collegeboard.org (although more helpful for US citizens that non-US citizens, there is a section on merit aid.)

Milestone 9: Update Your CV

While this Milestone looks to be brief, it may take some time. When was the last time you updated your CV? Time to refresh your memory of when you last did and update your activities, accomplishments, interests and involvement appropriately. Keep this fresh and as updated as you can. You'll be surprised how much your CV—and certainly a continually updated one—will come in handy.

IMPORTANT!

Niche students: For those of you who are decidedly niche applicants—this means that you'll be aiming to play sports competitively at a university (D1, 2 or 3),2 perhaps play an instrument with the intention of this someday being your profession, or focus on art or acting not just as a major but also as a potential profession—your work is going to become twofold at this stage. It's imperative that you are keeping an appropriate portfolio and separate CV based on your talent (and how that is done will depend on your area—a great book for this is Creative Colleges) continually updating this as you create, design, accomplish, and "do". Most of you will have to turn in a separate CV, portfolio, website and perhaps go in for live auditions or meetings with administration, professors and/or coaches. For the athletes, this is your time to start reaching out directly to coaches. Don't depend on them to find you. One of my good friends and a long-time D-1 football/soccer coach used to tell me that there was no way he and his staff could cover the world recruiting and so much would depend on the student's initiative to start the communication. Ultimately, that communication—whether it's with coaches or faculty or administration—will be one of the major deciding factors in your Admissions criteria as well.

I'll close the chapter with this quote from The Washington Post.[3] Nick Anderson writes, "Of all college statistics, the admission rate might be the most misleading…The admission rate looks straightforward enough: Admission offers divided by applications. But, what is an offer, and what is an application?"

---

[2] This is NCAA jargon—The National Collegiate Athletic Association, a behemoth of an organization that has jurisdiction over the majority of competitive, collegiate athletics in the US. There are three divisions—1, 2, 3—and each are very distinct in terms of their competition, how they recruit, if they offer scholarships, etc. There are other associations for athletes as well such as NAIA.

[3] Anderson, Nick. "College admission rates for Class of 2018: an imperfect but closely watched metric" *Washington Post,* 3 April 2014. https://www.washingtonpost.com/local/education/college-admission-rates-for-class-of-2018-an-imperfect-but-closely-watched-metric/2014/04/03/820ff578-b6af-11e3-8cc3-d4bf596577eb_story.html?utm_term=.d1ce78314d2c

Worksheet 3.1: My Long List, Stage 1

1	2	3	4	5	6
My Colleges	Research Pages completed for this university?	Location	Type of program that might interest me	Another type of program that might interest me	Another type of program that might interest me

7	8	9	10	11	12
Comments by me (e.g., I don't like it because…I love it because…I need to ask them about…)	Requirements: SAT, ACT, Subject Tests, TOEFL/IELTS,…	Admissions standards	Questions by me about the university/program/fit/etc.	Why I think it could be a fit	Deadlines

It's important that you understand better than anyone where you stand and what your own criteria and standards will be as you create your Long List. Every guide suggested will reference these factors and will help you to gauge if you should add it to your Long List.

Part 1: Black and White—Basic Information

Please fill out this chart with your grades and scores per year over your last three years of high school (considering 11 Grade is your penultimate and current year).

	9 Grade	10 Grade	11 Grade (penultimate year) *star if on upward trajectory
Final year/current grades by subject			
Final exam/exam grades by subject where applicable			
Stand-out teacher comments, both positive and negative			
Standardized test scores (SAT, ACT, Subject Tests, TOEFL/IELTS)			
Predicted/final scores (IB, AP, A-levels) if applicable			

Five questions for the family:

1. Finances. Do you have a restriction on finances? _____ Will you be looking for "best buy" schools? _____ This can be a reality and it's important to confirm that now. Also, keep in mind that guides like *Fiske* list "best buy" schools.

2. Factors that you know won't change. Refer to Chapter 2, Milestone 1. List here. (E.g., *I absolutely hate and am miserable in the cold.*)_____, _____, _____, _____, _____

3. Geographical restrictions. Don't list here if it's not a true restriction. Remember that the best and most successful Short Lists will not be geographically specific. _____

4. Do you truly know what you want to study? This is generally "known" by future engineers by junior year. List here if you absolutely know._____ _____ (Note: Most students think they have an idea but the reality is that you don't know…and frankly speaking that's even better. Remember you're only 17, or around this age. My point is that you shouldn't know and college should be the open opportunity to figuring that out!)

5. Your high school. It's no secret that Admissions offices will have "rankings" or opinions of high schools—how those "rankings" work depends on the Admissions office but a hierarchy exists—in your city or country or region and this will affect your application.

When you've completed Part 1, go straight on to Part 2.

Part 2: Gray Area—Individual Reflections

By this point many students may have changed their mind on a lot of factors and discussion points from Chapter 2. Please consider and reflect on the following and fill in accordingly in the corresponding column to the right.

Potential career interests	
What do I think I want from a university education? (Connections? Collaborating with faculty? Exploring?…)	
What do I think I want from a university experience? (Greek life? Strong community? Building awareness? Developing passion? Competitive student body?…)	
Which factors did I evaluate in Chapter 2 that I still feel are most important?	

Which factors from Chapter 2 are still up in the air for me?	
What type of student am I?*	

———————

*For this last question, it will be up to you to determine what type of student the universities on your list have and if you "fit" that.

Worksheet 3.3: Enlightened Guide to Researching Your Long List

There is no right or wrong way to investigate universities at this stage; the idea is to start looking, feeling what piques your interest and what does not, and recording everything by following my guidelines.

These are the four steps to begin your investigation:

1. **Take your Long List.** This is a real mix of universities—size, geography, location, and so on. That's the point! (And, hopefully this will spark your curiosity to look at others. Excellent! Please record everything.)

    You've noticed that the "Long List" also has several columns for your input that I'll request you populate as you do your research in Chapter 4. Those columns will eventually be critical information for you if you apply. We'll get to them and the terms in Chapter 4.

2. Worksheet 3.4: Research Pages will give you **tips on what to look out for as you start to research universities**. (Later, you'll become an expert on this and know exactly what you want to be looking for in each university depending on what you've defined as right for you.) Use these guidelines as you start to research each university on your Long List and begin with the university's website. Choose one to begin with.

    Remember that you are looking here for style of university, factors that you like, don't like, want or don't want. *You may choose to look at the university as a whole but what we're trying to do is examine parts of the whole so that we can use your feedback to create a better idea of things you'd like and need and things you would not.*

    Your feedback will lead you to figuring out universities to add or take off the List and finding the right fit for you.

3. **Use the resources I suggest** in Milestone 1. There are others but these are the ones I have in my own library.

4. **Adopt a sense of freedom** when you're doing this and record everything and anything. You'll be amazed at what even a trivial observation can do as you go deeper into this process.

Reproduce several copies of this blank Worksheet for each college you research.

Fill out the following information:

Restate and *confirm what is important to you. Remember factors discussed and what you rate highly. Write them here:* _____

Research for University _____ **(place name of university here)**

1. **Your Fit** Refer to your factors above. Search for these at this school. Record your feedback here.

   Consider questions that pop up as you are researching this university. If you had a student who attends this university or an Admissions officer in front of you right now, what questions would you have for him?

2. **General** What's the size of the undergraduate population?

   What is the percent of international students?

   How many students live on campus in freshman year? All four years?

   What is the population of students like/student profile like?

Where is the campus located? What's the size of the town/city it is located in?

What type of campus is it? Enclosed? Spread out?

What unique programs have you found that could be of interest? (E.g.: types of majors, minors, unique double degree programs, honors programs, scholarship opportunities, etc.)

3. **Campus Life**   What do students do outside of the classroom? What types of activities are on offer that are of interest to you and what do a lot of students seem to engage in?

What type of campus culture does the school have?

Where do you see yourself fitting in, if anywhere, and how?

What do you see lacking at the school, if anything? Does this present a potential problem or a potential opportunity?

4. **Academics**   Review a major/majors that could be of interest to you. What courses would you take and in what years? What electives can you take?

Is there a core requirement of every student? If so, what is it? What does that mean you would have to take your first, second and beyond years?

What are professors in your area/s of interest doing? Name one professor who sounds very interesting to you. Why is he/she interesting to you?

What opportunities are there for internships and/or research with faculty within areas that interest you?

Can you design your own major? Does that interest you?

Do you have an LD? What types of accommodations do you receive or will you need to receive? Does this school accommodate and to what extent?

5. **Other**   Follow whatever else interests you. Record anything and everything. I would like you to share this with your family regularly.

Please answer the following questions:

1. What are your priorities? We've discussed this earlier and it's critical: Is having a job and making money over your breaks something that is non-negotiable? Is taking care of a family member something that will occupy your breaks? Please list here those things you truly have no choice on doing during your breaks:

2. Considering the above, let's assume you have time to engage in a break/summer activity. What are your interests—both academic and outside of the classroom? (You may want to refer to Chapter 2, Worksheet 2.1: Self-assessment for Student and Parents.)

3. Is there anything you really want to learn or want to do during your break? (E.g.: writing poetry, learning a new code, volunteering with the mentally ill, or learning photography and developing your own prints.)

4. Is it possible to link what you wrote in 2 and 3 with a project over the break? Do you know of organizations or people with whom you could connect to discuss opportunities for internships or volunteering? What/who are they and how would you connect with them? Please connect with them appropriately.

5. Have you spoken with anyone in your school—teacher, coach, administrator, and so forth—who is connected to your interests/passions and who may have ideas of where and what to pursue for your break/summer plans? Who are they? Please send them an email to set up a time to meet to discuss.

Putting yourself out there—you'll find—will bring a whole lot back. Starting to engage in this practice now will help you rely on yourself and your fearless attitude of putting yourself out there at university as well.

Once you've gone through 1–5 above you should have some leads and potential opportunities to pursue. Please list them here with contact information and notes on follow-up.

CHAPTER 4

Your Goldilocks Moment

February, March, April

School is ramping up and you're busier than you've ever been. You're joining and leading clubs, going for extra help before and after school, doing sports, music or what you love outside of the classroom and have loads of homework. Thinking about university for some of you seems far from a priority. Many of you are attending high schools where the focus right now is not on applying to university but instead on grades and being active in your community. For those of you in high schools where suddenly the tide has shifted and everyone has a new rumor to spread about university Admissions, this has suddenly altered the momentum of high school as you knew it and it's an added stress. Regardless of your situation, you need to manage it by doing just the right amount for college Admissions. These are your Goldilocks moments—not too little, not too much, just the right amount.

More than anything, this is the stage in the process where I want you to be working on self-assessment, beginning or continuing your review of universities and focusing one hundred percent in classes and pursuing passions outside of the classroom. Some critical questions as you sit here reading this and thinking about your "right now":

- Are you being genuine with yourself?
- Are you doing what you want to do and approaching this process with your true self showing and shining?

Or...

- Are you doing what you think should be done and going through the motions, not exploring what is important to *you* but instead what you think is important to others?

- Equally paralyzing, are you lazing around, saying to yourself and others (as one of my students wrote to me today), "I'm just not a leadership kind of person"? I responded to the student by saying this: Don't do it for the applications. Do it for yourself. Have you ever dared try being a leader? Step out of the comfort zone of safety and not working too hard and try; usually you find that if you hadn't done it, you would have been disappointed in yourself looking back.

Remember that this is not a game. It's an important process of life. Everything I stress to you as being important will not only strengthen your applications and help you find your best fit university, but will also give you tools and experiences, character-building opportunities and discoveries that you'll go back to, depend on, use, and reflect upon as you go through the rest of your life.

On that note, let's focus on just the right amount in this chapter. Here are your Milestones that you'll need to complete before moving forward:

 Milestone 1: Factors [in a university that are most important to me]

 Milestone 2: Long List Research, Stage 2

 Milestone 3: EGI: Efforts of Genuine Interest

 Milestone 4: Look Who's Coming to Town

Milestone 5: Confirming Break Plans

 Milestone 6: Considering Recommenders and How

Case Study

Name: Maya

Gender: Female

Country: Philippines

Nationality: Japanese

Started process: 3.5 months prior to submissions (she did not do any Early submissions)

Program/Rigor: IBDP (HL: Economics, French, History; SL: Biology, English Literature, Mathematics)

Grades to date: Predicted 41

Standardized tests to date: SAT three times with highest composite reaching 1550

Subject Tests: Biology, French with Listening, World History.

TOEFL/IELTS: Not necessary

Challenges: Maya is lovely. Intelligence—both emotional and intellectual—oozes out of Maya the first time you meet her. She is a very smart young woman, yet motivated when she wants to be! Clearly, she self-motivates—you can see this in her work and activities. However, she started the process very, very late and ultimately decided not to go for any "Early" applications. A procrastinator, Maya certainly waited until the last minute. I was worried about her not taking advantage of any Early Admissions opportunities, considering how many highly selective institutions she had on her final list.

Strengths: Active member of a band and community service. Very strong grades and test scores. A very enthusiastic young woman, Maya is fun, smart and energetic. Anytime I was vexed by her not getting something in to me, as soon as we met or spoke, she made me smile. It was all genuine and you could not help but enjoy being in Maya's presence. She is also quite aware of herself and her strengths and weaknesses. Maya is a very smart writer.

Fit/Factors: An intellectually stimulating place with open-minded and energetic (physically and mentally) students. Maya was quite sure she wanted to study public health policy, yet as we got deeper into the process—as deep as one can go in a few months—she became more "flexible" in the program she was looking for; a positive sign in my view as she was learning her options as she went through and realizing there were a lot out there. Location—urban/suburban—and diversity were high on her "factors for fit" list, along with class sizes and course offerings.

Interests: Public health and policy, writing. Community service.

Essay topic: Maya wrote of being a bully as a little kid and how that came back to bite her as she moved countries and cultures and struggled to fit in, finding herself at the other end. This affected her life greatly and how she chose to get through it—essentially by becoming a more involved community member and helping those who are less fortunate.

(continued)

Short List: UCSD, UCLA, Boston University, Tufts, Northwestern, Barnard, University of California-Berkeley, Cornell, Columbia, University of Pennsylvania.

Interviews: The few from her Short List that offered them.

Visits: None.

EGI: Not thoroughly and was quite late in the game getting to this.

Dream school, if any: Maya didn't really have a number 1 "dream school", which is not a negative thing. She was excited about all of those on her Short List.

Application strategy: Maya decided she was not going to apply Early to any of the schools on her list, against my advice. That said, she was not convinced of one university that would fit an "ED" applicant and part of that perhaps was also due to starting late in the process and not having time to assess and prepare for such, even a university that offered a restrictive "Early Action".

MAYA'S ADVICE

"I think I would have definitely started the process much earlier if I could do it again and have considered applying Early—but at the end of the day I was not convinced of "one" university and many had ED, so that was not going to fit me. I will say that when I finally made my decision, it was based on this process and knowing what was a fit for me and not for anyone else. Don't forget those factors—they really impacted me up until I had to decide on where to go by May 1."

MILESTONES

Milestone 1: Factors [in a university that are most important to me]

At this stage, you'll want to revisit the factors in a university that you feel are most compelling to you and are what you will be looking for and feel you want and need.

At this stage I normally meet with my students once or twice per month. At the start of each meeting I ask (in this instance, Maya), "Maya, tell me what's most important to you in a university at this stage?" (And, for those of you who want to know what is important for Maya at this stage—and which may change a bit as we get closer to determining her Short List—her responses follow.)

So, I will ask you to do the same at this point, something I will ask you to confirm in the next chapter as you move from a Long List to a Short List. In essence, you'll be defending your fit. Please go to Worksheet 4.1: Confirming My Factors for University Fit.

★ ★ ★ ★ ★

Finishing Worksheet 4.1 will be key to moving on to the next Milestone. Do not jump around. Remember that this is a Milestone because it has an impact on the process.

Milestone 2: Long List Research, Stage 2

You'll need time for this Milestone and that includes concentration and energy. This is an important stage for your Long List as it's the final stage before you turn your Long List into your Short List. As this is a multi-layered Milestone, I'll guide you through it.

Worksheet 4.2: Your Long List, Stage 2 continues the work you did on your Long List from Chapter 3. You'll be completing columns 1–11 in this Milestone for all of the universities on your Long List. Here's my advice on how to attack each column:

Column from Worksheet 4.2	Advice
2. Rank	How would you rank this university now based on the rest of your List? Don't be overly precise but start to gauge where it would fall for you.
3. Resources utilized	I often have students "finishing" their research in a rather one-dimensional way. When I ask them to name their resources for me—think of this as your Extended Essay (EE) for those of you in International Baccalaureate (IB) needing primary sources, or for those of you writing research papers and needing to cite sources—a blank look comes over their faces and they tell me sheepishly, and only realizing their mistake in that moment, that they used the college's website. Only. I expect you to use *at least four resources* for each college as you research your Long List. Here is where you can remind yourself which ones you used as you justify to yourself why a college is going to remain on or leave your Long List in the near future. Again, don't shortcut this as it will only work against you. You're not playing against anyone but yourself.
4. Requirements	What are the requirements for the application to this university? What is highly recommended yet not required? Write these down.
5. Candidate Profile	What does the college tell you they look for in a candidate? What type of grades? Test scores? What about experiences or mindset? You can find this out from a college. And, if you cannot for some reason, mark this with a question mark. This may be something you choose to use as EGI in the very near future. And, yes, you can ask an Admissions officer this question!

6. What this university has that I want	Go back to Milestone 1.
7. What this university has that I need	Go back to Milestone 1.
8. Supplement essays and questions	Most universities will not have their supplement essays and questions published until the summer months—June, July and August. However, at this stage, it would be a great opportunity to look and see what was asked of applicants last year. I always ask my students to investigate this. The ones who are lazy and don't bother are always jolted when the supplement essays are eventually published for their year. Why skip this, then? Get a sense of what these universities are asking of their candidates as it will give you a very good idea of what they are looking for and if you like what you're being asked. Sometimes I'll have a student find out what they asked last year and not feel comfortable at all with the question—or vice versa, where they thought a college might be coming off their Long List and they took the time to review what the college asked of its applicants the year prior and *loved* it, compelling them to keep the university on through to their Short List and apply. So, do your work and find out. It's only going to work in your favor.
9. Specialty programs?	Does the college have any programs and scholarships you've seen or researched or come across that could be of interest to you? Do they have a separate application? What are they?
10. Reach, in range, likely?	Classify at this stage where each university on your Long List falls.
11. Will this university remain on my Long List today?	I am asking here if you've taken any off the Long List since this point in the process. If you have, remind yourself why and write that down. This is important for you to have as reference. Many times I've had it happen that a student will forget why they removed a university from their Long List, or they will be reminded later on as to why and then put it back on.

The last question here is critical: Which ones will you leave on the Long List? Which ones will you take away? Keep track of *why* you are taking any off the Long List and jot that down in the area provided.

IMPORTANT!

Continue to modify the Long List as you move through this time period. Keep your goal in mind: to develop a strategic, unique, thoughtful, balanced, "any of these will make me happy" Short List by the next chapter. You're not there yet and there's still lots of time to develop this. Make sure it's exhaustive.

Milestone 3: EGI: Efforts of Genuine Interest

"Efforts of Genuine Interest" (EGI) is, in fact, precisely what you think it means. While some counselors may call this "Demonstrated Interest", I prefer to be more direct in what it needs to incorporate: genuineness.

As we'll discover throughout the rest of this guide, EGI comes in many, many different forms, and you're going to express EGI in various ways. I'll include as a starter in the box below how those forms may look moving forward. But, as is always the case, this is personal and EGI for one student may look very different for another. But the very first EGI is the same for everyone and that is connecting with Admissions officers. Directly.

I can't begin to tell you how useful this particular EGI will be for you throughout the process if you engage in it genuinely from the start. In fact, I'll let my students tell you how and why it was so useful for them (see below). In the meantime, I'll go ahead and explain to you what your EGI intentions are at this stage:

1. To network. Yes, that's ultimately what this is and this is how you're going to do it. You're getting on someone's radar and introducing yourself. You're interested in them and their institution and hope they will someday be interested in you.

2. To share—in a subtle manner—some traits about you. Make this human and make this personal...but not too personal. See some of the examples that follow.

3. To ask questions you have and to seek answers you want and need. Refer to your Long List and Research Pages for this.

4. To begin to establish a "relationship". This will not be the first time you are in touch with this person and when you do need them in the future, it will be that much more beneficial to you—and more pleasant for them—to respond to someone they already know and who has made the effort early on (but not too early on...balance and moderation are key throughout this process...tread carefully).

Here are a few examples of EGI that I've taken from some of my students and my comments about why it was particularly good or what was lacking:

Dear Mr. Jameson,

I hope you enjoyed the rest of the summer. I know you will soon be enjoying some really nice Fall weather in [town], something I sure miss in Southeast Asia.

Comment: Reminding the Admissions officer of where he is.

I was incredibly impressed when I visited the [university] in July. It has so much to offer someone like me who is passionate about science but also has a lot of other academic interests, such as history and geography.

Comment: Reminding the Admissions officer that he made a visit to the university.

Comment: Sharing again his interests.

I am very interested in applying Early Decision to the [university], and I have some questions for you.

Comment: Giving a heads up that this uni is top of his list and he may in fact be applying ED.

1. I was really excited to learn more about the Fusion Science Center. This summer I was very fortunate to be able to visit CERN near Geneva when I was participating in the CERN summer programme. I hope to be able to pursue my interest in this area further when I am completing my undergraduate degree.

Comment: Connected a feature of the uni to something he did over the summer effectively and adroitly without just listing or "bragging".

2. I would like to know more about research opportunities at the [university]. Can you tell me more about funding for research? I would also like to know whether there are opportunities at the [university] to work collaboratively with industry. If so, can you give me some examples? If there are established programs, how hard is it to take part in them?

Comment: Shows a lot of things including eagerness, intellectual curiosity, needs, and specifics that will clearly allow this student to determine if this university is going to be his ED or not.

I look forward to hearing from you soon.

Comment: I would have liked Frank to write "Thank you very much for your time." or the like. Always thank them.

Regards,

Frank

frank@his.school.email

Class of 2018, School name and location/country

+mobile phone number

Here is another sample letter:

Dear Miss Martin,

My name is Patrizio and I am a junior at the [high school] in Barcelona, Spain. I am currently studying social sciences and liberal arts. I want to have the chance of studying in the US for university. I lived in San Francisco for three years where I completed 8th grade, my freshman and sophomore years. While researching universities I came across [your institution], and immediately it grasped my interest. I would really like to apply to your university this coming fall, and before doing so, if you don't mind I have a few questions:

- *Regarding the study abroad programs, I was looking for some insight on the specifics for requirements, student experiences and compatibility with students' majors?*

- *Regarding internships, I would like to know how this combines with a student's undergraduate studies, what types of internships are offered, and are they based on majors?*

- *Regarding possible interviews, I didn't find any information on interviews for international students, would that be a possibility?*

Thank you very much; I see that you travel and if you're ever in Europe it would be a pleasure to meet you.

Best regards,
Patrizio Lamont
Junior at [high school]
mobile: +34...

WORDS OF WISDOM: EMAILING FACULTY

One of my students, Rich, called me last week—he's in this very stage of the process—and asked me how he could effectively gauge the quality of a department in the academic arena he wishes to pursue. Rich happens to know what he wants to study, computer science and econometrics, and has determined that one of the most important factors for him in developing his List—one of his top "needs"—is the faculty and program itself in these academic areas. Aside from looking at the university websites and the programs offered, courses, and options for electives, he was looking for something more substantive.

I told him he has two options and I'd ask him to follow them in this order. Both are EGI.

First, he should contact his Admissions officer. *Who's that? I've never met them.* Well, time to introduce yourself. Just about every university Admissions office has a list of their staff somewhere for you to find. Sometimes these staff members are easily accessible with phone and email at your fingertips, along with which regions they cover, so you know exactly who will be reading your file and who you should be contacting with your EGI. Others are much more opaque, taking you through a convoluted path to find them. But, you will. It takes time. (See how both Patrizio and Frank did so in the examples covered earlier.)

So, Rich wrote an individual email to his Admissions officers at his Long Listed schools to ask a bit about these departments, if there were opportunities for undergraduate research and, if so, during which year and if there was any further information they could send to him. He made sure not to ask questions easily answered on the website.

The second step I told Rich to consider was to email the faculty. I only recommend this in certain cases and of course they need to be academically related, but here's why. A former Admissions officer at one of the country's most selective universities wrote this to me:

"When I was in XX Admissions there were times when some aspiring rocket scientist or musicologist found his/her way directly to a faculty member (maybe through a teacher, or more often through some external mentor). When this happened, the Admissions office inevitably heard from the faculty member in question, and if the professor liked what he/she saw, this kid would absolutely have a leg up in the process.

Occasionally the kid would simply have enough gumption to be in touch directly with a professor—and again, if the professor was favorably impressed, the kid had a better shot than someone who did not have faculty backing in the process.

So, if your student wants to reach out directly to a professor (or has someone external and legitimate to bring his case to the attention of a professor whose email can be easily found in the university directory online), I say go for it! The faculty contact has to be the "center of the bull's-eye—so if the kid has developed a water purification system, he should be in touch with the key professor in our department of Engineering/Public Health and not someone in the Classics Dept..."

Let's go to Worksheet 4.3 for EGI Record Keeping.

Write down the universities that you've decided to keep on your Long List from Worksheet 4.2. Now go and find the Admissions officer for your region and log that person's name and email address.

It's time now to consider EGI for your universities. This will take a while to do over the span of days and weeks.

IMPORTANT!

Remember that EGI should serve two important functions:
1. To get answers to questions you have and that are pressing to you; answers that you cannot find on the school's website.

2. To express or show something unique or compelling about you—by asking a question—as a candidate. This second function is more nuanced and of course requires you to be able to ask-something-while-showing with the right tone.

Here are some ways in which you may discover your EGI:

- *Candidate Profile question*: When you can't find this in your research—Column 5 from Worksheet 4.2—or you have questions about where you might fit in to the candidate profile, this could be a form of EGI. For instance, one of my students attends high school in a country that makes it very difficult for its students to take foreign language in the last two years. Yet, colleges will look for this on your transcript. He immediately wrote to the colleges on his Long List to ask about this discrepancy and if his application will be evaluated without the foreign language or if he should enroll immediately in an online course or a course at the local university.

- *Visiting your country or city*: Find out if your Admissions officer or the college will be visiting your country or city. (Don't email regarding this if your school has a list of visiting colleges or if it's posted on the university's website. This is poor strategy as it's like asking the question you know the answer to or should know the answer to. It won't get you far.)

- *A question you came up with during your research process*: One of my students is very interested in studying geology. He has discovered through doing research that he's very keen to study agriculture and environmental sciences. He is looking for courses on this and has found them in some of his universities but will ask if the others offer such programs or courses.

- *To request interviews* (such as Patrizio did earlier): This is not the stage in the process to request interviews and I will get to that in Chapters 5 and 6. However, by that time you will have established a "relationship" of sorts with your Admissions officer, making the communication both more at ease, more effective and more compelling at that stage. Trust me…you won't be disappointed if you follow my lead here.

Some poor examples of EGI (which are not genuine, don't pass muster and can in fact leave you with a red flag on your file):

- Not asking a question ("Hello! I really want to attend your university!").

- Asking a question that has an answer on the website ("Do you have Early Decision or Early Action?").

- Asking a silly question ("Do you take students from Turkey?").
- Asking a question that is clearly not one you care hearing the answer to. Admissions officers can read through any non-genuine script from students.

How to do EGI with your Admissions officer through email:

1. Find out the Admissions officer's name. Use his/her name, never misspell that name and find out if this person will go by "Mr." or "Ms.".

2. Be brief. Be prepared to write your email using bullet points. Your Admissions officer does not have that much time.

3. Introduce yourself—your name, where you attend school, what year you are in. Let them know you're excited about their school and why (but in a sentence!).

4. Ask them your questions. I always suggest you bullet them—it's much easier for them to read—and be concise and to the point.

5. Never, ever misspell words.

IMPORTANT!

Logan asked me today, as we were discussing his emails to Admissions officers, "And after all that research, what if I really don't have a question?" Don't force it. If you don't have a question, you don't have one. One will come up as you continue the process; and, when it does, ask it.

Logan then asked: "Do Admissions officers want me to tell them how much I love their university before asking them my questions or do I just go straight into my questions?" I told Logan to just be himself. If he is so excited about a university that it just comes out as he is writing, let it come out. Just don't tell that Admissions officer that you have had pictures of their university pasted all over your walls since you were 10 and you will do anything to get in. Think, and then use your common sense...

Other forms of EGI that run throughout the process:

1. Request material online and at fairs. If a university gives you the opportunity to "sign up" with them, of course you'll do that.

2. Follow any and all social media of the institution that you are also connected with.

3. Know the universities that interest you and know how to explain your fit.

4. See which university fairs or university visits are happening in your region and city. Attend and make sure you meet the representatives of those institutions that interest you.

5. Campus visits where and when possible. This is not easy for international families and we'll get to this later in the guide.

6. Interviews: Request one via Skype or in person if they offer them. If they don't, recognize this and ask if you can schedule an informal chat with the Admissions representative.

7. Write compelling supplement essays: They will never be able to be cut and pasted from one institution to the next. They are specific and show your fit.

8. Apply Early.

9. Thank you notes: Handwritten or email.

10. Deferral and waitlist: Communicate strategically with the university if you are wait-listed. (We will discuss this in Chapter 12!)

On Worksheet 4.3: EGI Record Keeping, I expect you to keep a log of your EGI and your contact with your Admissions officer moving forward. My students who do this risk failing to remember whom they contacted; and, when they are waiting for a response, for instance, they risk their efforts and could make a big mistake through the process.

Milestone 4: Look Who's Coming to Town

This is the time for you to check if universities on your Long List have plans to visit your country, region and/or city. These are useful for:

- Getting information from the source—always the most beneficial way to collect in-formation and data.

- Interaction. It's a human process. Are you more interested in something when you read it on a white piece of paper or when an enthusiastic human being tells it to you?

- Putting a name to a face. This works on both ends. For you and also for the Admissions Officer.

- Building your understanding of your Long Listed institutions.

Step outside of your comfort zone and look for more, ask questions and learn new things. You may make a lasting impression, a key connection, learn about a new program, or figure out a great-fit university for you that you hadn't earlier considered.

So, at this stage, I will ask you to complete this Milestone by doing the following:

1. Check with your guidance counselor or dean for a list of visiting institutions to your school.

2. Check on the university's webpage to see their travel schedule. Most universities post this.

3. Check university fairs—something we will discuss in future chapters—that travel internationally and are a great way to see a number of universities in one shot (although don't expect to have a lot of one-on-one intimate time to chat as lines can get long). Some international, traveling university fairs that may be in your region or city include:

   • Linden Tours

   • CIS tours

   • Education USA

4. Contact your Admissions officer and ask when they will visit.

IMPORTANT!

If you're going to reach out to Admissions to ask them when they will visit because you cannot find the information elsewhere, keep in mind two very critical points. First, give them some time to arrange a schedule. That means that you should be waiting until well into the spring semester/term to give them time to get this up and published. Second, if you're going to email them, do as my students have done and don't send your contact four different emails in one month, each with a different question. Consolidate and send one email with several questions. Be smart.

Finally, I've included a list of questions to get you thinking about what you might ask Admissions officers when you do meet with them on their visits in Worksheet 4.4. Use the worksheet as a guide for your plans at this stage. There's room to add your own.

Milestone 5: Confirming Break Plans

You've pondered. You've discussed. You've dissected. You've called. You've emailed. You've interviewed. You've gone through the pros and cons of each. You've questioned. You've done your due diligence.

You've decided.

You know what your options are for spending your break and what will both best suit you and your family, and satisfy what we discussed in Chapter 3. What will you do?

You'll want to finalize your break plans by the end of this chapter, including any courses, internships, community service, work and campus visits that you plan to do over the break. Now's the time to go back to Milestone 7 of Chapter 3 and confirm what is important and how to do it (quality over quantity, for instance—those one-week internships don't hold high value for you or for Admissions).

Take your decision and be prepared for a very busy but very momentous break. It's your last before your applications will be turned in...

Milestone 6: Considering Recommenders and How

Now is the time to start considering who you will ask to consider serving as one of your recommenders. A recommender will be a teacher, counsellor, coach or someone who knows you well and who you will ask to write a candid evaluation of you for your colleges. Remember that you want to assume the mentality, right now, that you will request a teacher to *consider*; you will not request a teacher to *be*. Writing a recommendation takes a lot of time, energy and dedication and you'll never want to assume that someone will do that for you—whether now for university or for a future job or graduate school.

First, some rules about recommenders:

1. You will probably have at least two recommenders for your US applications. This depends on the individual student and college, but for now assume you should have two.

2. Your recommenders will most likely be the teachers who teach you "core" subjects: mathematics, science, social science, literature/language, foreign language. In some cases, particularly if a student is going for computer science or engineering, and is taking AP or IB level courses in CS or Higher Level/AP science and mathematics courses or is pursuing an arts degree, he may want to consider these teachers.

3. Ideally, you are asking a teacher you have throughout your penultimate year of high school: someone that can speak to you "in the now" without having to try to remember you.

4. Your recommenders should be teachers who "know" you and not just you in the classroom. These are teachers who can speak to your character and persona.

5. Do not necessarily go for the teacher in whose class you are performing best. The best recommendation is a frank and deep assessment of the student citing both strengths and weaknesses and showing progress.

6. Have you struggled but given your absolute best? Does a teacher recognize your efforts, even if you're getting mediocre grades? Do you see this teacher outside of class and could he/she speak to you and about you beyond your test scores? This might be one to consider.

7. Often, you'll identify teachers that many other students have identified as well. The best recommenders tend to be some of the best teachers—those who know their students, love what they do, and are passionate about learning. It also means that they are writing loads of recommendations each year. This is why this step is so important to follow. Don't be just another recommendation to write.

I will ask you to go to Worksheet 4.5 to work out which recommenders you are considering and why. Before you do, also consider what may be asked of your recommenders as you consider who you would like to ask to write one for you:

- Specifics: Is there an instance or are there instances that you can draw out about this student specifically to show/prove their intellectual curiosity/conviction/whatever it is you said the student excels at?

- Can you speak to the student's character—beyond just academics—and how they interact with others, both in the classroom (classmates and you, the teacher) and outside? What have you *specifically* observed?

- The Admissions committee reviews hundreds/thousands of recommendations. Just as I tell students to make themselves stand out by recounting a story or incident to "back up their claims", the teacher, too, should absolutely include this. And, sometimes the simplest of anecdotes can be the most powerful.

- I advise recommenders to ask for their students' most up-to-date CVs and to meet for 20 minutes (although I tell my students they should be proactive in offering CVs and asking for a meeting, but I suspect not all do…). This type of meeting should help both parties—by understanding where the student is applying to and why, what they feel their fit is with these schools, and anything they want to draw out of their CV. Or there may be something from the past few years that the teacher could highlight, be it positive or something that they struggled with that the teacher should know about and perhaps consider before/when writing the recommendation.

By the end of this chapter you are well into the meat of the process. If you've done everything asked of you so far, you're committed. And, you're going to have success. Stay on track as the months to come actually become more and more busy but also—if you're dedicated to being true to yourself—more interesting and fun as you continue to explore and reach for what you really want.

Please answer the following and make sure you date this for your own reference.

Today's date: _____

Needs: These are less flexible from your perspective. Things you *need* are things *you know are of utmost importance to you and/or you cannot do without.*

So, what do you *need*?

What I need in a university at this stage

Me	Example: Maya's responses
1.	1. Small classes
2.	2. Professors who know me by name
3.	3. City or suburban
4.	4. Liberal mindset
5.	5. Course options
6.	6. Progressive—not stuck in tradition

Wants: These are a bit different than "needs", things that you would like to have at your university. Maybe they are not a killing factor at this stage, maybe someday they will be, maybe they will no longer become a "want" in three months.

For now, however, what do you *want*?

What I want in a university at this stage

Me	Example: Maya's responses
1.	1. Social awareness of student body but not obligatory and certainly not extreme
2.	2. Collaborative but not competitive student body
3.	3. Not rural, at least I don't think so
4.	4. Good food, healthy options
5.	5. Single room?

Worksheet 4.2: My Long List, Stage 2

1	2	3	4	5	6
My Colleges (taken from Worksheet 3.2)	Rank: If I were to apply today, where does this university rank?	Resources utilized	Requirements/ Candidate profile—grades, testing, other	Candidate profile	What this university has that I want

7	8	9	10	11
What this university has that I need	Supplement essays and questions (if not yet published, ones asked from last year)	Specialty programs, dual degrees, etc., that interest me	Reach, in-range or likely at this stage?	Remain on LL? If not, why not?

Worksheet 4.3: EGI Record Keeping

University	Admissions contact name and email	EGI and Date	Response?	EGI and Date	Response?	EGI and Date	Response?

Worksheet 4.4: Questions for Admissions Officers

1. What happens to graduates? What do they do?

2. What is the advising system like? When would I meet with an academic advisor once enrolled at your university?

3. How does the career counseling center work with students?

4. What is student pride like on campus and then with alumni?

5. What would a faculty member say about students who attend?

6. What is the relationship like between the faculty and students?

7. How does your university focus on undergraduate education (versus its graduate students and programs)?

8. How are international students integrated into the campus?

9. What is "campus life" like for students? What do they do socially and for extracurricular activities?

10. How easy is it to get into the classes for which you've registered?

11. How large are freshman and sophomore class sizes? Is that just for core classes or are those for all freshman/sophomore classes? Who teaches them? Full professors? Teaching assistants?

12. How rigorous are the studies? How are students evaluated by professors?

13. Do students stay on campus on the weekends? How many freshmen have cars?

14. How do you evaluate international applicants from my country/this region?

15. What LD accommodations do you have on campus and with whom can I speak to learn more about these?

16. Is the teaching method theory-based or more experiential?

17. My specific question for _____ university:

_____

_____

Please fill this out now as it will be referenced again in Chapter 5.

List all of your "core courses" here from last year, this year and next year (or what will/would be your last three years of high school) with teacher names for each:

10th grade	
Courses	**Teacher**

11th grade (penultimate year)	
Courses	**Teacher**

12th grade (final year)	
Courses	**Teacher**

Now place an ⋆ next to those teachers you feel could speak on your behalf regarding:

- Your progress in their class.
- Your intellectual curiosity.
- Your work ethic.
- How you deal with failure.
- How you interact with your peers in the classroom.
- Knowing you and your "reputation" outside of the classroom.
- Your uniqueness.
- Your potential for success and how that looks.

Feel free to add any comments to each teacher, respective of the points above and what was discussed in Milestone 6.

CHAPTER 5

Less Snap-Chatting and More Real-Chatting

May–June

For most of you, this chapter comes at the end of your school year. Things are busy, exciting, nerve-wracking and you're exhausted. You're looking forward to a break. Yet I'm sure I will not be the first to tell you that this summer won't be the break you're expecting. Campus visits, schoolwork, jobs, volunteer work, projects, classes and, ah yes, university applications are just a few of the things you'll be doing. I see it every summer and will say it to you straight: it will be easy for you to bury your head in your mobile phone when you do need that down time and break from life. Unfortunately, it doesn't do the trick. Just watch yourself in these months as you will need some down time and you'll also need to dedicate time to this process. Both can be usurped by the ease of diving into your devices.

But why am I giving you what sounds like a lecture on limiting your social media when you're here to learn about the next step in US university Admissions? Because, as any student who has been through the process will tell you, time management is going to be key from here on in. That includes working hard, but also giving yourself the down time that your mind and body need, which will rejuvenate you to keep pressing forward thoughtfully and with great results.

What will be key in these next two months will be drafting your Short List (very exciting!) and planning for your campus visits and interviews, whether the latter is in person or over Skype. Let's start with what requires the most depth of thought and reflects on your months of hard work and research: your Short List.

This chapter will consist of the following Milestones:

Milestone 1: Moving From Your Long List to Your Short List

Milestone 2: Mock Interview

Milestone 3: Planning Campus Visits

Milestone 4: EGI Progressing and Developing

Milestone 5: Standardized Testing: IELTS/TOEFL, ACT/SAT, SAT Subject Tests

Milestone 6: Requesting Recommendations From Your Recommenders

Milestone 7: Writing Workshop 1

Resources found outside of this book but which will be helpful for you to complete the Milestones in this chapter include:

- All guidebooks and map of colleges that you have in your Library
- ACT study guide
- SAT study guide
- The Official Study Guide for All SAT Subject Tests, by College Board

Case Study

Name: Michelle

Gender: Female

Country: Singapore and Indonesia

Nationality: Singaporean

Started process: 14 months prior to applying Early (November)

Program/Rigor: Mix of AP and IB courses along with general courses

Other: Michelle is a niche applicant. A highly talented musician, this is what Michelle was going to study.

Grades to date: Upward trajectory with some loose cannons; a range but overall pretty strong

Standardized tests to date: SAT taken twice: 1150 the first time; 1100 the second

Subject Tests: None

TOEFL/IELTS: Not applicable as she had always been in English language schools and spoke English at home.

Challenges: Clearly, the fact that Michelle had "bounced around", having been in three different high schools, with no transcript for the second half of her 10th grade, and she had switched from Northern to Southern to Northern Hemisphere calendars. She also started her last high school a month after classes started, entering into AP and IB classes late. There was a lot of catching up to do, not to mention the social challenges. Michelle is a niche candidate, a very talented musician, which made time management a challenge.

Strengths: About six months into the IBDP, Michelle "changed her chip" dramatically and started really prioritizing. She took Instagram off her phone. She wrote schedules for herself that even included dinner, when to go to bed, etc. A very social young woman, she was not a stereotype. And she was not willing to fit into any stereotype. But what that meant was learning how to manage time and to become very directed, not just with her instrument but with her studies as well. Michelle incorporated Korean dance and jazz into her routine as she became aware that she wanted to become a pop strings performer. Again, thanks to her time management, dedication and drive she was able to accomplish such a demanding schedule.

Fit/Factors: Absolutely did not want a conservatory. Did not want anything other than Boston, New York City or Los Angeles. Michelle was not even willing to look at some of the best music programs located outside of these geographic areas. Frustrating [for me], but she was determined! She also knew the risks involved in this strategy.

Interests: Niche candidate who was focusing on the strings but not to play in a chamber. Michelle wanted to be a performer and knew this.

Essay topic: Michelle grew up in Indonesia and Singapore. She related these two cities to her artistic/music style—contrasts and coincidences—as well as to her personality—many contrasts and then coincidences. This then tied to what she wants to do with her music as a career.

Short List: It was very short. University of Southern California (USC), Pepperdine, Berklee School of Music.

Interviews: Berklee. She flew to Korea for the audition and interview.

Visits: None.

(*continued*)

EGI: Very good. Very directed. In particular, with Berklee where she established a positive "working relationship" with the Admissions officer of her region.

Dream school, if any: After a long road, it ended up being Berklee, but was not determined until after her audition with them in November.

Application strategy: Michelle and I "fought" about this often but she was determined and knew by October what she wanted. I relinquished my appeals, seeing that she knew what she wanted. She would apply Berklee Early Action and complete the other two applications, request auditions and fill out the SlideRoom supplements as requested but she would not submit them, if possible, until she heard from Berklee if it was before the 1 January deadline. I would have much preferred she just send everything in for all of the reasons I discuss in this book. Michelle got her way in the end.

PARENT ADVICE

"Going through this process properly has shown me how powerful a timeline is as a tool to help plan and prepare for college applications. This was even more critical with the dual application track many musical applicants may encounter when applying. The timeline really helped to put in perspective when and what is needed for any pre-auditions/auditions and also when to submit the academic part of the application to general Admissions.

For a niche student like Michelle, ultimately it will be her performance that counts. A musician's success in the Admission process is not only about how well prepared they are but also how they feel, as that will clearly be translated into their performance for the review committee."

—Serene, Indonesia

MILESTONES

Milestone 1: Moving From Your Long List to Your Short List

You worked hard in the last chapter to weed out, highlight, add, modify and build depth and serious detail into your Long List. By now you should be prepared to convert that Long List into your Short List and I'll guide you through this.

I am assuming that you have completed every one of the Milestones leading up to now; without having done so, you won't be able to develop your Short List at this time.

I'd like you to understand clearly why you're creating a Short List and what this means. *Why a Short List?*

You've worked hard over the past months at researching, reviewing and opining on many, many universities. You've used multiple resources and have reached out to Admissions officers, spoken with your teachers and Guidance Counselor—truly done your due diligence to understand how each university has its own profile, character, and pros and cons vis à vis you being a fit.

You're now prepared to narrow down that Long List and create a balanced, comprehensive and thoughtful Short List.

You need a Short List to narrow down where you will apply to university. As we discussed in the last chapter, your Short List needs to be balanced, a true representation of your needs, wants, and pursuits and a "fit" for you on many levels. By now you could write a book on what "fit" means, so I won't waste your time.

Your Short List, which we will get to in a moment, will have the following components:

1. 10–15 universities.

2. A common Thread: These universities will have common traits that you'll be able to identify easily—and have identified as you researched them. It should "make sense".

3. A handful of "likely" institutions, a couple of "reach" institutions and a good majority of "in range" institutions. This is called a balanced or "well-rounded" List.

4. Universities that all appeal to you, where you'd be happy to attend and know how to defend your fit for each.

Let's create your Short List. Please go to Worksheet 5.1 and be prepared to fill in Columns 1–12.

Column from Worksheet 5.1	Advice
1.	Please refer to Worksheets 3.1 and 4.2 as you write down the names of the universities that you would like to see on your Short List.
2.	From your previous research, confirm what range each university falls into, whether it is likely, in range, or a reach. Keep in mind that these ranges may have shifted due to your testing or recent grade report. It's up to you to keep this updated and know where each falls.
3.	Explain here why each university is a fit. Get detailed. Basically, you're defending yourself and making the argument as to why it is a fit.
4.	Taking column 3 further—and one of the bases of your application—explain specifically what you would contribute to the university (a talent, a mindset, a deep interest, etc.) and what that university will provide for you. Why is this a perfect match?

5.	Confirm the requirements of this university for your application year. Do not just take them from your Long List. Go onto their website and confirm it. From now on you'll be using your Short List as a reference moving forward with applications, so make sure this information is accurate and up to date. If the university websites do not have updated information posted yet, make a note to go back, and I will remind you in later chapters as well.
6.	Confirm what the testing policy is for this application year for each of your universities. This will vary by institution and it's a critical part of the application, if not one of the most important parts. It is your responsibility to know what each policy is and to understand what that means (e.g., Super Score, test flexible, test optional, "highly recommend Subject Tests", etc.). Confirm that here and write the specifics in your Short List.
7.	What type of application does each university use? Or do they use multiple types? Options could be The Common Application, the UCA, or even a university's own application. The University of California system, for instance, has its own application portal. Note all of this here. You're not only saving yourself time in the future, but you're making yourself fully aware of each application and school's requirements, making you a very informed and eventually articulate candidate.
8.	Something we'll determine in the next chapter will be your Early application plan. Here, I'd like you to confirm the "Early" policy and deadline/s for each of your universities. Do they have ED? ED1 and ED2? Is it Single Choice Early Action? Do they have EA and ED? Maybe there is no Early plan. Know it and record it.
9.	Will the university have a writing supplement? At this stage some colleges will have published their writing supplement, or have said if there will be one, and some will not. I'd like you to review all the colleges on your Short List and record both whether they have one and what it is or when you will find out. The websites will inform you.
10.	Do they do interviews? How is one requested and when? In column 10 this is where you'll record this information—very important for you to know as you won't get prompted for this; it will be up to you to know and to make the request appropriately.
11.	Will you need to take TOEFL/IELTS? Again, every college is different in what they require of their international students; know if you have to take it or not as this is one of your Milestones for this chapter.
12.	Fill in your Admissions contact name and contact information. You probably know this by heart by now.

Milestone 2: Mock Interview

The US university Admissions interview is unlike those conducted by universities in other countries. We have a style of interviewing in general that is more conversational and informal, and for many of my students this comes as a surprise as we go through a mock interview. While I won't be doing your mock interview, that doesn't mean you should not and cannot prepare and engage in one; in fact, I'm making it a part of your Milestones, so you will need to do this.

First, identify someone and then ask that person to be your mock interviewer. The interviewer should use Worksheet 5.2a, while you, the student, will use Worksheet 5.2b. The interviewer should *not* be your parent or grandparent or anyone you live with. They will naturally be too biased and perhaps too controlling. Do not use a friend because they will not be able to give you an objective mock interview. I would suggest you consider a teacher, a counselor, a neighbor, or a family friend. So, choose your mock interviewer and ask this person for the following:

- Would this person be willing to spend 25–45 minutes giving you a mock interview *sans parents*, ideally in a classroom or neutral space, i.e., not in your bedroom or living room with your parents nearby.

- You will tell the mock interviewer which school they will be representing ahead of time. (You should choose one from your Short List that you know offers interviews.)

- Once the interviewer agrees, you can share Worksheet 5.2a: Mock Interview, Interviewer with them.

- The interviewer will not have to do much preparation, but it might be nice if they do a bit of research on the institution to understand the profile of the institution and its students prior to the mock.

- Please request—again, Parents, no offense to you and this is in your child's best interest—that the interview take place in private between you and the interviewer only. No parent, friend, acquaintance or otherwise should be lurking. This is not a "mock" situation.

- Settle a time and date for the mock interview.

For the student, prior to that mock interview, you will need to prepare. This preparation is the reason for this exercise.

A few pointers before you start working on Worksheet 5.2b:

1. Do your homework and know your school. Know why you are a fit and why you are applying.

2. What do you want to get across in this interview, for the interviewer to know about you?

3. You'll see that I am going to stress in the Worksheet 5.2b that you ask questions. Have at least three prepared.

4. Bring your CV to your interview. Hand it to the interviewer after you've shaken her hand and introduced yourself. You should also hand her your grade reports with comments from high school. Whether she chooses to read them there or not is not the objective; the objective is to be prepared and give the interviewer information about you without having been asked for it. (These are tips that you'll use throughout life...although for your job interview out of college, please don't bring your grade reports...)

5. Look your interviewer in the eye.

6. Laughing is fine; try to avoid giggling too much. I say the latter as I think there's an element of self-control involved. You want to smile a lot and be as relaxed as you can (I know, it's nerve-wracking, so how can you be relaxed?!), but you also want to show a mature and serious side.

7. Stumbling is also fine; if you want to re-word something or find you don't know the answer, ask your interviewer, "Would you mind if I started that answer again?" or "Would you mind if I took a minute to think about my answer?"

8. Take notes. (That means you should have a notebook.)

9. I never had a student tell me that their interview was too serious or formal with a US university (when contrasted with, for example, Cambridge in the UK). Most tell me that they loved the experience, in fact.

10. Finally, yes, it's a little awkward since you know your interviewer and you're both going into "mock" mode. After the first question, it will be fine. Just go with it. And stay in your role until the end. Your interviewer knows this and will guide you through it.

Please go to Worksheet 5.2b to prepare for and execute the mock interview. Everything is in the actual Worksheet 5.2b itself.

Good luck with your mock interview and follow the instructions on each corresponding Worksheet.

★ ★ ★ ★ ★

Milestone 3: Planning Campus Visits

Many students will be fortunate enough to visit campuses over this coming "summer" break. This is something that should be planned well ahead of time and *take a lot of time to do*. Any parent who has done this will tell you the coordination and planning of these visits is a huge effort. And one that is well worth it.

In Chapter 6, I will guide you through the visits themselves, indicating what to record, where, and questions you may have or pose to Admissions while you're there. This chapter we're focusing on determining where you'll visit and preparing for those visits. (Preparing for those visits? Oh, yes indeed! This is a well-oiled machine that requires that you plan ahead, register for dates and times of your visit, and so on.)

You will absolutely need and want the map of colleges from your Library, purchased in Chapter 1, by your side as you plan, along with a calendar and your laptop to search universities and their visit schedule.

1. The major factor in college visits, as I tell all of my parents, is time and money. You don't force these if either is limited. Colleges will not expect that you visit them from far away. It will benefit you by being on campus—not just for EGI which some schools track, but more so for the feeling you get from being there. There's nothing like spending some time on campus to see what it is like if you are able to go.

IMPORTANT!

At the time of printing, Amtrak, the national passenger train service in the US, offers special discounts to families who are doing campus visits at certain times of the year. For more information: http://www.campusvisit.com/amtrak/.

---

2. Be realistic. I would suggest no more than two university campus visits per day, maximum.

3. Distances can be wide and far in the US; there might be a lot of driving. Keep this in mind.

4. Also keep in mind that even with Google Maps, give yourself two extra hours to get lost, find your way and deal with parking. Stress on these trips is inevitable and so avoiding where you can control a reduction in stress (by giving yourself more time and less campuses to visit) will benefit everyone.

5. Use the map of colleges to gauge which campuses on your Short List could be visited in one trip.

6. Finally, while you want to visit the colleges on the Short List, here are two rules to live by:

a. You will not visit every college on your Short List. I had one family do this and it took 3.5 weeks, cost a lot of money, and a very stressful summer.

b. *While you're in the area*...even if a college never made your Long List but is in the area and you have time and it is not way off (e.g., an all-women's college and you are male), go visit! There's nothing like feeding the mind and spirit with options and ideas. I'm not saying that this college may then make it to your Short List, but it will give you a better perspective and more understanding of your fit.

You have your calendar and your list of schools that you're going to visit—no more than two per day—and the Internet. Now it's time to organize your visit. This is where patience is required.

1. You will want to sign up for the following for each campus visit: Campus Tour, Campus Information Session, Interview (where applicable).
2. Please go to Worksheet 5.3: Planning Campus Visits.
3. Check out Jacquie's advice on Parent Advice!

PARENT ADVICE

"We have triplets and so our planning needed to be extra organized when it came to campus visits. Here's my advice to any parent:

- Plan, plan, plan, and plan again! Then spend a day mapping your plan. We literally sat down with a map of the US and decided what could be feasibly covered in the time we had.

- Create a spreadsheet [see Worksheet 5.3] to help with planning. We planned right down to the minutia with the kids so they knew where we'd be on any given day and when they'd be forced to tag along with a sibling to a university that might not be on their List.

- Find out what the schools offer to potential students, and when. Schools offer information sessions, tours and interviews. Prepare your student for the interviews. Our son was extremely reluctant to ask for interviews and we had to insist he do so. Much to his surprise, he found out the process was fun and interesting.

- Some schools offer opportunities to attend classes and stay overnight in residence. Seize these opportunities if you can. Our children all ended up at universities where they had spent time going to classes and in residence to see whether they were a good fit.

- Encourage your children to ask to speak with the faculty who teach in their areas of interest. Universities are also looking to "sell themselves" and will be happy to find professors your child can talk to.

- Limit the number of universities you visit in one day. You may be selecting a university, but they are also assessing you. Students need to take the time to make an impression, and should try to arrive fresh and prepared. We found that visiting three universities in one day was too much, so we limited it to two per day.

- Take good notes—what you like, what you didn't like. The facilities, the faculty, the campus and environments. We visited one school, and the boys said it felt "like high school".

- Compare notes as soon as you can, so you don't forget the key take-aways."

—Jacquie, Singapore

Milestone 4: EGI Progressing and Developing

This should be organic and natural, something that will not stop until the end of this process.

In Chapter 4 you wrote to your universities and by now have received responses from the Admissions officers. You've adjusted, if need be, who your Admissions contact is in your Short List from Milestone 1. Did you need to respond to the replies you received? Did you thank the Admissions person for taking the time to write to you? Were your questions answered?

As I've mentioned to you in earlier chapters, EGI is something that requires your finesse, a sense of social awareness, being adept and true commitment. One of the keys to networking in life is "staying in touch" but without being overbearing or lacking genuine initiative.

Then, how, do you ask, would you move into "organic" mode with EGI? Since you've just planned your campus visits, you might want to let your Admissions officer know you'll be on campus and when and that you've signed up for an interview. Will the Admissions officer be interviewing you? If not, try to stop in and introduce yourself in person regardless.

Again, moderation is key as is being socially adept. If you have your nose stuck in your mobile phone all day, you'll lose the social adeptness and natural behavior that you'll need throughout life. Please continue to keep track of this in Worksheet 4.3.

Be smart and diligent about your EGI. Here's what a student said about EGI efforts.

"It takes some practice but if you start when you're asked to, this can really pay off. I ended up getting a very prestigious award from my high school after my Early applications were sent in. It didn't hurt that I had already been in touch with and developed a cordial relationship with my Admissions officer at the school I applied Early to—I wrote to her to tell her about the award, knowing it was unofficial but in case it was helpful I could send in more official information about it. I think it worked in my favor and if I had not been in touch with her earlier I never would have even written to her to tell her about this award when it happened."

—*Ella, Vietnam*

Milestone 5: Standardized Testing: IELTS/TOEFL, ACT/SAT, SAT Subject Tests

You will know from working on Worksheet 5.1: My Short List what your testing requirements are for each of the schools on your Short List. By now all testing policies should be posted by universities for your application year. While I will briefly remind you of this again later, it's best to know now so that you can plan ahead, particularly if you need to take Subject Tests, IELTS/TOEFL and to understand how the reporting of ACT/SAT are done.

Make sure you've done your due diligence and have signed up for your proper tests or reminders for registration, and have your study plan laid out for each.

Milestone 6: Requesting Recommendations From Your Recommenders

This is a rite of passage! You've been planning for this one for a while and now's the time to actually put that planning into practice by approaching your intended recommenders and asking them directly to write a recommendation for you.

Reflect on what you wrote and determined and why in Worksheet 4.5: Considering Your Recommenders, before you tackle this one.

To complete this Milestone, here's what you will need to do:

1. Set up a time to meet with your recommender:
   a. If you're able to ask your recommender in person—for example, if she is a teacher in your school—set up a time to speak with them and not while passing in the

hall. Give this moment respect and time, something that is transmitted to the recommender personally if you do.

b. If you're unable to see this person in person, the next best thing is to ask for a brief Skype call. You see that I am urging you to ask your recommender face-to-face where and when possible. Humans respond more positively to other humans, less so to words that are transmitted electronically in black and white. Any human knows it takes more effort to do this than to write a quick email. Go for the method that requires more effort. You're helping yourself if you do.

c. The last option is writing an email if there is absolutely no way to see this person. Be careful! If you choose this option and the teacher is someone you see every day, it can almost have the reverse effect and reflect on you poorly.

2. Ask for the recommendation:

a. Please review Worksheet 5.4: Helping Your Recommender Help You.

b. Let your recommender know why you're meeting and that you'd like to ask him to *consider* (a key word!) being your recommender. Never assume a teacher will and can do this…and by asking for consideration you are implying you understand this is not a "given".

c. Tell your recommender where you are thinking of applying and show them your Short List. Tell him why you're applying to those schools.

d. Tell the recommender why you are reaching out to him/her as a recommender. Why did you select him/her? Go back to Worksheet 4.4: Considering Your Recommenders to refresh your memory.

e. Let your recommender know that you don't need an answer now; you'll follow up in August (Chapter 8) with your updated CV and final List.

f. Let the recommender speak.

3. Follow up. Send a thank you note to your recommender for meeting with you.

WORDS OF WISDOM: RUMOR OR FACT?

Every year the same rumor regurgitates itself in some form or fashion about that "other" recommender—someone beyond the general two required by universities and perhaps outside of the framework. Indeed some universities—again, case-by-case, as always—will allow for additional recommenders. You'll know this by being aware of your universities and their specific requirements. Yet, every year, I get a student who has the option to submit an additional recommender and I am asked what to do. First, we look at the institution. What are they saying on their Admissions pages about that "other" recommender? Read between the lines if you have to. Does it sound like it only happens in extreme circumstances, perhaps to explain something that will show up in your application? Or do they encourage you outright to get your debate coach or community service leader to submit a recommendation for you? You'll have to gauge this and if you're doing your EGI well enough through the process, you will also want to ask your Admissions officer if it's unclear. The next point is the one a student brought up with me as he considers asking an additional recommender: "But my friend told me my school discourages it and only if it's someone famous or on the board." In fact, I told my student this can be more harmful than helpful in most circumstances (does the "famous" person know the candidate well and are they an appropriate recommender? This is what will be evaluated by any solid Admissions officer—alongside whether or not the candidate is just trying to show his or her social circle, which could come back to hinder his chances if not done appropriately) than a solid "other" recommendation by someone who truly knows you and can speak about you from a unique perspective that a teacher recommendation will not grasp.

A few lessons here:

1. Don't overload on recommendations only because you have the opportunity; instead, consider if an additional recommender will give more depth and breadth to your application.

2. Know your institution and by doing so gauge what they want from you; if you don't know, ask.

3. While I'm sure you have great friends, they are not the experts; go to the source and ask.

Milestone 7: Writing Workshop 1

Writing is so essential to this process that I've developed a separate but complete Writing Handbook to guide you through. You'll start the writing process in this chapter by completing Workshop 1, Part 1 and Part 2 located in the Writing Handbook.

You'll need at least an hour to complete Writing Workshop 1. Please turn to this section and complete it before moving on.

★ ★ ★ ★ ★

Once all of the seven Milestones have been completed in this chapter, it's time to take a short break, commend yourself for the hard work you've done, and to reflect on why you're going through this process.

My sense—and hope—is that both parents and students are learning more than simply how to apply to universities in the US and that you are all also learning more about one another.

You should also be learning about what you really want and more about who you really are. Your experiences coming up in Chapter 6 will be unlike any you've experienced in life before. Get ready, as they may be some of your most exciting moments in life yet!

Worksheet 5.1: My Short List

1	2	3	4	5	6	7
University	Range: likely, in-range, reach	Why it's a fit	What I will give; what it will give me	Confirm requirements	Testing policy	Type of application

* Also use Worksheet 6.3 Interview Contact/Schedule and Questions

8	9	10	11	12	13
Early application policy (Chapter 5 and 8)	Writing supplement	Interview?*	TOEFL/IELTS?	Admissions contact	Chapter 6: Will I apply Early?

14	15	16	17	18	19
Chapter 7: Specific requirements (e.g., Subject Tests, portfolio, etc.)	Chapter 7: Supplement questions (verbatim)	Chapter 8: In range, likely or reach	Chapter 8: Deadlines by university for application	Chapter 8: My deadline for each application (Early)	Chapter 10: Schedule for ED2, Regular and other applications, submission deadline

Scheduled for _____ [date and time] at _____
[location]

   University selected: _____

A quick note for the Interviewer: *You're giving this student a great opportunity by taking the time to do this! You can follow these questions, if you like, and hopefully you've taken a look at the university you'll be "representing". A few points*:

- I suggest you say hello to the student and let him/her know when you'll be going into "interviewer" mode and, once you do, you're in it the entire time.

- Please introduce yourself with a name and what you do at the university.

- I suggest you ask at least one question from the ones given below. The student has also received these questions in my guide and is preparing for these. This is not "real-life" in the sense that they will get a list of questions prior to a university interview; that's why this is practice.

- There is a spot after each question for your notes. Please jot down notes as you ask questions regarding the student's response. I suggest you wait to go over these notes until the end of the interview.

- These interviews are generally quite relaxed and are an opportunity to get to know the student by the Admissions staff or alumnus and not for a right or wrong answer. That said, I have advised the student to bring you their CV and his/her grade reports at the start of the interview and shake your hand, look you in the eye and introduce himself/herself.

- Finally, I have asked your student to prepare at least three questions to ask you at the end of the interview. You should expect these. You do not have to answer them, of course, but just guide the student through his/her other questions.

Questions for the student:

The Fit

- What are you interested in studying?

- How did you determine your "List" of schools?

- Describe your dream university.

- What is most important to you in your university?

- What aspects of X university do you find attractive?

- How will X university help you achieve your goals?

- Where do you see yourself at age 30?

- What can you give to X university as a student here?

Curriculum
- Tell me about your high school experience thus far.

- What are the most positive/least positive aspects of your final year/this past year in high school?

- What is your favorite/least favorite class and why?

- What do you like/dislike about your high school and why?

- Describe your favorite teacher to me.

- Describe your ideal college professor.

- Looking at your high school performance to date, is it an accurate reflection of your ability and potential? Explain.

Extracurricular/Commitments/Talents
- What do you enjoy doing during your free time?

- Describe your day today to me.

- What activities do you hope to be a part of at our college?

- What might you try that is new when you are at college?

Other

- Current events: Choose one and tell me what is going on.

- Case study: You have been assigned a known-to-be difficult professor for your Intro to Creative Writing class. You've tried your best to change to another professor but it's not possible. You go to see him during office hours and either he's not there or he is very brusque with you. You failed the first quiz. How do you handle this?

- Tell me why I should admit you to X university.

- What have you learned from your parents? What have they learned from you?

- What is your top university on your list?

Your own questions for the student:

Scheduled for _____ [date and time] at _____ [location]

University selected: _____

Student, a quick note to you: *Please fill out your answers to each question in order to prepare for the mock interview. Then, leave these questions and answers aside when you go for the actual mock interview. It's important that you prepare but that you don't regurgitate. The best interviews are the most natural ones.*

- Always bring to the interview or submit via email to your interviewer at least a couple of days prior to the interview your updated, proofread and grammatically correct one-page CV. Bring a notebook to take notes and your list of questions.

- As part of your Short List preparation, you checked to see if the college has its supplement essay/questions published yet; this will give you a good idea of where the interview questions may go.

- I have given you pointers and tips below where applicable in parenthesis.

Questions for you to prepare to answer

The Fit

- What are you interested in studying? (This is based on your review of their academic programs, majors, minors, special programs prior.)

- How did you determine your "List" of schools? (The interviewer wants to see that you have assessed your fit and are applying to "similar" schools in terms of culture, style, academics…your fit.)

- Describe your dream university.

- What are you looking for in a college? (Be as personal as you can; of course, you want to make sure this ties in to the school for which you are interviewing.)

- What aspects of X university do you find attractive? (Make sure you've done your homework. Be specific. Is it a particular program? The style of students who attend? What you hope to do when you finish and you see the school is strong with internship and job placement in that field?)

- How will X university help you achieve your goals? (Again, be as specific as you can; if you are going in undeclared, you may focus on how the university provides a very liberal arts-style, holistic education for you to try different things that you are passionate about. What are those things?)

- Where do you see yourself at age 30? (Feel free not to focus on your career, especially if you don't know what that will be! Perhaps it's just to be happy, in a creative job, having climbed Mt. Everest...)

- What can you give to X university as a student here? (What will you give back as a student while there? Politically active? You want to start a club you know they don't have but are passionate about?)

Curriculum

- Tell me about your high school experience thus far. (Narrate and pull out any high and any low points. Any struggles or successes you've had. Remember that humility goes a long way when you're also praising yourself.)

- What are the most positive/least positive aspects of your final year/this past year in high school? (Self-explanatory.)

- What is your favorite/least favorite class and why? (Self-explanatory.)

- What do you like/dislike about your high school and why? (It goes without saying that the positives and negatives that you focus on reflect your character and values.)

- Describe your favorite teacher to me. (Self-explanatory.)

- Describe your ideal college professor. (Self-explanatory.)

- Looking at your high school performance to date, is it an accurate reflection of your ability and potential? Explain. (Self-explanatory.)

Extracurricular/Commitments/Talents
What do you enjoy doing during your free time? (Expound upon this! Even if you're crazy about movies! Even if you love baking a different cake every Saturday. Share who you are.)

- Describe your day today to me. (I always asked this one. I wanted to know at the heart as much as possible what the student was like.)

- What activities do you hope to be a part of at our college? (This is based on your research on what their student life activities are, what their students are involved in, etc.)

- What might you try that is new when you are at college? (Great question! This is based on your research and the things that the college offers that are of interest to you!)

- Describe one thing that may surprise me to know about you. (Self-explanatory.)

Other

- Current events: Choose one and tell me what is going on. (Have you read the news lately?)

- Case study: You have been assigned a known-to-be difficult professor for your Intro to Creative Writing class. You've tried your best to change to another professor but it's not possible. You go to his office hours and either he's not there or he is very brusque with you. You failed the first quiz. How do you handle this? (I won't tell you how but you can imagine that the interviewer is looking for some negotiating tactics on your end and your ability to address your own faults.)

- Tell me why I should admit you to X university. (Make your case for why you're a fit. You should have this written down after researching for every college for which you are interviewing.)

- What have you learned from your parents? What have they learned from you? (There is no right or wrong answer here but your answer will show your maturity—the capacity for introspection and awareness of others—in this case your parents.)

- What is your top university on your list? (Don't ever say that the school you are interviewing for is not somewhere near the top. It does not have to be the first, but it should be close to the top or that you're able to explain why you are so keen on this institution without saying it's number one.)

Sample Questions to Pose

*Note that posing a question having shown you did the homework is much more effective and powerful. Please have three ready for your interview.

- What is your job placement rate and how does career advising work? (I saw that your job placement rate is X—what does that mean? How does your career advising work?)

- How many courses are taught by full professors and what level courses are they?

- The average class size is said to be X as per your website. What about lecture halls?

- How involved, if at all, are professors in internship placements?

- In what ways do professors collaborate with students?

- What types of clubs have students been known to launch on their own when they arrive at X university?

- I'm very keen to study X. Can you tell me a bit about this major, the types of students in it, and what types of careers students take after graduating from it? (I saw on your website the types of careers and was curious to know specifically what companies recruit on campus for this major?)

- How many internships convert to full-time job offers?

- Do you think I stand a strong chance of being admitted into X university? Is there anything you can advise me to do at this point to be a stronger candidate? (Find a way to tell them about your niche areas vis-à-vis your fit with X university.)

- Tell them about a time you showed intellectual curiosity, fitting this into one of their interview questions.

- There have been some recent events involving your university in the press. May I ask a few questions about this?

- Don't let the interview end without telling them what you want them to know about you. (You've planned this ahead of time!)

- Your own questions:

Worksheet 5.3: Setting Up Campus Visits

Here are some important points for you to note as you start to set these up:

1. Note that some universities do a campus tour and information session in one, while others require that you sign up for each individually.

2. Every university has their own way of having you review and schedule a visit. Visit their website in order to do so.

3. Have your map beside you to mark the location.

4. I would recommend you arrange your visits in the order that you will visit them.

5. Remember the golden rule of giving yourself two hours more than you think you need to locate the university, find parking and find the building on campus.

6. When planning the time it takes to leave one campus and arrive at the next campus visit or location, double the amount of time Google Maps tells you to deal with traffic, parking, getting lost, etc.

7. When in metropolises, use public transport whenever possible, for example, in Boston, NYC, DC, and Chicago. LA will require the use of a car to get around, unfortunately.

8. Check each tour, information session and interview when confirmed in the table that follows. Do the same for your lodging once confirmed.

University	Date planned to visit	Location and number on map (Indicate this on your map)	On Short List?	Campus Tour preferred date and time	Info Session preferred date	Interviews offered and requested by me?	Comments (ie: priority visit, etc.)	Departure time: (to arrive next visit/ location at arrival time of:___)	Hotel/ accommodation

When you meet with your recommender, share the following information to help them understand you better and be able to write a more thoughtful recommendation if they agree to do so:

1. Explain any inconsistencies in your academic career to date:

    a. Help them understand why you have gaps.

    b. Explain the weaknesses on your record and what you do to work to improve them.

2. Character reference:

    a. Speak to your social abilities and what you've done at school or in your community that reflects on your character positively.

    b. Give examples.

3. Fit for the schools to which you are applying:

    a. Explain schools on your Short List and why they are on there.

    b. The recommender will need to be able to speak to you and your fit for the school in their recommendation.

4. Academic Achievements: This is self-explanatory. State these.

5. Strengths (as a person and student): What do you feel your strengths are as a person? Share this.

6. Interests and Passions. Your recommender probably doesn't know many of them. Share these.

7. Why you are unique. Self-explanatory!

8. Explain some of your career goals and/or ideas with your recommender.

CHAPTER 6

School's [Not] Out for Summer!

June—July

This is what the next couple of months of your life will consist of: writing, reflecting, writing, writing, summer project and activity, writing, reflecting, maybe some campus visits. Hopefully, you will get some sleep, some time with friends, and eventually, some down time. But expect a very intense couple of months. You can make it the best summer of your life or you can make it a very treacherous one. Let's make it the former. This is the most important and probably the most intense summer of your life to date!

Writing will be the bulk of what you are focusing on vis-à-vis college applications during this period. As you know, writing is one of the most critical aspects of your university applications to the US. But you don't need to be a Hemmingway. And you are not expected to write like Proust. You probably won't reflect as profoundly as Thoreau and you [hopefully] will not be as stuffy as Shakespeare. (Sorry to all you Shakespeare fans! We all have favorites!)

No one is expecting you to be the next Man Booker finalist. (Note: When you do have the time after high school, check out some of the finalists. Some of the best books for you to read come out of this competition.) What is expected of you, however, is to write, and it's now that the writing begins. Don't tell me you're not a writer; every single one of you can write. And, surely, every single one of you can write about yourselves—much more interesting and fun than writing another literary assessment of that book that put you to sleep from last year's Lit class!

So, I ask you not to go into this step of the process with a negative attitude, saying you can't write or don't know how to write. This will be the bulk of this chapter's Milestones in terms of time and commitment and I expect that you'll manage your time as such appropriately.

Last year, I had a mother who contacted me at the start of this stage regarding her son. "Jen, Marshall doesn't write."

"What do you mean he doesn't write?"

"I mean, I don't think he's every written one introspective thing about himself in his life. He can't do it. What will we do?"

He'll learn. And, he'll write.

Marshall ended up learning; he ended up writing; and, he ended up delivering one of the most introspective, telling and beautiful essays that I read that year. Profound? No, it wasn't. Smart? Yes, it was. Simple and honest? You bet. Did it answer the question? Yes. Did he use fancy words? Not one. Did his mother help him with the essay? You better believe she didn't. (It would have been imbued with fancier words and more "profound" themes if so. That's one of the ways I knew.) And, he was accepted to his ED school. I'm quite certain the essay had a big part in that acceptance.

So, you get my point on how I want you starting off this process—with an open, positive and can-do mindset.

The rest will be taken care of if you follow my guidance and commit to working as hard and as thoughtfully as you can.

There's a lot of fun to be had in these Milestones:

 Milestone 1: Confirming Your Short List (Again!)

 Milestone 2: Campus Visits and Interviews

 Milestone 3: Executing Summer Plans

 Milestone 4: Writing Workshop 2

 Milestone 5: Writing Workshop 3, Part 1

Milestone 6: Standardized Testing (This month's advice builds on previous months' work, so don't skip it!)

The resources you will be using for this chapter:

- Guidebooks you have been using from your Library
- Standardized Testing study guides

Name: Sacha

Gender: Female

Country: France and Singapore

Nationality: French/Singaporean

Started process: Late! September before applications were submitted. Determining that she was going to submit Early applications, that gave her less than two months to do the entire process! Luckily, she was on a gap year, so all of her time was essentially dedicated to US university Admissions.

Program/Rigor: Lycée—French Baccalaureate. Very high rigor.

Grades to date: Sacha finished her secondary school career and the Baccalaureate and was taking a pre-planned gap year. She therefore had all of her scores and grade reports completed. She scored a 16/20 on the Baccalaureate with a "mention très bien"—a very strong score.

Standardized tests: She came to me never having taking an SAT or ACT and never having prepared for one. It was September and she was going to apply to university by November. . .She ended up taking both the SAT and the ACT (see below) with the following scores: ACT 21; SAT 1020.

Subject Tests: None. She did not end up taking any, as they were not required, and also because of her timeline.

TOEFL/IELTS: She absolutely would have to take the IELTS. (She was applying to UK universities as well, so instead of having to take both and confirming that her Short List of colleges would take the IELTS, she only took this.) Sacha came from a French system her whole life and while living in a country where English is widely spoken (Singapore), we were pretty certain that regardless of her list, she would have this as her requirement for all of her universities.

Challenges: There were several. First, Sacha was starting the process very late. Second, because she came from the French system, the whole "US university Admissions process" was totally unfamiliar to her. Introspection, showing a relaxed yet thoughtful essay, writing in a less structured way than she had been taught her whole education, researching universities, and EGI, were all very foreign to her as this was the first time she had ever really been exposed to such a unique process. She had also never prepared for, seen or taken a US standardized test. Considering she wanted to apply "Early", something we determined right away, she would have one chance with the

(continued)

SAT in September and one chance with the ACT in October. To further challenge her, she was able to get a seat in the SAT with one week to prepare; the ACT was fully booked through to the end of the year in her region, so that was no longer an option. It was stressful. Also, as the French system does not incorporate community service or involvement in many clubs and activities, she was perhaps lacking in these areas. There were also no strong summer experiences or projects that went along with her "story".

Strengths: Sacha was both bright and a hard worker. She was diligent and dedicated to this process from the moment she began to the moment she ended. So, for all of you saying, *Why would I have to start this process when Jennifer tells me when she's had a student have success with it starting just two months before applications were due?* I say this: If Sacha had known what she did before September, she would have started a year prior, as she told me just about every time we met. These were not the most fun months of her life, and certainly not stress free. Sacha was a good listener and was eager; she was also not afraid to ask questions and to try things. She was organized, took notes, made lists and followed deadlines. Sacha was also very humble and thoughtful. The latter two attributes helped her a lot through the process. Sacha was also embarking on her gap year, one that would be filled with some internships and pursuing her Chinese studies.

Fit/Factors: The Boston area and New York City were going to be her only geographical regions, it was determined. She was keen on studying entrepreneurship and business but also enjoyed political science and international relations, the latter coming to light as she went through the self-evaluation process. A medium-sized school was best for Sacha and one that had diversity of students. She determined she did not want an all-women's college. She also wanted a college that valued sports at any level as she knew she would participate.

Interests: Love of baking, love of sports, love of cultures and love of family. Sacha needed all of those parts balanced in her life along with friends and learning. She was very interested in how countries interact politically and interculturally and was finding as she went through the process that she was drawn to articles in the press on the nuances of diplomatic relations among countries with current and past events related to culture, religion and socioeconomics.

Essay topic: She wrote about the tie to her baking—and learning this from her mother—to the importance of having a passion in life and putting love and effort and risk into it. She went through over 15 drafts of this essay until it was finalized.

Short List: Boston College, NYU, Boston University, Tufts, Bentley, Babson, Northeastern, Bryant. The last three she applied Early Action.

Interviews: She was able to interview with Bentley, Babson and with Bryant.

Visits: Sacha went to Boston, DC and NYC for a week in early September when we first began. It was a quick trip and we certainly did not have a Short List prepared. She visited: Bentley, Babson, Tufts BC, American, GWU, NYU and Fordham. From the visits she was able to better formulate her Short List.

EGI: Very good considering her challenges.

Dream school, if any: Not truly one school as she loved all of those on her final List.

Application strategy: SAT results came back very poor, absolutely discouraging for someone like Sacha and considering her success with the "Bac". We knew that these would greatly affect her candidacy at any institution requiring standardized testing scores. She submitted them to her one EA school that required them—Babson—and (thank goodness for her previous and thoughtful EGI) had long conversations with her Admissions contact on whether they would consider her taking the SAT in November, which she was able to get into. The Admissions contact said to send them and she did in a screen shot immediately when she received them, well after the 1 November EA deadline. While her father initially thought it would be a bad move to take the SAT again—further setting her up for failure and suggesting that we should leave all US universities out and just focus on the UK, what with her initial SAT results—we eventually went with the approach that trying again will only help, and show Sacha herself that she gave it her all, and then to show Admissions. This was a positive move in the end.

SACHA'S ADVICE

"Start earlier than I did! And, when you're coming from a totally different type of academic system—how I learned and wrote and spoke with teachers in the French system was totally different to what I was doing with my US applications!—make sure you keep an open mind to really try to understand what you need to do and **how** you need to do it. And, be yourself!"

MILESTONES

Milestone 1: Confirming Your Short List (Again!)

Although we did this in the last chapter, your thoughts change from day-to-day and week-to-week and this can and is the case for many of you regarding your Short List.

Where do you stand with it today?

I won't ask you to confirm this until after your campus visits, if you're doing them and once the summer ends and school begins. But, this step is a critical one, so please don't skip it.

Please go back to Worksheet 5.1: My Short List. There are three things I'd like you to complete in this Milestone:

1. Review your Short List itself and the columns you adroitly filled in from Chapter 5. What information is left blank that you could not find while working through the last chapter? Go ahead and find that information now. It will be readily available.

2. I'm sure you've been considering this ever since we started talking about Early Admissions and the pros and cons and idea of it. Now is the time I would like you to consider and record in Column 13 with the heading "Chapter 6: Will I Apply Early?" which university on your Short List you plan to apply to Early. Discuss this with your family.

3. Finally, reconfirm requirements for those early schools you just indicated and confirm/adjust accordingly in the Short List itself.

In Chapters 7 and 8 you will confirm and begin writing your Early application essays. Right now it's exciting to know what you plan to do and all of the research you've done to lead up to this thoughtful choice of yours. In just a couple of months you'll have your first applications submitted. And, I think the next Milestone will help you further confirm or not what you just added to your Short List.

IMPORTANT!

Don't forget what we discussed in Chapter 3 about merit-aid strategy and creating a unique list!

Milestone 2: Campus Visits and Interviews

For those of you visiting campuses, this Milestone is for you. I'd also ask those of you not visiting campuses to make sure you read through this Milestone—it won't take you long—and also to review the corresponding Worksheets. It will give anyone going through this process—with or without visits—a greater understanding of the breadth and depth of thinking that should go into confirming your Short List. I also think anyone who reviews this Milestone will learn from it.

In Chapter 5 you arranged all of your campus visits and schedule. Now you're about to actually "do" them. I have four parts to this Milestone and will ask you to complete all of them.

Campus Visits

Please refer to Worksheet 6.1: Campus Visit Guide. I've prepared for you a Guide that I give to my families prior to their visits. I ask that they follow this guide for each college visit and that their reflections are not combined. Rather, I would like everyone on the visit, even your younger siblings if you have any, to contribute—after all they are going through this process with you and might have seen or noticed something you did not! They should each take a Guide and report their own notes on each. There is a space for Campus Visit Notes within each Guide. I will expect you to be filling this out as you go.

WORDS OF WISDOM: RECORDING YOUR CAMPUS VISIT FEEDBACK

Veena's feedback from her campus visits (Chapter 10 Case Study):

Amherst: "It wasn't a fit for me. It's a lovely campus, yet the location, for me, is something I cannot overlook. I thought it would work as part of the Five College Consortium and prominence of college students, but not for me. It seems much more academically focused and driven—let's see how the others go."

Wesleyan: "This visit was the one that really did show me the value of college visits. Everything was perfect. The people were friendly, there was a vibrant arts community, the five most common majors are all interests of mine, the academic program is so flexible with majors, minors and certificate options, housing options are among the best I've seen, the campus is lovely, I could go on. But I couldn't picture myself there. I didn't get that click or that gut feeling. It was so annoying and worrying and strange because I liked the school itself, I really did. I wish I felt that "click" that you should feel when you set foot on an awesome campus that you love. Everything about it is great, except for reasons that I just can't explain or put my finger on, I didn't feel the click. I think I'll definitely still apply because I like it and I could make it work for myself if I had to."

Yale: "This is such a problem now, but I've fallen in love with my first Ivy League school and it hurts. It hurts because it's so out of reach and unachievable and I almost want to slap myself for falling into the Ivy League trap, but I loved Yale so much and understand the hype of it now. I'm just scared that I'm not good enough for Yale and similarly to a girl's fear of heartbreak, I'll confess to an apprehension for falling too hard for something I can't have and will only end up getting hurt by. (This is probably not the right arena to feel such emotional attachment, but I'm a teenage girl and I think I've already subconsciously invested considerable love and attachment to Yale, oops). Mom and I fell in love with everything about it—the college system, the beauty of the campus amidst New Haven, the arts inclination, the diversity and just the easy-going yet academic feel of it. Seeing the students chilling on a Sunday in the coffee shop and seeing them walk around just made me feel so happy and comfortable with the location of Yale, despite New Haven's bad rep. I could see myself there. I felt like I was a part of it already, and it's scaled my list to the top now. This could easily change over the next few days as I see more colleges, but I'll keep you posted on those when I see them. For now, my heart is in New Haven (and I don't quite know how I feel about that)."

Tufts: "Tufts made me smile, if anything. Literally the happiest campus ever, and somewhere I am *definitely* applying regular decision to. I met with a student there who's a family friend and everything I took from our conversation was reinforced when I visited. It's such a happy, bustling place. I felt like I could go there and make remarkable friends—I loved everyone I met on campus and got such a good feel for the place from the genuinely wonderful tour guides I had. The campus was nice, in a good location, and I have no complaints about Tufts. It wouldn't be my bet for Early Decision, but I would be perfectly happy here, no doubt."

Mei's feedback from her campus visits (Chapter 3, Case Study):

Pitzer: "It was actually a really nice place to be. At first when I stepped into the grounds I was surprised about how much like a desert it was. Compared to the other Claremont colleges like Pomona and Scripps where they are covered in green, Pitzer was covered in cacti. But once I got used to it, it brought this new atmosphere which I enjoyed. A few things I liked about Pitzer was how they have great study abroad programs and more than half of the students go visit. Also I liked their vegan/vegetarian/gluten-free option meals. Something I really liked about Pitzer was their mission/values. Out of the five, eco-friendly (environmental sustainability), social responsibility and intercultural understanding really made me fall in love. As you probably already know, I'm a huge service person and Pitzer actually requires 40 hours of service for all students and more if they are willing. So I think the people I will meet here will be more or less passionate in giving back to the society and I think that that school environment will make the place special. Also, Pitzer respects all cultures, which I thought was nice. I loved how the school was built in a super sustainable way (for example, AC in the dorms turn off when the window opens). They also have free rental bikes, so students will use them instead of cars, which I thought was pretty awesome. (Oh and they don't require SAT/ACTs!)"

Scripps: "Again, I can't emphasize this more but it was *gorgeous*. Very different from Pitzer (where all you see are cacti), Scripps was very green with roses and gave off an old

European-style vibe. Indeed, was pretty small compared to the other Claremonts but they get to share facilities and sports and classes and everything, so I thought that it was nice having a calm, home-like place in the big area (whole of Claremont colleges). Also, because it is all-girls, I heard that the dorms don't get crazy and it's pretty clean all the time (which is really nice, compared to Pomona where some dorms share bathroom areas between both genders). Another great thing about Scripps was their tradition. The graffiti wall (a wall where each year the graduating class writes their name on) was what really got me because I think its great to leave a mark where you spent four years of your life.

I looked through their yearbook and I realized how small each year group was. But at the same time that means we get a lot of attention from the professors, so I think that's a great thing. I was talking to an Admissions officer, actually my interviewer who happened to be the Admissions officer for international students (me), and she told me quite positive things about Scripps (of course she will be positive but it was pretty persuasive). I liked how she emphasized that although it's all-girls, there are always guys walking in and out of campus and taking classes together. She even told me that when I know my ACT score, I can email her asking whether its a good enough score or not to just make sure."

Chapman: "Clean, good size, friendly people, nice building and more. I think I'm super biased towards the Claremonts because I just really really, really want to go there, but actually Chapman was pretty awesome as well. I liked their campus; it was flat and easy to walk around with modern buildings and good facilities. I liked how students can casually jump into any of the fountains on campus if they are hot. Also, it's pretty near the downtown area and even if you don't go all the way, it's located in old Orange, so there were nice restaurants and shops around campus.

The place itself didn't have anything sparkling or jumping out but in general it was a beautiful place and easy to get around. I liked one of their study abroad programs where students go on a large ship for a semester and take classes while travelling around the world (how awesome is that). Also, their gym was really nice, so I would take advantage of that if I go."

Pepperdine: "I just visited Pepperdine today. It was a gorgeous campus—as everyone who visits will probably say. It's located in Malibu and you can see the beach from the campus and it was really pretty. The downside was that there were lots of stairs and up and down hills (since its located in the mountains). I guess it makes you fit but I don't want to imagine myself running up the hill trying to get to class. Also it was actually the first college I came across—apart from Scripps—where the dorms were gender separate (which makes sense considering that it's a Christian school). When I talked to my Admissions officer he told me that the practice of Christianity is not serious but about 90% of the students are more or less Christian and I'm not sure if I'll like that atmosphere or not. Yes, the people were great, the view was great, but the only thing about the school is Christianity and how much that will affect me. I'm not too sure at the moment and I am glad to have visited!"

Pomona: "I think that Pomona has a great campus with lots of green and beautiful architecture. Walking through the college gave me this feeling of calmness and I really, really liked it. However, I felt that it was not exactly a 'fit' for me in the sense that I feel that the academics are the top priority in the school—of course students are involved in numerous other things. Also it gave me the feeling that everyone in their subconscious mind had a pride that they were better than the other Claremont schools (which is true in the sense of prestige and selectivity, but still). Yet at the same time I can see myself taking classes there and I would love to take classes there, so perhaps I am a better fit in another school; however, I will still take advantage of the classes offered in Pomona."

Claremont McKenna College (CMC): "I still think that this is the school for me. Firstly, compared to other schools CMC actually sent me 2 emails saying I have a campus tour and an interview on the day before and already, they have sent me an email saying thank you for the visit. It is very modern and 'concrete' compared to Pomona and Scripps, I would have to say, but still it gives me this feeling of home. Also, going on a campus tour, I really liked the dorm rooms and the classrooms. The people were also very friendly to talk to and they all really seem to like the school, too. Another thing is CMC's philosophy of balancing work and play—or things outside the classroom. I love how CMC provides many, many different opportunities to students from internships to sports to clubs to study abroad programs. It's just great. Just one thing about CMC. . . well actually *all* the Claremont colleges, is that it has *no Japanese food near school!* Our whole family is craving Japanese food right now but unfortunately there is only Thai and an Asian fusion place. . . but yes, that is the only thing against CMC so far."

Interview

After every Campus Visit Guide, you should use Worksheet 6.2 to prepare for the actual interview. You should be reviewing Worksheet 5.2b: Mock Interview (Student) for each university, preparing your notes, and completing Worksheet 6.2 prior to every interview.

You can also go to your actual interview with this book and worksheet in hand.

IMPORTANT!

Those of you doing Skype or phone interviews will want to use this Worksheet as well!

Interview Master Schedule

Worksheet 6.3 is a master schedule of your interviews where you will be putting the time and date and interviewer details in one safe place. You'll reference this and populate this now and in future chapters.

Post Campus Visit and Interview

Two critical steps to take after each visit and interview, regardless of if they fall on the same day:

1. *Sharing reflections*: Share your feedback with your family after you've written it in the Guide and after your interview. Try to do this every evening after your visits or in the car on the way to another university visit. Try not to wait more than 24 hours to do this; do it while you're fresh (if not exhausted, I realize).

2. *Thank you notes*: Send your interviewer a thank you note the evening after the interview. Don't delay on this. You know what to say by now.

Milestone 3: Executing Summer Plans

There's a Milestone just to tell me to go forth and "do" the summer plans I worked so hard at identifying, securing and now executing? Of course. This is a very important step in the overall process—the most important summer of your life to date—and I have some points that I'd like you to review as you embark upon your summer project:

Embrace it. Don't just "do it". Jump in. This means I expect you to:

1. Ask questions.
2. Be open.
3. Be thoughtful.
4. Be selfless.
5. Listen.
6. Make new friends.
7. Find a mentor.
8. Be curious.
9. Don't be lazy.
10. Turn off your mobile.
11. Take a risk.
12. Try something new.

13. Take someone under your wing.

14. Recognize a peer's contributions.

15. Recognize a challenge you need to improve in yourself.

16. Set a goal.

17. See what makes you happy. (And what does not.)

This summer will "go on record" in your applications, but the most important part about it is the impact it makes on you and your ability to grow from that and reflect on it beyond the moment.

STUDENT ADVICE

"What I did during the summer before my senior year was that I went to California and Vancouver for three weeks to look at five different schools. During these three weeks, in addition to college visits, I also explored the cities of California and Vancouver. Once I came back from this, I interned at an animal welfare organization for a month. This still allowed me a few weeks to enjoy my summer with my friends, and trust me, it isn't as hectic as it sounds!"

—*Mei, Japan*

Milestone 4: Writing Workshop 2

In Chapter 5 you began your writing by doing Writing Workshop 1. As the goal of this chapter is to have your Common Application or main application (applications for US state schools, UCA, Coalition Application, etc.) essay drafted and finished in at least its first form, I'll ask you to get started on this in early June. This may take you a month or it may take you three. Everyone writes differently, at a different pace and with different motivators. I can't write, for instance, in my office. I need a lot of light and a span of hours without meetings, calls or email. What type of environment do you need to write? Respect that in yourself and give yourself a lot of time. Know the timeline.

Go ahead and turn to Writing Handbook, Writing Workshop 2. Please work on and complete both Parts 1 and 2. You can do this in one sitting and I suggest you do. Give yourself at least an hour. You'll then move on to the next Milestone. Don't let more than a week come between finishing this Milestone and moving on to Milestone 5.

★ ★ ★ ★ ★

Milestone 5: Writing Workshop 3, Part 1

You'll move into Writing Workshop 3, Part 1, of the Writing Handbook while you're still in this chapter. Part 1 focuses on the main college essay. You will complete this Milestone when you have written your full first draft of this essay.

The first part of this Workshop is to review the prompts, regardless of the application portal you are using. The prompts in all applications are very similar to one another and the advice here is relevant to all. Part 1 of Writing Workshop 3 takes you through some simple exercises to determine which type of prompt is right for you. This will take at least an hour, perhaps a couple.

Go ahead and complete Writing Workshop 3, Part 1 now.

★ ★ ★ ★ ★

At the end of this Milestone you are directed to write your first draft. You've been preparing for this and don't need me to say much more at this stage. You have the entire Writing Handbook to refer to, but by now you are ready to write. You know what you're writing about. You know what to include. You know what not to include. Now is the time to sit and write.

IMPORTANT!

For most, writing this essay will not happen in one sitting. You'll write. You'll stop. You'll perhaps go back to it that same day. Perhaps you'll go back to it the next day. Whatever your style and preference—there is no right or wrong way—do yourself the favor of committing to writing over a certain week span—I suggest a month—and starting and finishing in that month. This is your first draft and you'll be working on it to make it final at the end of Chapter 7.

WORDS OF WISDOM: THE ESSAY THAT NEVER CAME

At this stage in the process I expect of my students, as I am expecting of you, that they sit down, write and deliver. One of my students, Hamilton, did not turn in his first draft to me on the deadline.

I asked him for it. He said he didn't have time. I gave him a new deadline.

Nothing.

I started getting annoyed, reasonably so. His mother asked me to have another meeting with him. I told her I would if he had questions.

When we got on Skype, Hamilton asked me how to write. I told him there was no way I was going to go over the entire Writing Workshop again to save him some time. Did he have questions? Yes.

"How do I begin?" he asked.

I told him, "It is not a 'how'. You just do it. I'm not asking you to walk a tightrope. I'm asking you to write. How many things did you write today?"

"38" he said, "including some SMS messages."

When I asked him if he tried to write, he said, "Yeah."

I asked him how and he said, "Well, I just tried."

I asked him to tell me about his setting and he simply replied, "Just, you know, at my desk."

Hamilton was really pushing it. I told him, "I don't want to hear from you until you have a full first draft to hand in to me. I want you to turn off your phone—in fact, leave it upstairs and you go downstairs—disconnect your laptop from the Internet, grab a drink, grab your Writing Handbook with all of your notes and lock yourself in the bathroom and don't come out until you've written. The. Whole. Thing. Then, once it's in a first draft form, send it to me."

I had it two days later.

Milestone 6: Standardized Testing (This month's advice builds on previous months, so don't skip it!)

I have two very important points during this stage on Standardized Testing:

1. Sign up for Subject Tests if you need to retake them, if you are thinking you will want to take them, or if you are considering taking them for your Early applications. If you change your mind about a subject, you can change to a different subject on test day, with the exception of language with listening, which cannot be changed.

IMPORTANT!

Always sign up "with listening" for the Subject Tests if you're doing a language Subject Test!

2. Review with yourself and your family what your "strategy" is, keeping in mind what we've been discussing all along and the requirements of your institutions, their "Testing Policy", in particular for the one/s you have placed currently as your Early schools. This may affect whether or not you need to register or prepare for further testing.

IMPORTANT!

I've tried to keep the tone down throughout this guide on testing. Now is not the time to get heated up about it or to change your own strategy based on what anyone else is doing. This is individual and you know how testing is assessed and used in the Admissions process. Many don't, or have an inflated or unrealistic understanding of how it is used. Yes, it can be important. No, it is not the most important thing on an application. Don't over-test.

The Enlightened Insider: UCA and The Coalition Registration

UCA and The Coalition (two other application portals) registrations are not discussed here as few international students use these application portals at the time of publication. These portals are likely to increase the number of universities under their umbrella, so it would be a good idea to keep informed about them.

As you finish up Chapter 6, it will confirm that you can, and do, in fact, write. You are, in essence, a writer. Another life skill that you have learned is burying the excuses for self-doubt. We will continue at a brisk pace for the next several months yet, if you have completed all of your Milestones so far, you are making excellent progress!

Worksheet 6.1: Campus Visit Guide

University name:

Visit date and time:

People I am scheduled to meet by name:

Before your visit:

1. You've registered for the campus tour where applicable and also for your interview.

2. What's the most recent book you've read? It is always wise to have one you're ready to talk about in an interview. Read the news consistently a few weeks prior, too. Remember, these are hubs of thought and intellect!

3. Refer to all of the research you have done in this guide before your visit. You've done this hard work for a reason.

4. Using this guide, you have already identified why you're a fit. Review what you said before you hit campus.

5. Have this guide with you. Be prepared to take notes. Log the questions you would like to have answered in the space provided below.

6. Get a good night's rest before your visit. Be excited and have an open mind. Plan to give yourself some time to explore the campus and before and after your interview.

During your visit:

1. Always have this guide and a pen in hand!

2. Plan time before or after (I always like doing it before to get my own sense of the place before the red carpet tour begins...) to walk around the campus and explore.

• Pick up a student newspaper. What are the hot topics? Take this with you.

• Go to the departments of those majors that potentially interest you. Look at the bulletin boards. What are on the faculty doors? Look around.

- Go to the "quad" and student centers. What's going on there? What are the students doing?

- Sit and have a coffee in the café, a bite to eat in one of the cafeterias. Sit near some students. Eavesdrop. Yes! What are students talking about? Look around. Who's interacting with whom? People-watch.

- Go to the bookstore: What's for sale (besides books)? What's put out front? Academic things? Toys? Look around. Compare it to the bookstores on other campuses you visit.

3. Take the tour.

- Ask questions but don't hog the forum.

- Take lots of notes (and don't let your parents take them for you—a terrible offence).

- Be interested. You'd be amazed at how many students who go on tours look bored to death. That is not you.

4. Interview (see Worksheet 6.2): Have a copy of your CV and transcripts to share.

5. Ask yourself: How can you contribute to this campus? Do you want to? Do you see yourself here?

6. Is there Greek life on campus (fraternities and sororities)? Ask about it and look at how it's treated on campus: Are there Greek-life dorms? Is everyone involved? Is it community service-based or not?

Post-visit:

1. Email and thank anyone with whom you had valuable contact. Didn't get their card? Find their contact information.

2. Any further questions immediately after the visit? Send them to your Admissions contact.

3. Gauge where this university sits in your pecking order. Why is it ranked that way? Log it by writing it down. I'll ask you in the next chapter to confirm your Short List.

4. Are you still a fit? Go back and adjust and comment where necessary in the Short List.

5. Share your feedback! It's important that you and your family share your feedback after each visit.

Some questions to consider asking during your visit:

- What percentage of the students have cars?

- Are freshmen and sophomores allowed cars? (If so, get a gauge on how many leave campus on the weekends.)

- What do students [really] do on weekends? (Ask your guide or if feeling relaxed ask someone randomly in the cafeteria for a non-doctored up response.)

- Can you transfer from one school to another internally? How?

- What's the most popular major? (This can give insight into a college's culture and student body.) By what percentage?

- What examples do you have of students doing research with faculty (in humanities, in business, in science…)?

- (For your tour guide) As a freshman/sophomore, which classes did you not get into (in which departments and for which requirements) due to classes being full?

- Who hangs out with whom on this campus?

- What percentage of undergraduates do community service and what examples can you offer?

- What's the biggest issue on campus right now? Positive or negative. How's it being handled?

- Your own questions you want to ask list here. . .

My post visit reflections on this university:

Write this within 24 hours of your visit and not after you have visited another institution. It may change what you really felt.

Worksheet 6.2: Interview Worksheet

(Use in conjunction with Worksheet 6.3)

University name:

Interviewer name and title:

Time and location of interview:

Phone number and contact information of interviewer:

Do I have a CV to present to interviewer?

Do I have my transcripts to present to interviewer?

Things to point out or notes from Mock Interview regarding this university:

Questions I have for interviewer:

1.

2.

3.

4.

5.

. . .

Notes during interview:

Worksheet 6.3: Interview Contact/Schedule and Questions

University	Interview scheduled: time and date	Interviewer name	Interviewer contact details	Additional notes

CHAPTER 7

You Can't Fake It

August

S ummer, for those of you on the Northern Hemisphere calendar, is coming to a close. And for those of you on the Southern Hemisphere calendar, your July break went by in a flash. I hear it from *every* student regardless of where they live, what program they do in high school, or what they did during the summer. It was the quickest and busiest summer of their life...so far. It was filled with summer activities, work, volunteering, visiting campuses and working on school projects. Now that August is here, the dial goes from "drive" to "overdrive". It is time to get organized and set deadlines for specific days of this month.

Just about everything is critical this month in your Milestones. You're starting to review your university-specific applications, confirming important requirements and continuing your writing. Writing should never be put on the back burner, yet it's the easiest thing to ignore. It can be difficult, time-consuming and, you just can't fake it! If it's rushed, the reader will see it. If it's not your own voice, the reader will see it. If it's not given the care and attention it needs, the reader will see it!

You have lots of Milestones to accomplish in this step. If you complete them, you'll be raring to turn in your first applications in just a couple of months!

These are the Milestones for this chapter:

    Milestone 1: Registering With Application Portals

    Milestone 2: Other Universities and Their Applications

Milestone 3: Confirming Recommenders

 **Milestone 4:** Finalizing Your Main College Essay

 Milestone 5: Confirming the Universities on Your Short List

 Milestone 6: Confirming All Requirements and Deadlines

Milestone 7: (Re-)preparing for Standardized Testing

 Milestone 8: Requesting Interviews

Milestone 9: Continuing EGI

Milestone 10: Writing Workshop 3, Parts 2 & 3: Organizing and Brainstorming Supplement Essays

These are the resources you should have to hand during this chapter:

- Fiske Guide and/or other college guides from your Library
- The appropriate standardized testing prep books.

Case Study

Name: Sara

Gender: Female

Country: Hong Kong

Nationality: Turkish

Started process: A full 14 months before early applications (November) were due

Program/Rigor: IBDP Predicted 41

Standardized tests: Lots. Took SAT three times. SAT highest composite: 1510

Subject Tests: Biology 720, Spanish with Listening 700, and Literature 780

TOEFL/IELTS: Not required

Challenges: Smart as a whip and with an EQ beyond many adults my age, Sara was a massive procrastinator. She did not enjoy the US university application process and

---

having to "play the game". Likewise, Sara was hesitant to make any definitive decisions as to which universities she really loved, although we knew deep down she had her own "List".

Strengths: A fluid and avid writer, Sara has tremendous writing talent. (Still, this worried me as she was behind in her Milestones and fighting the process.) Sara is also very bright and got very good grades and is a strong test-taker with very strong interests in the arts and politics. Because Sara had opinions I knew she could more easily find her college fit (even though she wasn't letting any of us have it at this stage!). All of her interests were pursued with depth and she was genuine in her pursuance of them. Finally, Sara was respectful and eager to learn.

Fit/Factors: Politically active campus; not a huge party school; Liberal Arts education; East or West coast USA, nothing in between (save Chicago); ability to study her loves: literature, theatre, politics, perhaps a new language.

Interests: Sara has so many interests. Perhaps some of the deeper ones are music, people, theatre, literature and languages, leadership and current events.

Essay topic: As prolific a writer Sara is, she struggled with her essay topic as do most students and hers came late in the game as she procrastinated. Sara tied her summer work experience in a newsroom in Turkey—her home country—to her acting and directing of riskier theatre projects at school and the impact of this connection to her own life and how she views the world.

Short List: It was decided a few days before the deadline (and known by her parents and me but dragged out for weeks) that she would apply ED to Barnard. Luckily the supplement essays for Barnard had been completed before the deadline struck. University of Chicago—EA; Tufts; Pomona (possibly ED-2); Northwestern; USC; University of California Berkeley and San Diego; Wesleyan.

Interviews: Done at every university on her very Long List that allowed for interviews, both in person and over Skype.

Visits: She and her family did a whirlwind tour of the US in July between her junior and senior years to visit universities in California, Chicago and throughout the Northeast corridor of the US over four weeks.

EGI: For every school on her Long List. Well done here.

Dream school, if any: Barnard was her true fit and that came through in the application she wrote for them.

Application strategy: ED to Barnard. EA to University of Chicago. Pomona for ED-2.

MILESTONES

Milestone 1: Registering With Application Portals

Many of you will be using The Common Application for most of your applications. While registration for The Common Application has been opening earlier and earlier every year, it is about this time when applications are ready in full, which means that each university that houses its application under The Common Application (CA) will have its application ready to go in all its glory, including supplement questions and essays. To the latter point, it's here where you find out about all of the other university-specific questions each college has and will be requiring of you.

WORDS OF WISDOM: PUSHING BACK ON THE HYPE

Even though The Common Application and other applications are being made available to students earlier and earlier, I still think this is the right time to get to work on it. You're well into the process now and have a more strategic and thoughtful mind vis-à-vis US university Admission than you did a few months ago, where you may have started to approach the applications in a different, and perhaps less "thoughtful" way. Don't be swayed (or pressured) by those who are "getting in the game" earlier than you are. You're doing just fine and are getting in the game at the right time.

Please go to the applications you plan to apply to from your Short List and register. This is an exciting step! Take some time to get this done—it's simple but you don't want to rush this. There's nothing about this process you want to rush—start to use it by poking around those universities that are on your Short List, perhaps even selecting them to sit on your Dashboard/in your account. Here's what I would take an hour to do:

1. Register on The Common Application/other application portals you are using. Use your school email address.

2. Start to see how the program is set up and the dynamics of it. Becoming familiar with the interface is critical. Nothing you do now is going to be sent to any college; you have to pay [for most!] before you submit, so no worries about doing so by mistake at this point!

3. Take your Short List and go to those universities' applications. What are they asking? How do they look to you? You don't need to take any notes in this Milestone. Just review.

4. Register your Short List universities on your Dashboard for The Common Application/select your Short List universities in the application portals.

Milestone 2: Other Universities and Their Applications

Not all universities—but most—fall under The Common Application. Some universities have their own applications or prefer you use a different portal. This means that you'll be filling out more than just The Common Application as an application itself. It's more work but it must be done. Just because a university on your Short List has its own application does not mean you will not apply to it.

Please make sure you do the following for this Milestone:

1. List which universities on your Short List are not on The Common Application or on the UCA or Coalition application (which you registered for, if applicable, in July). You did this in Chapters 5 and 6 and have it noted in Worksheet 5.1 Column 7.

2. Please go to those universities' websites and register for their applications today. As with The Common Application, use your school email address.

Milestone 3: Confirming Your Recommenders

When you spoke to your potential recommenders face-to-face to ask them if they would consider writing a recommendation for you, for most of you, the teacher gave you an immediate answer; and, in most cases, this was a "yes". (For those who received the "no" from a potential recommender, you asked an alternate and should have continued doing so strategically until you received a positive response.)

I would like you to take the following action steps to confirm with your recommender at this stage that he/she will be writing for you soon, and to continue helping him/her to help you.

1. Draft an email to each of your recommenders and, in your own words, welcome them back from summer holiday and remind them of the conversation you both had prior to the break about them writing a recommendation for US universities on your behalf. If you had not yet received a confirmed "yes", you should ask them outright if they are willing.

2. In this same email, you can give them an idea of where you believe you will be applying, what institutions you are most excited about and why, and update them on your summer.

3. You can go ahead and attach your updated CV to this email for them "as an FYI".

4. Finally, in this same email I would suggest you request a meeting with them when you return to school or in the upcoming weeks to discuss your applications, their recommendation for you, and why you are planning to apply to the universities you have on your Short List.

IMPORTANT!

Many of you will be in high schools whose guidance offices also coordinate with the recommenders you have chosen, keeping them on the timeline and sending out a reminder to them. That's very helpful. I still recommend you do this Milestone as it's individual and part of you making and showing the effort to your recommender. Don't discredit the power and benefit of not relying on the system or another person and making your own effort! (You can refer back to Worksheet 5.4: Helping your Recommender Help You as a refresher.)

Then, I would go ahead and have this meeting and conversation with them. It won't be long but it will be memorable to them. Help them understand why you are applying to the schools you are and anything you've done or want to update them on since you last spoke. Also let the teacher know your timeline, in particular if you are applying to any university "early", which means they should be prepared to get the prompt from the university/application portal as soon as you register them as a recommender, and the deadline for getting this in.

After this meeting with your recommender I would like you to:

1. Please send a follow up email to the teacher/recommender to say thank you for their time.

2. Let them know when you plan to submit and what the deadlines are. You would appreciate it if they can get theirs in at least two weeks prior to the deadline.

3. Remind the recommender that the prompt for the recommendation will come directly from the university/CA/UCA and not from you. Advise that you have waived your right (which you will do and colleges expect you to do) to see his/her recommendation, assuring a most ethical and honest evaluation on his/her part.

4. You can go ahead and register these recommenders in your applications.

Milestone 4: Finalizing Your Main College Essay

Now that you have gone through several drafts of your first essay—The Common Application essay prompt that you chose to write about in Chapter 6—it's time to finalize that essay. You'll want to start to shift your focus to the applications themselves and the myriad supplement questions and essays from the specific universities on your Short List.

Please go ahead and finalize your essay, referring to the Writing Handbook for guidance. You should have the main college essay—whether it be the CA, UCA, Coalition or university-specific—ready to upload at this stage.

You can go ahead and share this final draft with the person who has been reviewing your essay all along. As I've said before, don't ask for too many opinions; one person's honest feedback and suggestions is enough.

Milestone 5: Confirming the Universities on Your Short List

Before you begin this Milestone, please note that it should be done at the same time as Milestone 6.

You've worked hard to get to this point and now you should be close to certain on the universities that have made your Short List, and why. For this Milestone, I would like you to do the following in a methodical and thoughtful way. That means thinking about why you are doing it and checking in with your gut and feelings as you do it:

1. Please go back to Worksheet 5.1: My Short List

2. Make sure that all of your universities listed on Worksheet 5.1 are also uploaded in each of the application portals. That means, for instance, if you are using The Common Application, all of your universities should show up right now on the Dashboard.

3. Review Column 3 in Worksheet 5.1: My Short List and your reasons for fit for each.

Now move on to the next Milestone. These two should be done together.

Milestone 6: Confirming All Requirements and Deadlines

With all of your university applications available from having completed Milestone 5, please do the following:

1. Refer to Worksheet 5.1. Go ahead and log all of the requirements for each university currently in Column 14.

2. You can find the requirements in the application itself (e.g., two supplement essays, both required) and online on the university's website (e.g., two Subject Tests recommended).

3. For Column 15, copy verbatim the supplement prompts and questions onto Worksheet 5.1. If there is a supplement that consists of several short or one-word answers, you do not need to copy that directly into the Short List. Instead, indicate what it is and what is expected of you.

4. When you have finished, you should have both "Chapter 7" columns completed and filled out for each university on Worksheet 5.1.

Milestone 7: (Re-)preparing for Standardized Testing

You have just finished confirming your requirements for each university on Worksheet 5.1. Now is the time to confirm what you're planning to do about standardized testing, perhaps again.

Remember to check in with the universities where you plan to apply under their Early policy and find out about their testing policy. Some will want you to take all standardized testing and have the results before the application deadline. Others will ask that you simply complete the testing prior to the deadline, knowing that your results will not come in and therefore not be sent to them until after the strict deadline. It's your responsibility to know this for each university. When in doubt, go to the university website. Still confused? Ask your university contact or give them a quick call to make sure. I always like my students to have things in writing unless there's a time issue and then calling is the best bet. If you do call, follow up with an email to confirm what was concluded in the call.

IMPORTANT!

Rushing scores: Be careful of "rushing" any scores—this means paying an extra fee to get your scores "rushed" to a specified university, presumably to make a deadline. Some universities will not accept rushed scores. It is your responsibility to know every individual university's policy.

TOEFL—and in many cases IELTS—will be required of non-native English speakers. In other cases, one of these two tests may be required of an applicant who was born speaking a language other than English, even if English currently is his/her strongest language and considered his/her main language. Call it what you like, but each university has its own policy on this and it's your responsibility to know what the policy is and abide by it, keeping in mind deadlines and the time it takes to receive results and send scores. For many of my students who also apply to UK universities, I recommend they take IELTS as this is now the test of English as a foreign language that is required by UK universities. And if they are applying to both countries it prevents them from having to take what is essentially a similar test twice; but, of course you want to make sure that your US universities will all accept IELTS instead of TOEFL.

A few reminders at this stage about standardized testing:

1. If you need to take the TOEFL/IELTS, do it now. It can be determined by going to a university's requirements page and/or by talking to your Admissions officer at said university. You will need to determine if you should study for this or not.

2. How many times have you already taken the SAT or ACT? Generally speaking, I am hesitant advising my students to take it a third time, unless the first time was a shot-in-the-dark with zero preparation. Very rarely do students do better the third time around if they've prepared for previous sittings. In addition, it's expensive and means more stress during an already stressful time. Bottom line, are you using your limited time and energy most efficiently?

3. Make sure you understand terms like "super scoring", "score choice", "test-optional" and "single-sitting" and "test-flexible" and which is the policy of each of your colleges.

WORDS OF WISDOM: SENDING ALL TEST SCORES

Some schools will say they will only consider your highest score on the ACT or SAT but want to know all of your scores. I have parents and students ask me one question about this: "Do I have to send in my other tests, then?" My response is this: "What are they asking you? They want to know if you've taken the test other times and, if so, what you've scored." To me it's clear, you send them. If you worry that the other tests you did poorly on will negatively affect you, you should have faith in the system and what the institution is telling you. Why would you start off by being less than one hundred percent transparent in your application? They ask for a reason and you should be transparent for a reason.

Milestone 8: Requesting Interviews

Don't disregard this Milestone even if you went on campus visits during the past months and did interviews back in the last chapter (Chapter 6)! This is your time to triple-check that you've requested interviews at every university on your Short List, so please pay careful attention to this Milestone. Every year one of my students misses one.

For those of you who have not yet done interviews, now's your time to start requesting them when applicable, if you have not already completed that by the last chapter in Milestone 2. Before I outline the steps in this Milestone, let me tell you why I tell my students to request interviews whenever they can.

It's no secret that not every university will make interviews a part of their Admissions process. Abiding by the case-by-case rule with everything, each institution is different in how they handle interviews. Some institutions—usually the larger ones who receive tens of thousands of applications—will not conduct interviews. Make sure you know this before you ask a university for an interview! Nothing is more "lazy" than getting in touch with your Admissions representative to request an interview when he turns around and sends you a link to their application pages saying, "USC does not conduct interviews."

Know your schools.

For those that do conduct interviews, there is no "set way" that a student requests one. Some universities will ask students to register via an online portal. Some just say they do conduct interviews but leave it to the student to figure out how to request one (i.e. send a personal email). Some institutions only conduct them during certain periods and some will only have alumni conduct interviews and only if they are located in your country. Some require that international students pay a fee for an interview.

All in all, the interview is most often an optional part of the process. And, when you have this option, take it! I vividly recall being in Saigon recruiting for a US university and meeting students in my hotel lobby for 45-minute interviews. The 14 students that made the effort to contact me to arrange an interview, clearly stayed in my mind once it came time to review their applications.

You see yet again just how subjective this process can be.

Remember to use Worksheet 6.2 and Worksheet 6.3 for the preparation for the interview and during the interview itself, whether it is in person, on campus, or over Skype.

IMPORTANT!

With colleges, there are always exceptions! For instance, Boston College does not interview candidates. It is not a part of their holistic process. However, you may hear of someone who has interviewed at BC. Those candidates who apply to BC's restrictive early action program are considered for their Presidential Scholar program. This is a highly selective program whereby the top 2% of the REA applicant pool is invited to campus from around the globe (all costs covered by BC) to have a weekend of interviews, seminars, talks and discussions. Depending on the year, a few handfuls of students will ultimately be chosen for a full-ride scholarship, with grants, travel money, exclusive seminars and opportunities. So make sure you're looking closely at all the opportunities and possibilities of those schools that make your List.

Now for your steps in this Milestone:

1. Please refer to Column 10 in Worksheet 5.1: My Short List.

2. Find out if each school is visiting your high school or country/city in the next month and if so, request an interview in person. It doesn't matter if the Admissions representative does not make a formal visit to your high school; you can still meet with her/him and most will be thrilled to find a time to meet with you. This is what I did, for instance, in Saigon as I mentioned above. Students whose high schools I did not formally visit and who contacted me, I met in my hotel lobby for the interview.

3. Request interviews at *every* university that conducts them on your Short List. Not sure if you're going to apply or not? Still request an interview. You want to get

in front of another human being in this process. Follow the institution's specific guidelines for requesting interviews. Each one is distinct!

4. Follow up with an institution after 10 days if you don't hear back from them.

Don't forget to record—once confirmed—the time and date and contact details of the interviewer in your master list, Worksheet 6.3: Interview Contact/Schedule and Questions.

In Chapter 8, we'll discuss how you prepare for your interviews and how to follow up.

IMPORTANT!

If you already have interviews scheduled and will be doing them shortly, please skip to Milestone 7 in Chapter 8 to prepare for these interviews appropriately. This is the only time in this entire book I'll tell you that you can skip forward to a Milestone. Once you have dealt with this, I will see you back here to continue the process.

WORDS OF WISDOM: PARENTS REQUESTING ON BEHALF OF THEIR CHILD—NO!

A mother called me and asked if it would "be ok" if she requested all of the interview appointments for her daughter, as her daughter was "in the middle of tons of work this summer". My response: Absolutely not. There are myriad reasons for this very quick and direct answer, the most valuable being the following:

1. No Admissions office wants to receive calls from parents requesting things for their child. This is the first strike against the applicant and that can end up on their file.

2. Parents write differently than young adults. Trying to pass as your child in writing is a big mess just waiting to happen, and it will happen. Don't try it.

3. All children will have millions of tasks awaiting them, both in this process and in life. What would this teach them? Doing the tasks they should be doing themselves is setting them up for failure in many ways.

Milestone 9: Continuing EGI

It is extremely important to note that some universities track what we call EGI (and what the field calls Demonstrated Interest) and some do not. You can refer back to Chapters 4 and 5 for what EGI entails and why you do it. The point I want to make here is to not worry about who tracks it and who does not. It does not mean that if they do not track it, you won't ask your questions you have for the university.

I have my students connect with their Admissions officer at every single one of their Short List universities to show their genuine interest, but also to ask their specific questions and to start to learn how to network. You never know when that contact—and the ability to connect with that person—will be someone you need to ask a question of in the future, and it is a sure bet that you will. There's a lot more to come in this process and a lot more case-specific questions you'll very likely have.

So, for this Milestone, you should review the EGI you have to date with each university on your Short List (Worksheet 4.2). Check whether you need to follow up with any of them.

Milestone 10: Writing Workshop 3, Parts 2 and 3—Organizing and Brainstorming Supplement Essays

The last Milestone in this Chapter is not a simple one, so I suggest you start this when you're fresh and rested, without distractions.

We will be referring to the Writing Handbook for this Milestone. However, before you get moving on organizing and brainstorming your supplement essays and questions for each university on your Short List, I'd like to make a few points about these "university-specific" essays and questions.

Hundreds of universities will want to know more about their applicants beyond what The Common Application or other applications require. Usually this comes in the form of additional and university-specific essays, questions or requests of the applicant. It's a more in-depth way for the university to understand the applicant, his/her reasoning for applying to that university, his/her fit, and to make a more accurate determination on their end if that student is someone they want on their campus.

If you were a university and required the applicant to answer some of your specific questions about fit, about your passions, about, perhaps, your favorite snack food (yes, this has been asked before!), do you think that the college would pay close attention to these answers?

It is not only in your best interest but absolutely expected of you that you'll put time, dedication and individual attention into these questions. What's a sure-fire way to tell if you have or have not? I always say to a student when reviewing his/her supplement essay for a university, "If I can cut and paste this for another institution, you have not done your job at writing this well enough. Try again."

The supplement essays and questions require precision, dedication, thoughtfulness and show that you've done your research, and that you know the institution and why you are applying to that institution. This is another reason for all of the work you did in earlier chapters in defending your choices.

Please go to your Writing Handbook, Writing Workshop 3 Parts 2 and 3, and begin your outline and brainstorming for each supplement section for each university on your Short List. Drafts should be completed by the end of this month in order to prepare for full first and second draft editions of each supplement for your "early" schools in September. If you have a video option, this is where you'll also be completing Part 3 of Writing Workshop 3.

★ ★ ★ ★ ★

Once you've completed all of the Milestones from this chapter, go and take a short break. Go and do something that relaxes you and makes you smile. After that, be prepared to start Chapter 8 in earnest. The next two months will be the busiest of this process for you. You're making good progress, though, so nothing should be too much to handle at this point!

CHAPTER 8

The Pressure Is On!

September

As we move into September, there's excitement in the air; you are probably happy, nervous and thrilled to be back at school for your final year and university Admissions are at the forefront. . .yet you have no idea what this part of the process will really be like when it hits.

Preparing yourself in September means heeding the advice here and following your Milestones just as you have been doing; this "class" called university Admissions is soon to be graded.

The list of Milestones for this month is one of the longest, yet the busiest month to come will be next month! Here's the most important thing for you to know about this month moving forward—and that's for Northern Hemisphere students and for Southern Hemisphere students reaching graduation shortly: the scrutiny put forth by Admissions officers vis-à-vis your academic performance in these months will never be as high. This is your time to commit to doing your best, focusing and telling yourself you won't settle until you know you've given your full effort. You owe it to yourself. This is what it means to make a commitment—it feels great to start down the path knowing you will have no regrets.

I ask you to keep that in mind as you go through this month's Milestones, as there are many. You'll have a load of schoolwork as well, so you will likely have to decrease the amount of social or leisure activities. This is just for the short term, so use this as an opportunity to learn some self-control.

Here are your Milestones for September:

 Milestone 1: Re-confirming Your Short List: The most important column

 Milestone 2: Confirming Requirements and Your Own Application Deadlines for Each University on Your Short List

 Milestone 3: Confirming Your Early Applications and Schedule

 Milestone 4: Completing Supplements for Your Early Applications

 Milestone 5: Filling in Your Applications

Milestone 6: Reminding Your Recommenders

 Milestone 7: Completing Your Interviews for Early Applications

 Milestone 8: Sitting Standardized Tests

These are the resources you should have to hand during this chapter:

- Standardized testing guides from your Library

- You may also like to refer to Khan Academy online. Khan Academy is a free education portal that offers free SAT prep: www.khanacademy.org.

Case Study

Name: Xavier

Gender: Male

Country: Spain

Nationality: Swiss and Spanish

Started process: 12 months prior to Early application submissions (November).

Program/Rigor: US public high school for one year; Spanish public high school, final three years of high school.

Grades to date: Some very strong, some fairly weak. Inconsistent. Many on an upward trajectory from grade 10 to grade 12 but a few that were not. Some inconsistency in the same subject areas when Xavier moved from the US to Spain.

Standardized tests: ACT twice with self-prep, 26 and 28 composite score

Subject tests: None

TOEFL/IELTS: He ended up taking IELTS to make sure, since he did spend time in high school in the US but English was not his home language.

Challenges: The obvious ones are Xavier's inconsistent grades and not very strong test scores. Neither match his intellect, which is very high. He has been in two very different and also quite rigorous public secondary school systems, where the latter is particularly known to be very difficult to receive "high grades". Xavier is also very new to this process and the expectations and "norms" of the US application. In his final educational system (Spain), community service, sport, and extracurriculars are not embedded into the curriculum, giving him fewer opportunities to take part.

Strengths: Xavier is very smart, dedicated, and is a hard worker. He loves to write and to play football (but is not of the level or interest to play competitively in college). He is passionate about history and, he thinks, economics. He has a playful personality and is drawn to new experiences and cultures and languages.

Fit/Factors: It became quite clear and obvious after just a few months that a liberal arts college would be critical. Focus on undergraduate education and a liberal student body were important. Xavier wanted to know his professors and for them to know him. He was also seeking an embracing environment, one where the student body is accepting of new thoughts, people and ideas, but where he could take risks and explore new things.

Interests: History, writing, some photography and travel.

Essay topic: Xavier wrote about self-identity through his interests in casual photography and assessing what he learned about himself by evaluating his own photographs, something he had never done prior to having to sit down and write an essay.

Short List: Lewis & Clark, Willamette, Bates, Reed, Colby, Goucher, Kalamazoo, Connecticut College, Elon, Lawrence, Bowdoin.

Interviews: With all colleges on his Short List.

Visits: Visited his Short List schools on the West and East coasts.

EGI: This was very strong. He struggled at first but learned to manage this with ease.

Dream school, if any: Bowdoin at the end of the day.

Application strategy: ED to Bowdoin.

MILESTONES

Milestone 1: Re-confirming Your Short List: The Most Important Column

Please do this here and now without having to refer to your notes or previous work. Your answers should come easily and naturally to you:

What I need in a university:

_____   _____   _____
_____   _____   _____

What I want in a university:

_____   _____   _____
_____   _____   _____
_____

Once done, go to Worksheet 5.1: My Short List, Column 3. Confirm all of the universities in that column that make your Short List at this stage again.

Compare what you have in Column 3 to the exercise you just did above: do they meet/fit with your needs and with your wants? *They absolutely should.* You're rounding out your List and for many of you little will change after this stage and once you set yourself to applying. Your choices are just about set. The answer to this question will help us with those to come.

The information in Column 3 is the most important information you have and is the culmination of months of hard work on your part. It is when your months of research come back to serve you. Can you define your fit for each university? What does it look like for Elon University? It's a different answer for Goucher College, which is also on your list. Maybe it overlaps a bit with Juniata College—as you're keen on community service, have demonstrated that throughout high school, and want to make that a big part of your university career—but it won't be the exact same response. Think about what I have been hammering away at this the entire process: *Your reason for fit for a particular institution will be unique to that institution.*

Think of them as different people: Why are Helena and Arun great friends of yours? They are both loyal, true friends and they both make you laugh. Helena will tell you when you're out of line; you want that and need that in friendship. Arun pushes you in everything you do, makes you a better person and friend. You want and need that as well. Your ability to distinguish what makes them unique to you as friends is critical in showing them that you know and understand them, and why you need them as friends. This is the same when it comes to your relationship with the individual universities on your List. Show them they are right for you—why you need them and why they need you.

IMPORTANT!

Let's remember a very important point from Chapter 5. When I say "rounding out" your List, I am talking about creating a realistic, thoughtful List based on fit, whereby the majority of those institutions on the List will be in range for you in terms of academic profile, campus culture and, while you are not sure to get in anywhere, they are neither too far in either direction for a possible admission. Then you should have a few on either side, both those that you would be thrilled to get into and are a reach for you academically or statistically, and those few that you would be thrilled to get into and where you will present yourself as quite strong vis-à-vis their academic profile.

As I've said earlier, many high schools will limit the number of universities to which their students can apply to about 10. This is reasonable.

What is not reasonable is when a high school tries to manipulate their students' choice based on their own objectives, which could be statistics. There are many high schools who will promote themselves based on their college Admissions standards and acceptances. This is a product of immense competition between schools. One high school might say: "Ninety percent of our students are admitted into their five top colleges!" When you see such a claim, you should dig into stats. How were their lists determined?

I have had many students who were told not to apply to a certain college. The intention was not in their best interest but instead in the interest of the high school. They did not want to get too many rejections that year, which would alter their own stats. I find this unethical and tell my students to push against it; they cannot be told by their high school where they should or should not apply.

You can be guided but at the end of the day, it's up to you. If you want to apply to Bowdoin but know it's a reach yet within your profile and have taken that into consideration in your Short List, apply! Don't let anyone tell you not to apply unless it's in *your own* best interest.

So, you've reconfirmed your Short List, questioned those institutions that you cannot come up with a legitimate fit for and have replaced them, where and when possible, with another. You should now have about 8–12 universities on Worksheet 5.1.

Now, please confirm your colleges again in Column 16 on Worksheet 5.1, indicating which universities fall into a reach category (1–3), which are in-range (the majority) and which are likely (2–3).

IMPORTANT!

Don't forget to check out and confirm which fairs will be visiting your country/city this month and during this period. This is high season for Admissions officers to do their traveling and many cannot make a visit to every individual high school, so they'll join a tour instead to try to meet with as many students as possible in the region/area. It's only natural that you cannot visit all of the institutions that make your Short List and this is a great opportunity to meet with Admissions officers (usually the ones who will be reading your application and making the decision on it!) and university representatives, quite possibly even setting up an official interview with them while they are in town. So, go and check out university fairs that will be swinging by your region. Some to look out for include: Linden Fairs, CIS Tours, Education USA Tours, and so on.

Milestone 2: Confirming Requirements and Your Own Application Deadlines for Each University on Your Short List

Please stay on Worksheet 5.1. You should reconfirm the requirements in Column 5 with two sources:

1. The Common Application/application portal.
2. The university's website.

IMPORTANT!

This is a reminder from our discussions in Chapters 5 and 6. What if a university on your Short List is test-optional or "highly recommends" a Subject Test? How will you gauge this gray area? I have some suggestions:

First, you should read what the university's website says about this. Usually they will explain what "test-optional" means to them. Some universities will ask you to still send test scores if you've taken them, but say they won't take them into consideration then. Some will ask you to submit a project or paper in lieu of a standardized test. Sometimes I have students who have decent test scores but perhaps just on the lower end of the middle 50% range that colleges and guidebooks like the *Fiske Guide* publish to give a range. Do you submit them? It's going to depend. Look at your grades. Look at your courses and their rigor. Look at what the strengths of your application will be. Do you think it can stand strong without any tests considered?

Finally, when in doubt, go ahead and ask your Admissions contact. By now you've shown ample EGI and can send her a note perhaps asking her opinion. Be strategic about this, but I've found that in every case of my student having done this, the outcome has been positive—whether it was to ask if he should sit a Subject Test or submit his ACT scores or otherwise. Remember: There is no black-and-white answer. You really have to feel out the problem to get to a solution that works for you. Don't overanalyze and always review on a case-by-case basis. It will be more work but you'll be guaranteed a more thoughtful outcome, and less chance of feeling like you passed something over.

WORDS OF WISDOM: COURSES YOU'RE TAKING THIS YEAR

While many students confirmed the courses they would take before their final year of high school before the break—or even earlier for IB diploma candidates—some students are still selecting as they start their final year. It's critical that you evaluate your course load accurately and thoughtfully. Selective universities will expect that you are taking/have taken five core courses for the four years of your high school career—that's English, Mathematics, Science (with lab), Foreign Language, and Social Science and if you drop one, you will need to look at taking a course that would be of equal "rigor". Every institution is different, so be sure you look at requirements or what is highly recommended in their Admissions standards. Some universities will require four years of English and Mathematics but three for Social Sciences, Foreign Language and Science (with lab). Of course, this may also depend on what field you are interested in going into and the institution. As usual, there's no solid black and white answer, but there is a way to gauge and understand which decision will be best for you. Go back to the discussions in the earlier chapters (particularly Chapter 2) of how applications are reviewed; grades are one thing, yet rigor is just as important. Admissions officers want to see that you have challenged yourself considering the types of courses offered at your high school.

Milestone 3: Confirming Your Early Applications and Schedule

Will you apply Early to any of your universities? And more importantly, why?

Please have Worksheet 5.1 in front of you for this Milestone. Which schools are you planning to apply to under their Early policy? What are their deadlines? Please confirm that now in Column 17. Do you understand the policies of each?

How are you making this decision? So much depends on so many things. Let's take Early Admissions in general. That includes all types of Early applications. Here are some factors to consider:

- *Time management*

    If you have prepared yourself well, this month your Milestones match up with what is in this chapter. If you're able to manage what is asked of you this month, I'd ask you to consider applying Early to at least one institution (considering what your "Early" options are for each). The reason is that since you're already well prepared, it will help space out your applications. This should help you get at least one, or perhaps several, applications out by November. This way you don't leave all of your applications for December; this is called time management. This must be more deeply considered for Early Decision (ED) applications. More on that below.

- *EGI*

    Also, by applying Early to an institution you are in fact telling that institution that they are your first choice, or one of the first. You're showing a lot of love and that's also showing some EGI. The school will take this into consideration. You're showing them that they are topping your List.

- *Your clear first choice*

    The other reason will be this: Do you have an institution that you can answer yes to this question? "I would love to attend X University and can see myself there and would absolutely (this would be for ED)/highly consider (more EA) attending if they accepted me. It's at the very top of my Short List." The key word for an ED application being "absolutely". Without that confirmation to yourself, think again.

- *Statistics*

    Many students will look at the statistics of acceptance during an Early round versus the Regular round. One selective school filled half of their class last year with its ED round and had several fewer students applying Early than Regular, thus, indeed, making the admission rate quite a bit higher during the Early round. It is important to know this when you're considering where to apply. It's playing the game, for sure; but, if you are not aware of it, you're not fully educating yourself on how the process works and how to make a strategic and smart decision for yourself.

Which schools are at the top of your Short List? What policies do they have? Remember this: ED is binding. This means you must absolutely attend if you are accepted and—if the school's individual policy allows you to apply EA to other schools—you must unequivocally retract all EA applications if you are accepted to the accepting ED school immediately upon acceptance. (If you are denied or put into a RD pool, you do not retract the EA applications.)

WORDS OF WISDOM: EARLY DECISION (ED)

ED has become incredibly popular in this process and the option has, in my opinion, made the process less than healthy. As you determine your ED school, please consider this: Profiles by universities are not compromised when they choose from their ED pool of applicants so don't go hedging bets on it; you must stay within your fit.

Remember that "acceptance rates" are low because of the quantity of applicants that apply to these institutions, not because they are necessarily better than institutions with higher acceptance rates. It's a matter of numbers. Remember my earlier anecdote when a Dean of one of the most highly selective universities told me years ago, "Jennifer, we could have filled four classes with the quantity of applicants who fit us and who we wanted; we just are not big enough."

Finally, here is a quick anecdote about being accepted ED. My student Nikki was accepted ED to her top school. She sent me an email as soon as she found out—the middle of the night for both of us—and called me at an appropriate hour the next morning to say how thrilled she was. Once we both had calmed down from the excitement of it all, I told her that she had to email that very day all of her Admissions contacts at the schools to which she applied EA and tell them she was withdrawing her EA application immediately, giving the reason why and to thank that person for all of the time and energy they put towards her.

"I have to do it today?" she asked.

"Absolutely," I replied. "Imagine that they are considering accepting you for EA, and have chosen you over another very strong candidate. How dare you not give that opportunity to the other candidate now that you have no interest or ability to attend said university!"

She did so immediately and I would say the same to you if you are fortunate enough to be accepted ED by your first choice.

WORDS OF WISDOM: WHAT'S A POLYTECHNIC IN THE US?

The university that Nikki was accepted to has "Polytechnic" in its name. As I am writing this I am reminded of a discussion I had with her parents early on in our working together, about "polytechnics". Her mother told me after she saw Nikki's Long List, "We don't want a 'polytechnic'." In brief, there are many countries around the globe where a "polytechnic" has a stigma of being less than a university, or perhaps not the strongest academic institution in its class. In the US, there are several universities—4-year degree-granting accredited institutions that offer Bachelors, Masters, PhD programs—that have "polytechnic" in the name. In the same way that a university in the US having "college" in its name is still a full university, this is also the case for a "polytechnic" in the US. My point is that you should not dismiss anything until you know what you are dismissing.

IMPORTANT!

For the record, you can only apply to one ED school. You sign an agreement saying that you have done so and that, if accepted, you will attend said university. There is no question about doing this as your ethical reputation is on the line and you commit fraud by signing such an agreement and not abiding by it. Your parent agrees to this. Your counselor also agrees to this and will send only one transcript to one ED school on your behalf. If, for some reason, this is misunderstood or your counselor is not aware of how this works and agrees to send a transcript to more than one university for ED, the university will find out. Many other universities will inevitably find out. Admissions officers from different universities talk. . .a lot. You will forever put fellow classmates from your school at risk for attending that institution as the Admissions officers will look at your high school with an untrusting eye in the future.

I would say if you are prepared to apply to a maximum of three EA schools (due to the load and quality of time needed for each) without feeling unprepared or forcing it, go for it. At the same time we are seeing more and more schools going ED. Continue to watch the policies for each institution for Single-Choice-Early-Action or Restricted-Early-Action where you may not apply to another EA school. Only apply Early if you are ready. Not everyone does and not everyone should.

The Enlightened Insider: Some "Early" application options

Always check each individual university's policy on their website as none of these are standard and a university can adhere to whatever policy it chooses!

EA: Early Action. You apply Early and get the decision before the New Year (in most cases). You don't have to make your decision to accept the school back until 1 May*, and once, presumably you've heard from your RD schools.

ED: Early Decision. Apply Early and get the decision before the new year. Binding. You must be ready to attend if you are accepted. You can only apply to one ED school and in most cases—check your ED school's policy—can apply to other EA schools. But, if you get in, see my example on the previous page—notify and retract your applications from all of your EA schools (and RD if applicable).

ED2: Early Decision 2. Restrictions are the same as for ED(1) above, but the deadline is later and notification is therefore later. This allows a student to, presumably, apply to one school ED, and if she/he does not get accepted, go for ED2 at another school. Confused yet?

SCEA/REA: Single Choice Early Action/Restricted Early Action. Apply Early and get the decision before the New Year. You may not apply to another school Early Action. In other words, like ED, you apply to just one school EA, but unlike ED you are not bound to attend if you get in. You can still go through the RD round and take your decision on May 1*.

---

*May 1 is the agreed-upon deadline by all universities that students must "accept back" and inform their institution if they are going to attend, with a deposit. This does not pertain to ED accepted students.

To conclude this Milestone, please go to Worksheet 5.1, Column 18. Plan to get each application completed early. This is a critical Milestone to complete in order to keep you on pace moving through the rest of the chapter and month.

Milestone 4: Completing Supplements for Your Early Applications

Please have Worksheet 5.1 on hand for this Milestone, as you will be referring to the supplements confirmed for each of the schools that you completed in Chapter 7, Column 15.

In Chapter 7 you brainstormed and outlined the supplements for your Early schools. Now is the time to go ahead and finish the supplements for your Early universities, pacing them out according to the schedule you created earlier.

You should use this time now to work on your Early supplements. If you want to stay well paced, you should have them completed by the end of this chapter and month. This Milestone is one you'll come back to over the next few days and weeks in order to complete. We will revisit your supplements for your Early schools next month, but really just to tie them up and review them as you submit your Early applications.

IMPORTANT!

Your fit comes first. Without having articulated this to yourself—verbally, in writing, and thoughtfully—you will not be able to turn out a substantive supplement, whether it's an essay or a three-word response. The fit and how you articulate it for each institution is directly tied to the supplement questions. This is your opportunity to tell the individual institution why you are right for them, making your case to be considered and hopefully accepted. Do not take them lightly.

Remember, in Chapter 2 we discussed how to be a strong candidate and the importance of the following coming through in your applications:

- Intellectual curiosity
- Showing the real you: being true to yourself and honest
- Depth, both of character and in terms of interests and academics
- Showing your fit and EGI
- Doing your own work
- Staying clear of sounding privileged
- Strong essays and written components
- Leadership

- And, as a niche candidate, showing your depth of involvement. If you're going into engineering, for instance, this would be by discussing any true research that was done. If you're an artist, it would be by putting forth a well-thought-out and comprehensive portfolio.

To Parents and Guardians: While I know you're nervous right now, try to step aside and trust your child's ability to put forth a solid application. Keep in mind the Parent Advice! from Yasmine in Chapter 7. The more you interfere, the more you take away from an authentic application being put forth, and in the long run, putting your son or daughter at a disadvantage. Trust me on this. It's important that you give your child the ability to come through genuinely and properly in his or her application.

Milestone 5: Filling in Your Applications

As you tackle this Milestone, I would like you to have the following set up for yourself:

- At least 2 hours of time.
- You're in a quiet place—generally where you do your homework.
- You are using the computer—presumably your laptop—that you will do all of your essay writing on and submit your applications from.
- You're free from distractions. Turn off your phone and tell your friends to go home.

I would suggest you begin with The Common Application, if you're using it, or the application portal where you have the majority of your applications. You can then use this as your home base of information as you fill out other applications that require the same information.

About The Common Application or your main application portal

Please note that I will use The Common Application terms here as most of you will be using this at the time of publication. All advice is transferable to every portal since they all ask for similar information, perhaps using different terms from time to time.

1. **Log in**: Use your school email address and use the name that appears on your passport.
2. There are several tabs on The Common Application. Get familiar with them:
   a. **Dashboard/Main Tab**: This will give an overview of the colleges you've selected and where you are in the application process with each.
   b. **My Colleges/Your list of colleges**: Here are the college-specific applications. You'll have an opportunity to select recommenders for each college and you will find each college-specific essay(s) and question(s) here.

c. **Common Application/Application itself**: This is the application that all colleges to which you apply will see. I'll ask you to get started on it during this month.

d. **College Search**: Here's where you search for colleges to put on the Dashboard and on your My Colleges tab. We'll get to that now.

3. **My Colleges/Your list of colleges**: Start searching for the colleges that currently make your Short List in the College Search tab and select them—"add" them—so that they appear on your Dashboard. Do that for all the colleges that you have on your Short List to date, even the ones you are uncertain about. Once you've done this, go to the Dashboard and take a look at your List. Click over to My Colleges. Now, review each college's additional and supplement writing and their deadlines and testing policy.

4. **Common Application/Application itself**: Go to The Common App tab/to the main application page of the portal you are using and click through all of the side tabs on the left: Profile, Family, Education, Testing, Activities, and Writing. There will be a lot you need to do. Let's start with the overview and then divide them into what you will accomplish this month and the next:

a. **Profile/Candidate Information**: Fill this information in. Much of it is self-explanatory.

b. **Family**: This is also self-explanatory. Note that when they ask you about your siblings, as soon as you mention they attend or graduated from a university, they will ask which one.

c. **Education**: Finish this section by the end of the month. This section will take a little more time than the first two.

    i. Register your school in The Common App on the first part of this section. This will also link to the My Colleges tab and the **Recommendations** and **FERPA waiver** area for each. If your school uses Naviance (the American "college and career readiness software provider") this is registered within the Common App at this stage.

IMPORTANT!

The FERPA waiver (Family Educational Rights and Privacy Act waiver) tells the university that you waive the right to review the materials sent to the college by a recommender or counselor, ensuring that said recommender or counselor has written on your behalf freely, ensuring their truthfulness and honesty.

---

ii. Be precise about any changes or interruptions in your education, whether you attended a different school for a few months during your high school career or started at a different one and switched a year or two later to your current one. If this applies to you and you did receive grades and transcripts at a different school, you will most likely be asked to submit those as well, unless your current school and Guidance Counselor have access to those and can submit them all together. Please ask your Guidance Counselor about this to make sure you do not turn in an incomplete application.

iii. Pay careful attention when keying in your current year or most recent courses as they will be cross-referenced to the official transcripts sent by your counselor to each university. Be precise.

IMPORTANT!

If you're a dual citizen with an American passport, you must report that American passport. It would be considered illegal for you to do otherwise, and then request a student visa, only to arrive in the US and be found you also carry a US passport. You'll end up not going to university and will be sent back home.

---

d. **Activities**: These are evaluated closely. Here's your opportunity to set yourself apart. Some things to remember and to consider as you fill this out:

i. Generally it is advised—and I think for good reason—that you list those activities that you engage in with the most depth first, moving down the list in decreasing depth. Another way to think about it is which activities define you the most? Start with those that mean the most to you.

ii. Refer to your CV as you work through this on your applications. You may have forgotten something or it may remind you of what you don't want to forget to tell the Admissions office.

iii. Some of you will have far more than the allotted 10 activities. Here's my advice:

- Focus on those that are specific and that have most meaning to you here.

- Focus on those activities that you're engaged in/were engaged in with both depth and breadth.

- For those who have specific activities that also tie to others you've done with depth and breadth, consider adding this to your Additional Information section strategically. You don't want to do this if it just amounts to a list. No Admissions officer wants to see long lists that show a lot of activities but no depth. In one case, a student of mine added it to her Additional Information section with her reasoning—her whole persona is tied to theatre and community service even though she was not applying to a theatre major or program—and it made very good strategic sense.

iv. I also have plenty of students who do *not* have 10 activities to fill in. Not only is this not a problem but it can be to their advantage. By not filling in all 10 you may be showing the Admissions officer that you're committed to those you do and that you don't have that inclination to "fill in for the sake of filling in", a mistake many applicants make.

v. You're given a word limit and for good reason. You have to be concise; do not use slang, misspell, or make use of gross abbreviations.

5. **Writing/Application Essay**: This is where you will select the prompt you have chosen to write about and eventually—next month for your Early applications—cut and paste your finished essay into the appropriate box. You can go ahead and select your prompt here, but don't cut and paste your essay into the box unless you've truly completed it. That means it's been spell-checked a million times and you're ready to move away from it. If you are pasting it in here now, go ahead and review it for formatting and any typographical changes that may occur in placing it into The Common App. This sometimes happens with certain countries' keyboards or computer programs.

Do the same as above for each of your other applications at this time. We will not revisit this until you review your application before it is submitted. Dedicate time to do this and do it well.

IMPORTANT!

Most application portals have space for you to offer "additional information". In fact, this is what it is called in The Common Application—an open space for you to add something you feel the Admissions committee must know about you and that has not been properly addressed anywhere else in your application. I advise my students to consider this after they have completed each application in its entirety. After reviewing the entire application for that specific university, is there anything that they feel is truly missing that they feel compelled to share with Admissions?

This is not an opportunity to craft another creative essay or draw out your list of activities or to tell the Admissions committee why you are dying to attend their institution. You've had ample opportunity to do that in the application itself. Was there a massive dip in your grades at some stage in your high school career? Did you suffer a number of absences? Explain what happened. Give context to this information so that the Admissions committee can fill in the blanks. So, in essence, give Admissions more information than they ask for only where and when this is critical to your application and you feel like you have given them the fullest picture possible of who you are.

WORDS OF WISDOM: THE UNIVERSITY OF CALIFORNIA APPLICATION

Applying to a University of California school? The nine UC schools have their own application and application process—as do many state schools—which is very different from any other. First, their application has a very strict deadline of 30 November. In recent years the UC application has been opening earlier—meaning that you can register and begin the application now—yet all of their schools remain steadfast about the application deadline, which has not changed. You'll notice that the application is very different and their essay prompts will vary from what you'll find in The Common Application or other application portals, although often my students find that their main college essay can be tweaked or loosely modified to fit one of the UC or other state school prompts.

Milestone 6: Reminding Your Recommenders

This is a simpler Milestone than the others but one not to be taken lightly! In most cases, your recommenders will be the only "outside voice" the Admissions staff hears regarding your candidacy. and so you're correct in thinking that the Admissions staff will be paying close attention to what is written about you, by whom and to what extent, and how that fits into your application as a whole, what you've said about yourself, and your fit for the institution.

Admissions will take time to review the recommendations made for you, your relationship with this recommender, who she/he is, how many years you and she/he have known one another, and in what context.

Admissions will also compare the information they receive from this recommender against what you have given them. Is this the same person we are all talking about or do you paint a different picture of yourself vis-à-vis what the recommender says? All the more reason to request a recommender who knows you and to continue to work that relationship.

A strong recommender does not always sing your praises. They will also point out weaknesses and perhaps challenges you have had and overcome, or are dealing with currently. Admissions prefers to see this than to see all stars and glory; no one is all stars and glory. Another reason to ask someone you trust, who understands what is entailed in a recommendation for a US university.

IMPORTANT!

I have had students who have asked recommenders who have never previously written a recommendation for a US university. The application itself gives resources for the recommender along with guidelines and help. Don't worry if your recommender's first language is not English; Admissions staff are not looking at this—for you they are, not for your recommender! They are looking for solid, truthful, poignant insight into who you are both academically and as a person. However, if you need to get recommendations (and transcripts) translated, you must do this officially. WES is one such organization that does this (www.wes.org).

Your role in helping your recommender means taking time to share with them why you're applying to which institutions, give them an update on your activities, grades and any other pertinent information (including any hiccups). This does not mean kissing up, and in fact exposing some of your faults can go a long way. We're all imperfect, aren't we?

Consider the fact that your recommender will spend on average a couple of hours writing your recommendation. They are not getting paid extra for this and may have 60 others that they need to do. Your recommender also has lesson preps, correcting, exams to write and coaching to do. It would be wise to help them help you and this falls to you.

The more your recommender knows about you, the better their recommendation for you can be. The less they know, the less they can write in depth, and the less valuable the recommendation will be to Admissions. (Why did you choose *that particular person* to write a recommendation about *you*? What does it say about you, the candidate? It may say more than you think.)

Spend 20 minutes with your recommender at this stage to give them an update of where you're going to apply Early, and the reason why. Share your updated CV with them and give them a moment to ask you some questions. There is immense value in this.

Now, go to the My Colleges tab in The Common Application/recommendation tab in your application portal. Make sure you always "waive" the right to review your recommendation prior to the recommender sending it off. This is the FERPA agreement on your My Colleges tab for each individual university. Not waiving your right is analogous to your reviewing the results of the school election for this year's class president before you cast your vote. You don't do that. This question of waiving your right assures the Admissions staff that the recommender wrote what they did without any pressure of anyone having read it before it was submitted, that they were able to write freely and honestly, and without any repercussions in doing so.

If you are concerned about the recommendation, remember that rule number one is not to ask someone you think would write you a poor recommendation. Rule number two is, generally speaking, no recommender would accept the task if they were going to write a poor evaluation. An honest one including weaknesses and some things you need to work on? That makes it a stronger recommendation. A flat-out poor one? I've never seen it happen.

Once you input your recommenders into the application portal, you can assign them to each college and send a request for recommendation to them. It would be nice if you were to send an email to your recommenders right after you give the system the OK to send out the prompts alerting them to the fact that they will soon be receiving instructions on their recommendation for you and a reminder of when it will be due. Don't be lazy and not do this.

I always ask students to ask their recommenders to turn in their recommendation at least two weeks ahead of the deadline. You'll be able to see in your system through the portal when it was submitted, but it's nice to have a human reminder, and you taking charge of that on your end. After all, your recommenders are doing you a huge service and favor. Without them your application is incomplete.

WORDS OF WISDOM: MEETING YOUR GUIDANCE COUNSELOR

This is a great opportunity to set up an appointment with your Guidance Counselor at school, if you have not already done so. You'll want to share your Short List with them, tell them your reasons as to why these universities are on your List and share your CV. Remember that in almost every case, the counselor will be writing a recommendation for you as well, along with submitting all of your official files, such as transcripts for your applications. Ask your Guidance Counselor as well if any universities are planning to visit and when in the next couple of months. After this meeting, send them a quick thank you and advise them that you'll check in again next month. This little effort will go a long way. Your counselor would like to see you being proactive in this whole process, which also happens to be an extremely busy and stressful period for him/her!

Milestone 7: Completing Your Interviews for Early Applications

Please go back to Worksheet 6.3 where you have input whether your Early institutions do in fact interview candidates and where you may not already have requested or done an interview for that institution. Remember the golden rule: If they offer interviews to candidates, you request one.

Go ahead and confirm if this is the case for any of the universities to which you'll be applying Early. Then, take this time now to request those interviews. Remember that each university will have its own method of requesting interviews, whether online or through a personal email to your Admissions contact; and of conducting them, whether they do them online or have alumni in your area conduct them; and their limits, some will have a deadline for conducting interviews and once that's passed, the opportunity, too, has passed.

So, confirm the rest of your interviews for your Early applications, get them on your calendar, and update Worksheet 6.3 appropriately. You're not finished with this Milestone until you have those interview details in writing.

Remember to refer to your Worksheet 5.2b and Worksheet 6.2 to prepare and use when you are conducting those interviews in person or online!

Milestone 8: Sitting Standardized Tests

Many of you will be sitting standardized tests this month and next. And, for most of you, this will not be your first time. You know what to do at this point and preparation is key.

I have just one final bit of advice on this topic and of course, like all things in this process, will take some time to determine how to approach. When agencies—including testing agencies—ask you for personal information, or any information, try your best to find out why they are asking, how that information will be used, and if it is in your best interests to respond. (Unless it is mandatory, in which case you should also seek to understand how the information you are giving will be used.) This sounds like a lot of work and indeed it is. But, at the end of the day, these are businesses and you want to make sure that your information and what you submit is being used in your best interest, not the company's.

As I write this book and it goes to press, the process will continue to change. Keep up to date by always asking questions—on policies, requirements, rankings and numbers. Again, this is doing your "due diligence" and something that will not only help you come out of this process with success, but will also teach you a very important life skill.

CHAPTER 9

The Busiest Month of Your Life

October

For many, this will the busiest month of your lives. Considering the fact that you've now covered the most difficult aspects of this process, this month is about managing the workload and staying committed and present.

The biggest Milestone this month is turning in your Early applications. I like to advise my students to get them in at least two weeks ahead of the deadline. This is for two main reasons:

1. Like everyone else, Admissions appreciates a paper turned in early.
2. This would give you a cushion in case something comes up in life that sets you back a few days. It's a healthy approach to take and I'll be advising you to adhere to it as well.

However, note that every year more and more students feel pressured to push themselves to turn in their applications earlier and earlier. Do not jump on this bandwagon. Some of you will have completed some Early applications in September, which is good. However, I do not think there is value in completing applications prior to the summer that applications are due. I find that students learn a lot over that summer (or for the Southern Hemisphere students, the winter prior to submitting), which is reflected in the applications. Sometimes adults forget that as young adults, you grow quickly and what happens to you in a month can really impact you, make you consider new things, and perhaps even change your mind. So, while I do think it's important to get applications in at least a couple of weeks prior to the deadline—and I'll get to the reasoning on that shortly—I do not think it's helpful to sign up for the rat race.

IMPORTANT!

Some universities have a "rolling Admissions" policy. This means that as they receive applications they review them and thus also send out decisions at that time. There is an obvious advantage to getting applications in earlier as far as rolling Admissions are concerned. However, I stand by my statement that it is better not to get pulled into a rat race and submit a rushed, incomplete application, even with rolling Admissions. However, there are clear benefits to getting a complete, well-thought-out application submitted earlier rather than later.

Let's talk about why you're going to be busier than ever before this month and how to accomplish all that's on your plate. Here are your Milestones for the month:

Milestone 1: Meet With Your Guidance Counselor

Milestone 2: Finalize Writing for Early Applications

Milestone 3: Completing Your [Common] Application

Milestone 4: Standardized Testing: Submitting and Reporting Scores, and Retaking

Milestone 5: Submitting Your Early Application(s)

Milestone 6: Regular Decision Applications

Milestone 7: Checking Portals

For those of you taking any standardized tests, you may want to have your study guides on hand from your Library and also refer to Khan Academy online.

Name: Lori

Gender: Female

Country: Singapore

Nationality: Canadian

Started process: Six months before (in May) Early applications are due (November).

Program/Rigor: IBDP—HL courses: Biology, Chemistry, English Literature A; SL courses: Maths, French, Psychology.

Grades to date: All over the place. Literally. There is a full semester where Lori was not given grades due to a medical issue and where her transcript is blank. She jumps from high to low to high scores and there is no real scientific pattern following them throughout her high school career. (We like an upward swing if there were ever low grades on a student's record.)

Standardized tests to date: She took these for the first time in September of her senior year. Lori also needed accommodations due to her being hard of hearing, which drew out the process to sign up for the ACT and for her scores to be delivered. She ended up taking the ACT once. Scored a 34.

Subject Tests: None

TOEFL/IELTS: Not necessary.

Challenges: Her grades and the inconsistency in her performance academically showed throughout high school, along with having accumulated several weeks of absences in 10th grade. Missing grades—the teachers were unable to issue grades due to her string of absences—are not helpful to an application. Lori also started the process somewhat late and is a triplet—this means that the family was dealing with three applications at the same time in the same household! This meant lots of stress and anxiety. Lori's school provided little support by way of US university Admissions, so a factor here was that there was no counselor for the US, combined with conflicting information and advice. The slow process provided by the school added to the anxiety at the time of turning in applications.

Strengths: Very smart—EQ and IQ. Lori self-expressed very well and was a very good, honest writer who was true to herself. Lori did exceptionally well on her first and only attempt at the ACT, which let us tick that box and move on right away. She was also starting to level out her grades at the start of her senior year, showing a more

(continued)

reflective example of her ability. She also quickly and clearly recognized her "fit" for universities once she was exposed to what was out there. She could clearly articulate what she wanted in a university and had the opportunity to then go and visit. She also did a final "Open House" and "overnight" at her ED school in November maximizing the EGI she was capable of controlling.

Fit/Factors: An all-women's college was top of Lori's list. There were a handful that met her criteria and that she was really excited about. She was able to create a List that was very balanced having done her research, identified her own needs (liberal, community service edge, Northeast US, small to medium-sized, name brand not important, student body accepting of pink hair, etc.) and interests to pursue.

Interests: Many genuine interests! Science, gender studies, community service, poetry, writing, ice hockey.

Essay topic: Change and fear. From her move from small-town Canada to Singapore at the start of high school to working with autistic children to coming out—the fear involved in all of these allowed her to change and that change was something she was thankful for as she identified more closely with who she is and is becoming.

Short List: Wellesley (ED), Smith, Mt. Holyoke, Barnard, Bennington, Tufts, Northeastern.

Interviews: All schools that offered the opportunity.

Visits: All schools save Bennington.

EGI: From the start, Lori "got" how this was going to work. She established relationships even with the schools that did not offer interviews, which surely helped her candidacy.

Dream school, if any: After a final second visit for an open house and overnight, she decided to apply Wellesley over Smith ED.

Application strategy: Wellesley was going to be a real reach for Lori but she wanted it. She applied EA to Northeastern, which she liked, really drawn by her interactions with the Admissions staff, and where we also thought she would get in so that she would also have some "good news" in December—not relying on it, but considering this in terms of the strategy. The rest of the List was well-rounded based on her interests and needs, as well as her profile and where she may be considered a high priority candidate by the university based on what she could also bring to the institution (e.g., diversity, strength of character, connection/fit to the university's mission, etc.).

PARENT ADVICE

"We have triplets and I would strongly advise parents with twins or triplets to work with each child separately. They want to be treated individually. When our kids felt overwhelmed with the process we would sit down with them individually to help them get their bearings…It was madness—pure and simple. There's no getting around that when you have three kids considering 24 different colleges! Our children ultimately chose to attend universities on the same coast and now that we are visiting them from overseas we are delighted they are only 5 hours apart!"

—*Jacquie, Singapore*

WORDS OF WISDOM: OPEN HOUSE OVERNIGHTS AT YOUR UNIVERSITIES

At this stage some of my families are looking at Open Houses or overnights offered by universities that fall on their students' Short List. It's a big commitment—both in time and money—to go for a weekend Open House or overnight from abroad but some choose to do it. This may be something you consider as it can help, not just with the EGI aspect, but far more with the student's feel and understanding of the institution. However, it is far from required or expected. I have had students do this and be accepted to that university and also students who have done this and have been rejected. Remember that nothing will guarantee admission.

MILESTONES

Milestone 1: Meet With Your Guidance Counselor

Most of you will be obligated to meet with your Guidance Counselor around this time; some of you will not. If you fall into the latter category, don't waste your time wondering why it's not obligatory and go and set up a meeting! I've had students who have had to chase their counselor down and plead for a meeting. The meeting will always end up happening, but you may have to put in effort to get there.

Why is this meeting so important? It's the most critical one you'll have with your counselor. You want to confirm with him where you are applying and when you will be submitting your application and confirming what he needs to submit for your Early applications and, while you're there, for the rest of your applications. Please confirm the following when you meet with your counselor:

a. Where you are applying Early.

b. When you will be submitting—that means when you're literally going to press that submit button. I like to have my students do this both to give themselves a deadline (I have a lot of students who like to linger at this point, nervous to send in those first applications...) and I also like the student to tell the counselor their date of submission, to prompt that counselor to understand that their materials need to be sent in shortly, if not done already. Most counselors are on top of this but it's nice to give them a reminder and also show how organized you are. Remember, they are writing you a recommendation...

c. When, if not done already (you've checked this on your own applications prior to the meeting), the counselor's recommendation will be submitted.

d. When, if not done already, the counselor will submit supporting documents for you; transcripts/grade reports, and so on.

e. That your recommenders are well aware of their deadlines and have already submitted or are ready to submit. This is important both for those whose schools use Naviance as their recommendations go through the school, and for those who do not, as it's up to you to remind your teachers of these deadlines, too!

Finally, you will only complete this Milestone when you've thanked your counselor both at the end of this meeting and by sending him a brief and thoughtful thank you email. He does a lot of work behind the scenes for you and your thank you message will go a long way.

Milestone 2: Finalize Writing for Early Applications

This Milestone is what makes this month your busiest. As work on the final drafts of your writing for your Early applications, you will want to reference and review Writing Workshop 3 in the Writing Handbook, as well as both the advice and notes you've taken from the past chapters. Some points to note as you finish your supplement/s for your Early applications:

1. Now is not the time to second-guess your theme.

2. Avoid sharing the final draft with multiple reviewers; you're setting yourself up for confusion and strife, not to mention potentially deteriorating the quality of your essay(s).

3. There's no room for spelling or grammatical errors. Here's where perfection is expected.

4. Go back to the Do's and Don'ts of writing in Workshop 1 Part 1 in your Writing Handbook. Do your supplements follow suit?

5. If you are someone who is never quite satisfied, give yourself a day in the next week when you're going to give it one last revision and that's it. If you're the opposite and feel like things are always pretty good, be diligent about reviewing the Writing Workshops using your own supplements and check for proper spelling and grammar.

Save your final version of the supplements to a Word, Pages or other document and cut and paste it into the application itself. Review it again—margins and fonts and even some characters on non-US keyboards may not come out as expected once posted. It is easy enough to clean it up. Save it in the application portal.

WORDS OF WISDOM: PARENTS: NOW IS NOT THE TIME TO REVIEW THE ESSAY

A father wrote to me just a few days before his daughter was going to submit her Early application. Her application was done; she was giving herself a couple of days to regroup before sending it in. He said he read her final essay. He did not like it. What can happen at this stage is that a parent gets involved only now and asks to review the final application of their student, not understanding fully the objectives of the writing or the strategy of the application, which is essentially what was covered over the past eight chapters. Getting involved late in the process and second guessing the work that the student has done is not helpful. The father was transmitting his unhappiness with the final product not on his daughter—who was the author—but on me. Parents should avoid being their child's essay reviewer at this stage. I have *never* seen it be helpful. In the end, his daughter stuck to her original essay, submitted it and... got in.

Milestone 3: Completing Your [Common] Application

In Chapter 8 you toiled through The Common Application/other application portals. By this month and this chapter, you should have an application that is almost complete. Of course you've been reviewing it and adjusting it regularly; now is the time to "complete" it and make sure it's ready to go for your Early applications. I'll reiterate the things you should do but I'm sure you have identified all of these and will check every box as it's completed:

1. All sections are complete and have the appropriate green check mark or equivalent indicating such. ☐

2. Review each section. At this stage you're doing a final review, so you're reading first for content and then for grammar, spelling and syntax. ☐

3. As I said earlier, there is no room anywhere in this process for misspelling or grammatical mistakes. ☐

4. Make sure all information inputted is true to form and relevant. ☐

5. Consider having your parent review the content when you are finished. ☐

6. Have your parent sign the ED waiver where appropriate. ☐

7. When you've finished this Milestone, you're confirming to me and to yourself that the application(s) for your Early school(s) is complete. ☐

IMPORTANT!

Every year, a college decides it's a good idea (despite the fact that it is a bad one) to incorporate stealth essays into their applications. Essentially, these are hidden essays that pop up only when a student has just about completed their application and, all of a sudden, there's another essay to complete. Be aware that this can happen and usually if you've done your due diligence by comparing supplements from the portal application to the university's website on your Worksheet 5.1 Column 15, you know what will come.

Milestone 4: Standardized Testing: Submitting and Reporting Scores and Retaking

You must send in any scores officially. So, if you have not already done so, send those official scores via the official testing agency. This is critical.

Regarding the topic of "self-reporting", an option on The Common Application and other portals, how you report your standardized testing scores in your application needs to be strategic. If your Early college requires testing, you self-report on the application. That's an easy decision. Know the policy of your Early school on testing—you recorded this on Worksheet 5.1. Report accordingly and, of course, you've sent your official scores.

If you have colleges on your RD or ED2 list that do not require testing and you do not want them to see your testing, you can change this screen as many times as you like after submitting. That means you'll self-report now, and then change when you submit for those colleges that don't require testing.

For those of you who have taken standardized tests in October, but have not yet received scores and your colleges require those scores, you can self-report that you will take those at a future date (in the self-report section). I would then advise you *follow up with your Admissions contact* after submitting to explain what you have done. Your contact will appreciate your being proactive and organized and will take note.

For those of you taking the tests in November again, put it as a future testing date if you want it to be recorded as a test you are likely to send. I would rather have a student self-report their intention to take the November test if they have indeed signed up for it, to show they are trying once again, rather than to not self-report the upcoming test for fear of scoring poorly and having to report that score.

There is so much fear and over-strategizing with test scores that it becomes all-consuming. Test scores can be important. However, remember that this is a holistic process and test scores are not the only things considered. I have found that those who are overly strategic about sharing or not sharing test results are less open to the intricacies and actual strategy for developing a holistic application, which can negatively affect a candidate. This is my opinion but one that the students and families that I work with also follow successfully.

You should know if your Early school will consider your November scores after having reviewed and confirmed the Early testing policy over the past months.

Milestone 5: Submitting Your Early Application(s)

Check the following to make sure that you are ready:

- You've completed your essay and it's been uploaded and reviewed. ☐
- You've uploaded and reviewed and triple-checked your supplements. ☐
- The Common Application/Early application itself is complete and reviewed. ☐

Although this looks like the easiest Milestone yet, it's actually one of the hardest. All the work you did over all of the chapters has come to this point. Pay your fee (if the university requires one) and submit.

Note that you have received confirmation of your submission, time and date and confirmation.

You have now submitted your Early application(s)!

Before moving on to the final two Milestones in this chapter, please consider this: Now that you've submitted to your Early university, what kind of relationship did you develop with your Admissions contact at this Early school? Do you feel the person knows you? Did you have conversations or discussions about you applying Early? Would you be excited to tell your Admissions contact you've officially applied? Is this someone who would welcome that sort of news from you in an email? At this point, the "nuanced, socially-aware and observant you" should by now be able to gauge this. My advice is that if you answered positively to all of these questions, go ahead and write the contact a quick email, thank them for the opportunity and tell them how excited you are. This ultimately depends on where you stand with your Admissions contact after all of the EGI building up to this point. If you have any hesitation, don't do this. Most of my students know whether sending such an email is appropriate by this point after having heeded my advice on EGI through and through. It is entirely situational. You know best.

Take a short break (a day at most) after submitting your Earlies. There is still a lot to be done moving forward.

STUDENT ADVICE

"OK, I'll be honest. I had no idea what EGI was going to do for me and was pretty skeptical about it when I first started. I finally wrote to some of my Admissions officers (because my mom pretty much forced me to do it) and I have to say that it really helped my confidence and a few Admissions staff and I had some pretty regular back-and-forth emails. So, when I did apply ED and came across Jennifer's advice you just read above, I wrote to my Admissions officer. It was a pretty awesome feeling. He was really excited for me, too. (Oh, I got in!)"

—David, Italy

Milestone 6: Regular Decision Applications

Now is the time for you to go through Writing Workshop 3 in the Writing Handbook for all of your *Regular Decision applications*. You'll need to pace these out and I suggest you tackle one a day for your brainstorming of the remaining supplements. In the next chapter you'll be writing and completing your RD applications, so now the brainstorming is critical.

Please finish this Milestone for all of your college applications by the end of this month. You can go on to the next Milestone in between in order to stay on top of your Early application submission(s).

Milestone 7: Checking Portals

Ranging from as soon as you submit your Early application to within a week after submission, you'll receive confirmation from your Early institution(s) asking you to log in to their university-specific application portal. A few points to note:

1. Keep watch for this email and check spam regularly. If a week goes by and you have not received it, contact Admissions by calling them or email your Admissions contact.

2. As soon as you receive the portal login account, log on. I've had a few students tell me that they have not logged in even though they received the account details. In addition to the practical reasons to log on immediately, this is another way of showing EGI.

3. The portal will allow you to track your application. Your responsibility is to follow up on it. The last thing you want is to be told some items are missing and that you are not attending to them.

4. It is through your portal where you will eventually, for most colleges, receive the Admissions decision.

IMPORTANT!

Some of my students call me in a panic to say they are missing many things in their application! Before you panic, know what those items are first. One of my students forwarded to me the image below sent to her via one of her university's portals. She was panicked as she had one day to reply.

The solution was easy. These were the missing items:

- **First Marking Period Grades:** She was a gap year student, so First Marking Period Grades were not applicable. I did tell her, however, to write to her Admissions contact—whom she knows by first name—to remind him of such and to confirm it was an error of the system and not hers.

- **Certified Financial Resources Form:** This college asks international students to fill out a form confirming they have the financial resources to send their child to this university for four years. All universities require this, at some stage in the process, from international families and it will be case-by-case when they require it. In this case, the university requires it prior to giving a decision. Universities will need to know this information to provide to the government, in order to show that a visa can be issued for the sake of full-time education,

(continued)

Admissions Application Credentials

	Not Received	
⚠	First Marking Period Grades	
⚠	Cert. Financial Resources Form	
⚠	Sponsor Support Documentation	
⚠	Photocopy Passport Name Page	

	Received	Date
✓	Application Fee/Waiver	Nov 23
✓	Common Application Online	Nov 24
✓	Secondary School Transcript	Nov 24
✓	Recommendation	Nov 24
✓	Recommendation	Nov 24

and where the risk of that student coming to the US, dropping out of university due to financial constraints is low and thus the risk to the US government of that person staying in the US illegally is low. Now, there is another aspect of this document that I don't like and how it could be used and that's to try to confirm the family's financial worth and pass this information on to their development department for future fundraising possibilities. I used to run international fundraising for a university and whether it was because we were never organized enough or not, we never did this. There are other and much more sophisticated ways of finding out this information. Regardless, you must turn this information in.

- **Sponsor Support Documentation:** It will go by various names and this institution requires yet another form to show that she is fully supported financially and whoever "sponsors" her bears full responsibility for her.

- **Photocopy Passport Name Page:** This is self-explanatory. She needs to scan her passport and submit it.

It was completed in a moment. You may get other red flags too. Before you go into a panic, see if you can figure out the answer yourself without first contacting your Admissions officer for what might be an easy response. If you're confused and there's a deadline looming, call Admissions. They are used to these questions. The system often works more slowly than you do and they have not input all documents or they have a one-system-for-all, which in this student's case was the issue with the first-term grades and her being a gap year student.

Just like that—after months and months of preparation—you've become a university applicant. I think most of my students expect to feel a sense of relief and accomplishment at this point. They also tell me that there's little time to reflect on the feeling when there is still so much ahead to do. I encourage you to keep up the momentum. You've got a couple more months that are in your control and you want to make sure that after all this work you're still in control and not letting anything slow you down. A break is on the horizon!

CHAPTER 10

The Final Month of Writing College Applications...Ever?

November

Congratulations! You're officially a college applicant! While for most of my students, pressing that submit button the first time can take hours—perhaps days—to finally accomplish, moving forward you'll have much more confidence as you finish applications and submit them.

I said last month would be your busiest, but you still have one more month of work ahead of you before you can rest. There is a lot to do but you're on track and can consider yourself a pro by now. This month is all about writing.

Before we go into this month's Milestones, I'd like to mention a concern that many of my families sometimes have after having submitted Early applications. Do you continue submitting the Regular applications or do you wait until you have notification—if you know that that notification will come before the December holiday—before you submit? There are two answers to this question and what you do will depend on your own preference.

You certainly don't stop the process now. You'll be writing the rest of your applications this month and finish all of your applications by the end of November. That means that if you've applied ED and you get accepted next month—which we hope you do—it's true that these applications will have been written but not be reviewed by the receiving institution. That's part of the process. However, *when* you submit them depends on the situation.

Many of my students continue to submit all remaining applications throughout this month as the student finishes them. Parsing out the process to complete an application or two a week, depending on how many remain to be finished, my student submits an application once it is ready. And the student recognizes and "accepts" that the money paid for each application may be paid "in vain" if they do get into the ED school. I tend to recommend this option for those families who tell me they are fine with the money being spent as I like for my students not to wait until the last minute to send applications, for reasons we've already discussed. The other important point here is that we know by now that we try to get applications in before their deadline—to keep you paced and, in some cases, to show the school your interest by turning it in early. In general, I don't like my students to sit on their applications they have already completed; I prefer that they submit them.

The other option is to continue to write as per your own internal timeline and finish each application appropriately and completely. However, you will wait until you receive notification from your ED school—this depends on the school and you will know by now when your ED school plans to notify you (usually within the first two weeks of December)—and to submit if you do not get in to your ED school. This is recommended for those who do not wish to pay the additional application fees as they can add up. A secondary reason is that it simplifies things if you do get into your ED school; you don't have to then retract all of those applications—but to me this is not a good enough reason to wait.

Consider what is best for you, and not what your best friend or the mother who seems to know everything about Admissions is doing.

For those of you applying to the University of California schools, applications are due (as of the time of publication of this book) at the end of this month. This is a separate application process and application and can be quite time consuming—not just because there are additional essay prompts aside from your Common App/main college essay and supplements, but also because there are very detailed, California-system-specific questions to be addressed. Make sure you embed time for this into your deadlines for this month, as per Milestone 2 below.

Let's go over the Milestones for this month:

> **Milestone 1:** Checking Portals (and don't skip this just because it was in last month's chapter!)

 Milestone 2: Determining Your Internal Deadlines for Each Remaining Application to be Completed This Month

 Milestone 3: Retaking Standardized Tests

Milestone 4: Sending Official Standardized Test Scores

Milestone 5: Meeting With Your Guidance Counselor

Milestone 6: Reviewing Common Application/Main Application Before Next Submissions

Milestone 7: Finishing Interviews/Final Requests

Milestone 8: Final Writing!

If you are retaking any standardized tests (ACT/SAT), you may consider not doing a course and doing your own refresher course through self-study. If this is the case, remember the resources to consider using:

- ACT or SAT prep books
- Khan Academy
- College Board's *The Official Guide for all SAT Subject Tests*

Go ahead and get the College Board's *The Official Guide for all SAT Subject Tests* if you're signed up for taking any of these tests, so you are well aware of what will be covered in the exam and how.

Case Study

Name: Veena

Gender: Female

Country: England

Nationality: Irish

Started process: Veena started this process literally when she could, which meant starting to research universities and criteria and so on years before her application was going to be sent. (Whether you're like Veena or just the opposite, you can learn from her Case Study!)

Program/Rigor: Biology, SL Chinese, SL Math, SL Psychology

Grades to date: Predicted IB score: 45/45

(continued)

Standardized tests: Took SAT three times with highest composite of 1560

Subject Tests: Biology (760), Chinese (700), English Literature (670)

TOEFL/IELTS: N/A

Challenges going into the process: Veena was at the top of her game and was thus going to compete with all of the other thousands who are also at the top of their game. This meant going for the most highly selective schools where the outcomes depend on luck at the end of the day. Everyone she would be competing against would have her same test scores, grades and rigor, along with stellar extracurriculars. Veena also did not like mathematics and called me up one day at the start of the IB program to tell me she was switching to Math Studies, giving me the tiniest leeway to talk her out of it. Somehow her mom and I did. This, I believe, became a positive (that she did not resort to Math Studies). Veena did not have a lot of strength in the areas of community service or sport and this was a concern of hers. (My response was that she can't do everything with depth. Focus and go hard and strong.) Finally, Veena was attending a top British boarding school where the bar was set high. Perhaps too high. A predicted 45 was outstanding, but not totally unique. Veena says her challenges were managing time between schoolwork and SAT prep.

Strengths going into the process: Veena says, "Having a roadmap early on so I wasn't making important decisions last minute." I will say that because Veena started the process properly early in her penultimate year, she was able to figure out adroitly what she wanted. She took notes during her campus visits. She focused on fit and feel. Veena wanted liberal arts with perhaps a focus on journalism as a career path. She had launched a fashion blog that was already monetized well before she started applying to university. Her fit for journalism—she was already writing outside of school—and a highly intellectualized environment could be "proven" by what she had been doing in the years leading up to applications, so there was a lot of depth associated with her passion and strengths. Veena also had very good grades and test scores, and would not stop at just taking it twice (which I found to be sufficient), pushing through her senior year to study and take them yet again just to prove that she could get those ten or so points more. Note that not everyone will work like this. I like to encourage my students to weigh the pros and cons. Will it be worth it to have to study again for these tests while that time could or should be put to classwork, applications, passions, etc.? In Veena's case, she was able to fit it all in. For others, it might not be possible.

Fit/Factors: East Coast, Liberal Arts, medium-sized university, limited Greek life, easy access to major city/cities, large international population. Veena visited almost every university that made her final List and kept a very detailed log of her visits, which she referred to at the time of determining her List. She went for feel after visiting and from this was able to clearly cross off some institutions based on such. Studying liberal arts was what Veena was going to do, and preferably in a highly rigorous environment. Writing for student publications and being given opportunities to become heavily involved in the institution as a freshman were high on Veena's list.

Interests: Journalism, dance, creative arts, business.

Common App essay topic: Her experience as a young fashion blogger in Singapore.

Short List: Boston College, Georgetown, Brown, Yale (SCEA), Penn, Stanford, Tufts, Northwestern (Medill).

Interviews: Alumni interviews at every institution that offered the opportunity.

Visits: Penn, Yale, Brown, Tufts, Harvard.

EGI: Yes, but not extensively. Most of the institutions on her List state that they do not take EGI into consideration (but again, you know my take on this). She did expressly request interviews whenever the opportunity was available and visited all campuses possible. Veena gave the Yale Admissions officer a tour of her high school when she visited.

Dream School: Yale.

Application strategy: Veena, having started the process so early and then having been in school with classmates who were all "well-versed" in the process, knew that most of her schools were going to depend on luck at the end of the day. She did truly look for strength in liberal arts (save Northwestern, to whose journalism program she applied) combined with rigor and selectivity of program. She applied to Yale SCEA and applied to a selection of schools (safety, match and reach) RD.

VEENA'S ADVICE

"Worrying about an application once it's in is the worst thing you can do! Focus on making your Regular Decision applications the best they can be. Remember to keep an open mind during this stage of uncertainty and don't let this be a time of speculation; both Early and Regular Decisions make room for successes and failures, so don't assume you'll end up at your Early college—or that you will get rejected from your top RD schools!"

MILESTONES

Milestone 1: Checking Portals (and don't skip this just because it was in last month's chapter!)

The first thing I'd like you to do is write yourself a daily reminder to look out for any emails from your Early universities. Within, sometimes, a day and sometimes a week (no longer), your "Earlies" will send you an email with a link to their university-specific site where you can track your application. Log on and get in there the day it is sent to you. The reasons to do so:

1. The university can see when you log on. If you wait a month, you're not really interested in them, are you?
2. To make sure your application is complete. Is anything missing?

Email or call your Admissions contact if you see anything that does not match up. It often takes a few days for them to log everything that has been submitted for a file. Be conscientious but not so much that you're calling Admissions every day. Be smart about this.

If you have not received a portal after a week of having applied, check in with Admissions by giving them a call and inquiring if you've missed something or if they have yet to send it out.

Remember that this is an active part of the Admissions process and one that falls fully on your plate.

IMPORTANT!

In very rare instances, I have had a student who applies ED and, prior to getting that response back from the university, regrets having applied ED and would like to change that application to RD. We've gone over the steps of determining if you're ready for ED and the importance of *knowing,* but we're past that point. I hope you're not in this frame of mind but a few may be. The advice I give on this is the following: Confirm why you are reconsidering ED (usually this will deal with family finances but it can be one of myriad reasons). Call the Admissions office and explain if what you are asking is possible. Follow that call up with an email—having this in writing is key—to your Admissions contact reiterating why you would like to change to RD and the summary of your phone call to Admissions. Most often a college will comply but this is case-by-case. And, of course, this must be done as far before decision time as possible for ED applicants.

Milestone 2: Determining Your Internal Deadlines for Each Remaining Application to be Completed This Month

Please refer to Worksheet 5.1: My Short List. In Chapters 5–8 you populated and confirmed this List with all the supplements required by all the universities on your list. What you need to do now:

1. Review your Short List. Are all of your Regular universities on the Short List Worksheet 5.1, Column 1? How about an ED2 school? Please update.

2. Review each university's supplements *again*, comparing what you have on Worksheet 5.1, Column 15 to what is on The Common Application/the university's application. Please update with any changes or new supplements.

3. Finally, sit down now and determine when you will have each supplemental completed, in final draft form, throughout this month, for all remaining applications including ED2, Regular Decision and other applications, and record your deadline in Column 19 of Worksheet 5.1. Keep a few things in mind:

    a. From my experience, each supplement will have at least three revisions. Some of my students go through three; some of my students go through twelve. You know by now how you write and should be able to gauge how long each will take you to complete (that means through to final draft form).

    b. The month of November has 30 days. You'll need to parse this out accordingly, along with your other deadlines and commitments.

    c. Be realistic and be demanding of yourself. You will need to be finished by the last day of this month.

    d. ED2 has the same restrictions as ED1 (of course you'll review this on a case-by-case basis with your university), just with a different deadline.

Remember that this guide is set up so that you are finishing all applications by 1 December. That means that you are prepared to send in every application by then. All of my students manage this and so can you. It makes good sense for getting your applications in before the deadline without last minute stresses and starting your holiday (or graduation for Southern Hemisphere students!) with your university application work behind you.

Milestone 3: Retaking Standardized Tests

There's not too much to tell you about retaking standardized tests at this stage other than to plan for it. Many of you will be taking standardized tests this month for a final or penultimate time. What is important is for you to have determined if any of your "Earlies" will consider these results. You should know this. If you're reading this and don't, connect with your Admissions officer today to ask. Be thoughtful about it. Don't ask if it clearly already says so on the website; you're wasting your Admissions contact's time, and affecting your own standing. Do the work at your end and if you still don't know, connect with Admissions.

As for retaking or taking a test in English as a foreign language, this is not so much strategic as it is necessary. Remember that if you're also applying to UK schools, at the time of writing UCAS requires IELTS over TOEFL. Many US institutions will prefer TOEFL but will take IELTS. Knowing this is your responsibility. Make sure by checking in on each university on a case-by-case basis.

Also, and as you've been trained to do by now, *make certain* when your schools need the IELTS/TOEFL results in order to assess your file. Some schools are very strict about this, meaning that if they have a deadline of 15 November and say all materials must be in and that includes IELTS/TOEFL and you have not sent in your official scores by then, you *simply will not be considered*. Be smart about this and also take responsibility for it.

September, was not to her advantage. She was on a gap year and luckily while working did have a bit more time on her hands during these months than if she had been finishing up her Bac diploma. But, by the time she went to sign up for the ACT, it was full for the entire rest of the year in all of Southeast Asia. She could only arrange to take the SAT and only in November and December. This meant that her first test-taking would happen in November, with little preparation, while also coming from a very different system. This jeopardized her chances for any Early school she was interested in. She was left with very few choices and ended up being allowed to screenshot her results from November's test to her EA school (after having started her EGI right away in September and it having worked to her advantage to have these relationships built).

Milestone 4: Sending Official Standardized Test Scores

Just as your transcripts need to be sent "officially" so does your testing. You will need to log on to your standardized testing portals to send in the official scores, as we've discussed in earlier chapters. I can't tell you how many times students or families forget this critical step in the process. Your application will not be complete without attending to this Milestone.

Milestone 5: Meeting With Your Guidance Counselor

This is an opportune moment to meet with your Guidance Counselor and have a quick face-to-face. Some things I would like you to confirm and discuss at that meeting include:

- Confirmation of all materials sent for your Early schools.

- Confirmation of your Regular/ED2 schools and when you plan to submit each application. Feel free to share your schedule; your counselor will see just how dedicated and organized you are.

- Ask your counselor if there is anything further needed from you in order to finish up what they need to do on your behalf for your applications.

- By now this last reminder comes naturally to you: Yes, say thank you. Your counselor will be grateful to hear those words as this is one of his or her busiest times of the year.

"I don't have a 'counselor' at my high school in Spain and so this Milestone is not so easy for me. I ended up asking around at my school about who I should talk to about these points and for me it ended up being the 'head' of my high school. I think for many students like me who don't have a high school set up like this serving the needs of students who are going on to university they will need to figure out who to ask. In the end it worked out but it took me a while to figure it out!"

—Román, Valencia

Milestone 6: Reviewing Common Application/Main Application Before Next Submissions

At the time of publication, you are able to change your Common Application any number of times as you submit one application to the next. What this means is that you can change your entire CA essay. This is something I have never advised a student to do—after all of that work and commitment, it's ready to go. You can also go in and change other things in the application itself that may not be relevant to a college you are applying to at this stage to see or review.

For instance, many of my students determine with my guidance that it is important for them to include information for the Admissions Committee in the Additional Information section of an application. Usually the information they have decided to include is relevant for all of their applications and for all Admissions to see. However, in some cases students have written about standardized testing in this Additional Information section. I can oftentimes see value in addressing this when I have a student who is very bright and very dedicated to the entire process, but is simply not a strong standardized test taker. The student may address why they did not do well or simply be straightforward with the committee to avoid not addressing an obvious hole in their application.

That being said, that information is not relevant for applications that do not require standardized testing or for schools that the student has decided not to submit scores to under the school's specific policy.

It is important at this stage that you:

1. Review your Common Application (i.e. those remaining applications that you still have to submit).

2. Determine what is relevant, what is not, and perhaps what you may want to add for each remaining application.

3. Keep track of this information for each application so that you are not confused and accidentally send what should have gone to one university to another.

Go ahead and organize this now. If you have to, group your remaining universities so that you don't have to continually change The Common Application back and forth as you submit and do them in chunks, where necessary.

Milestone 7: Finishing Interviews/Final Requests

This is the last time I'll mention this as it's already getting late in the process to do so. Some time ago you completed your research on determining which universities on your Short List offer interviews and requested them as per the guidelines of that particular institution.

Please refer to your Interview Contact Sheet and Schedule Worksheet 6.3.

You will also want to refer to your Worksheet 5.2b: Mock Interview, Student and review those notes. You should be using Worksheet 6.2: Interview Worksheet to prepare for and use during all interviews, as discussed in earlier chapters. Are there any institutions on My Short List Worksheet 5.1 who offer interviews and with whom you have not had one or—gasp— have yet to request one? Please take a moment today to not only confirm this, but to tie up any loose ends and request an interview in any and all cases where that was overlooked.

Milestone 8: Final Writing!

While it's the final Milestone in this chapter, writing is what this month is really all about in terms of your remaining applications. A few steps as you go through the writing process throughout the month:

1. Please refer to your Writing Handbook, Workshop 3. As you did in earlier chapters, this will refresh your understanding of what is being asked of you and why. Don't skip this step. Go back and read it. Now.

2. Now refer to Worksheet 5.1 with all of the supplements clearly listed and get moving on them.

By this stage, my students usually "get it" and simply need to make the time, devote the energy and commit to writing the supplements and finishing each application. What you want to avoid here are the following:

1. Being lazy. There is nothing worse for an Admissions officer to read than a lazily crafted essay, basically telling that Admissions officer that their institution and time are not a priority for you.

2. Not going the extra mile and reviewing resources—the school's website, publications, and so on—that can help you craft the "why this school" response specifically and elegantly. Remember the cut and paste rule.

3. Thinking you will get in to your "Earlies" and *assuming* these supplements will never be read. This past year we saw record low numbers in terms of acceptance rates for ED, EA, REA, SCEA applications at highly selective institutions. My colleagues and I would, daily, throw out another message saying "It happened again—next to ideal candidate rejected ED from...". You do not have the luxury to be sure of a system that is subjective.

4. And, finally, being lazy. Did I mention this? Laziness, when put into an application, is more obvious than the words you've typed on the page. This is not the adult's white lie to try to keep you working your hardest. It's clear as day to the reader, who is trying to get through hundreds and thousands of well-thought-out essays and short answers, and comes across the dud that can reduce their time and effort of going through another application and put it directly into the "reject" pile. DON'T BE LAZY.

In terms of when to submit these remaining applications, you should go with whichever option you've chosen from what I outlined at the beginning of this chapter and submit accordingly. If you're going to wait until December, give yourself a reminder and follow through appropriately and attentively.

By the time you get to the next chapter, you will have completed every one of your US university applications! Congratulations!

The Enlightened Insider: Video and your application

More and more universities are allowing applicants to use video in some way in their applications. If you have this option, I suggest you go for it, keeping a few things in mind: Admissions is not interested in seeing a professionally developed video. Admissions is not interested in seeing you all primped up. On the other hand, Admissions is really not interested in seeing your messy room in the background. Subtle "mistakes" are natural and I advise you to keep them in there; be natural, be yourself and remember that if Admissions, upon seeing your video, wants to "see" more, there is always social media for them to turn to, so make sure that looks presentable and representative of you. Give Admissions the respect of being prepared, dressing appropriately and being genuine.

The Enlightened Insider: Your Counselor Talking to Your Universities

I had a family who asked the principal of their son's school to please write to his top choice university to put in a good word. The principal refused. The family was confused. I told them the principal should not be doing this and had made the right decision. At the end of the day, there will be discussions "behind closed doors" among school officials—counselors for the most part—and university Admissions staff. (Go ahead and read *The Gatekeepers*, if you have not already.) You won't know what is discussed and really should not. However, I will say that in many cases a counselor will share with Admissions where else the student is applying, who from that class might be the stronger applicant or fit for said university among those seniors applying or, in the worst cases (few and far between, but I've seen it happen) where a counselor simply did not like a student and so struggled to put in a good word for my student to any Admissions staff on my student's list until it looked like it could help that counselor (as the student was applying for a scholarship and if she got it, the counselor would be praised in this case). If this sounds unfair or unethical or wrong, please remember that in any human-driven process, there will be things that are unfair or unethical or wrong that happen. Remember: Control what you can control and leave the rest.

PARENT ADVICE

"I would like to say that communication [between you, the parent, and your child] is the key. Keep talking to your son/daughter about what they're going through, what the expectations are, what is going on in their lives… This is a long process and it gets quite intense. We never feel like we're doing it totally 'right' but the more you communicate, the better this works."

—*Ariane, Switzerland*

CHAPTER 11

A Rite of Passage in the Making

December

When you read this, you'll have officially submitted all of your US university applications. You must be feeling proud, excited, exhausted and relieved with a tinge (or pang) of anxiety, knowing that what is next is not in your control. And this is how life works. Remember that throughout this process you controlled as best you could those parts that were in your control—and with the highest of quality standards—and now it's time to let go and let, well, Admissions "do their thing".

What you'll experience in the upcoming weeks and months is like something you've never experienced before in your life. And, regardless of the decision(s) that you receive, it's a rite of passage that you'll go through, an experience that you'll never forget. Enjoy the fact that you have this opportunity.

So, while your applications have been submitted, December continues to be a very busy, critical, and active month with regards to US university Admissions. Waiting for those decision letters is the most passive Milestone you'll have (although it appears active as you feel anxious and moody, with your parents perhaps experiencing the same if not more intense phenomena), yet as soon as you do receive them, there are action items you must attend to right away.

You'll be surprised as to how much there is to do this month. Your milestones:

 Milestone 1: Managing "Early" Decisions

Milestone 2: Reviewing Your Active "To-do's"

Milestone 3: No Stopping Now

For those of you taking any standardized tests, you may want to have your study guides on hand from your Library and also refer to Khan Academy online.

Case Study

Name: Matthew

Gender: Male

Country: Indonesia and Malaysia

Nationality: British/Chinese/Australian

Started process: Six months prior (May) to submitting Early applications in November

Program/Rigor: Homeschool

Grades to date: 3.9/4.0 GPA

Standardized tests: SAT 1530

Subject Tests: Biology (800), Maths 2 (800), Physics (760), Maths 1 (760)

TOEFL/IELTS: Not necessary

Challenges: Homeschooling outside of the US is still not widely "accepted" and this was a huge challenge, not just for Matthew and his family in terms of going through the university Admissions process, but also due to the fact that the standards internationally for homeschooling could be looked at differently by Admissions—we were cognizant of this being a possibility—than what has become more standard in the US. Likewise, Matthew was a high school graduate at age 15. He was very young in age but not in maturity. However, some universities could be reticent with such a young candidate (or the opposite and quite eager).

Strengths: Clearly, Matthew was a special candidate. He had an exceptionally high IQ and was unquestionably unique in his very genuine interests, experiences and expertise (already at a young age). His grades and test scores were very high. He was very eager and ready and excited about this entire process, embracing every moment truly as an opportunity. Matthew was happy throughout.

Fit/Factors: Academically rigorous, challenging, and yet also a campus and environment that would be accepting and open to Matthew's ideas (see Interests below). Matthew knew at a young age that he would be pursuing a terminal degree, so he also wanted

---

and needed a campus that would allow him to interact with the faculty as an undergraduate, possibly even as a freshman, in terms of research and collaboration.

Interests: Film, literature. Cosmology, Buddhism. Matthew spent a gap year in Nepal learning Buddhism and living with monks. He also likes video games and hanging out with friends.

Common App essay topic: It combined Matthew's aspirations in the realm of pure physics and cosmology with the evolution of his philosophy of the world as developed through his various life experiences. It was very personal and very, very true to Matthew's beliefs and experiences in life.

Short List: I usually do not recommend a student apply to more than 10 universities. Matthew's case was very unique, being homeschooled internationally and our not knowing very well what the response would be from universities to such an atypical candidate. He was also eager to apply to several and was clearly up for the task: Boston College (SCEA), Carleton, Carnegie Mellon, Johns Hopkins, Swarthmore, UCLA, UC-Santa Barbara, UC-Berkeley, Brown, Caltech, Chicago, Columbia, Harvard, MIT, Princeton, Stanford.

Visits: None, except when invited to attend BC's Presidential Scholar weekend and University of Rochester's Renaissance Scholar weekend.

EGI: Every school on that very long Short List!

Dream School: None. Very excited about all. Scholarship was of great interest.

Application strategy: SCEA Boston College to be considered (which he was) for Presidential Scholar award.

MATTHEW'S ADVICE

"As a rule of thumb, homeschooling allows for preemptive subject specialization and exotic academic experiences well outside the scope of "ordinary" school and this holds true in the international sphere. Although one will be compared with better-prepared applicants—IB and AP programs—success will follow if one is passionate and possesses the initiative to seize command of available resources (however thin!) to further one's academic exposure through unconventional means. While it is established that international homeschooling (particularly when one is stationed in developing countries) lacks the ease of access to college-level material and program opportunities possessed by its US-based counterpart, this provides one the ability to distinguish by contrast: any amount of ingenuity in weaving together the cultural, religious, and technical components of one's background has unlimited boundaries, I believe."

MILESTONES

Milestone 1: Managing "Early" Decisions

When you receive your first responses to your US university applications, it will be an emotional experience.

This is the Milestone that everyone skips to and the only one anyone wants to know about for this month. Here is my advice:

1. Know when your Early schools will be sending decisions. This was told to you in some form or other—either when you applied, on the college's website or in the portal that you've linked to after applying. *You should not be bothering your Admissions contact with this question.* Know when to expect this news.

2. Think about where you want to be and with whom you want to be when you receive the news. Most of you will be in very different time zones from the US, waiting for the notification email; perhaps you'll be on the bus going to school. Do you really want to open it in front of the 6th grader sitting next to you? Perhaps you'll be heading to sports practice. Do you really want to open it before a scrimmage? Discuss this with your family and know where you want to be and with whom when you open the decision letter.

3. Be kind to yourself and to others. You may be one of the fortunate ones. Your best friend may not. Of course you should celebrate good news but be considerate of those who may not or have not received good news. You'll see that this is a very emotional time at school and among peers.

4. *I have a note for parents.* I received a call from one of my parents this year as we were waiting on her child's Early decisions. She is an "expert mom" who is also anxious, competitive and lovely. She needed to vent. Another mom at her son's school was posting to her own Facebook page for the past few days every college her son got into early until finally she posted something akin to "If we have another acceptance I don't know if we'll have the energy to keep rejoicing!" I don't need to tell you that this is obnoxious. This is an emotional time for everyone and no one is perfect. The emotion and competition can get to the parents as well. Parents should be kind to one another. Overly exuberant shows will only hurt your child in the end.

Once you do receive the news—and I do hope you were accepted but in many cases this won't happen—you have a few next steps depending on the decision:

- *You have been accepted.*

    Congratulations! It's truly something incredible and you have every right to celebrate! Review the entire acceptance letter and any action items that are sent to you by your institution. Don't delay on attending to them.

    If you have been accepted ED by a school, you must at this point contact all of your EA and/or RD schools via email or by phone (preferably by email, but I want you to confirm getting a response within 24 hours and if you don't, to phone) *to withdraw your application.* There are many styles of doing this but I would suggest you simply thank them for the opportunity, that you've been accepted by your ED school (no need to name the school), and to thank them for all of their help along the way. You know how to write by now.

    And, of course, go and share the fantastic news with your Guidance Counselor and with your recommenders. They will want to know!

STUDENT ADVICE

"We are all coached to not 'expect' this news but I have to admit it was difficult to not be hopeful. My college sent the news in the middle of my night here in Jakarta. I planned to get up a bit earlier than usual but not in the middle of the night. My parents were already up and waiting when I got up. So, when I logged on and saw that I was accepted ED, I really can't explain how amazing it felt. We celebrated over breakfast and I kept it to myself all day until the end of the day when a friend told me he, too, had been accepted by his ED school. There were a lot of students who had not been accepted, so it was a pretty emotional day at school. I feel pretty lucky."

—*Hector, Jakarta*

- *You have been deferred.*

    You'll be disappointed, of course. That's only natural and human. We all want to be accepted to anything we apply for or go after.

    You can, in many cases, find out the percentage of deferred from Early application status that get accepted in the Regular round. I'm not a big fan of this as I feel it really doesn't "help"—theoretically or practically. If you find out that "only" 20% of deferred ED candidates finally do get accepted RD, what does that do? Makes you more anxious? It obviously means that the institution is highly competitive in the first place, so that you knew from the beginning how challenging it would be, and this really doesn't change anything.

There are things you can and should do in this middle ground of having been deferred:

- The college has deferred you as they want to see how you fare compared to their Regular Decision pool and, most likely, to see how you do in your mid-year or next term grades (which will be sent by your school counselor to your RD colleges). I don't need to tell you that you need to work hard to do the best you absolutely can in your classes.

- You have an opportunity here to share with the college anything that may have changed in your application since they reviewed it, and touch base again with your Admissions contact in a strategic and meaningful way.

  1. *Don't*: Just write to them right away to tell them you are going to try really hard for the rest of the year or just wrote a new poem that should be published in your school's publication.

  2. *Do*: Wait some weeks before you reconnect.

  3. *Do*: Assess your application and yourself vis-à-vis the institution around late January. Do you have a relevant accomplishment you want to share? Have you done something that would be of interest to this college vis-à-vis your application? Have you taken your HL Biology grade from a 5 to a strong 7 and why?

  4. *Do*: Craft a thoughtful, short, concise note to your Admissions contact late January to share with them any updates on your end. Don't exaggerate and don't suddenly become involved in five new activities—at this stage the Admissions contact is looking for depth, purpose and relevance in anything new you want to share with him.

  5. *Do*: Let the Admissions contact know if this college is your very top choice and if you get in you will attend—*but only if this is one hundred percent the case*. Admissions is concerned about yield and knowing that you will accept back after being accepted *may* be of interest to them (or may not).

IMPORTANT!

If you truly have one college that is at the very top of your list and that *you know you will attend* if you are accepted, you can tell that college. Don't think that being strategic is telling this to every college. It's unethical, not true, and may get you in hot water. Remember that the Admissions world is one of its own and is quite insular. Admissions officers know one another. They know school counselors. They talk. They are human. Be smart and be honest and ethical. That will come through in your application and throughout the rest of this process.

You knew the rules of the game when you got into it, so you *can* be disappointed or annoyed, *but surprised, no.* Take a day or two to process the disappointment and then tell yourself to move forward. Life gives you no other alternative!

WORDS OF WISDOM: DEFERMENT FROM EARLY TO REGULAR

One of my colleagues tells all of his students that if they are deferred from Early to Regular, to try not to even have that college on your radar any longer. I actually don't do this, but I understand where he is coming from and why he does this—to set expectations and to help his students focus on the rest of their List. Bottom line is that there are many cases where a student went from Early to Regular and was accepted, and where a student went from Early to Regular and was rejected.

STUDENT ADVICE

"I prepared for this as best I could but it was devastating to be deferred. I really struggled with the news even though I knew it was very possible! I think I spent a full day feeling sorry for myself. My advice is to go through that but then to come back to life pretty quickly. It's truly not the end of the world and you may, like me, end up getting in to that school in the Regular round."

—*Deborah, England*

- *You have been rejected.*

     It's not easy news to receive and of course you'll be disappointed. I tell my students to take a couple of days to go through that feeling of being rejected. Even if you've prepared yourself—"I know it's such a long shot that they will accept me!"— you'll be disappointed if they don't. It's natural for humans to feel this way. We are wired to look for the gratification of being "accepted" and wanted by another and when we're not, even if it would have been the worst match made this year, it's disappointing. I still feel disappointment at some of life's rejections even now. So feel it and recognize it, but give yourself a maximum of two days for this, and then wake up, brush it off and move on.

I sometimes see this affecting parents even more than the students. I "get it" intellectually—it's a mix of feeling empathy towards your child's feelings of feeling rejected and also frustration or even anger towards an institution that could possibly reject your amazing child! Your child is still amazing! As a parent—and in particular if the rejection comes before any other notification of any other college—it is often a reaction to second-guess the entire strategy and process and decisions you and your child have been making since you began. Emotions may also usurp rational thoughts at this stage. I urge you to recognize when this hits and, above all, to not get into the discussion with fellow parents about who got in, who didn't, what the "expert parent's" reasoning was for another's acceptance and your child's rejection. None of this helps. Try your best to walk away from it and not find a reason. You will never find an answer.

IMPORTANT!

If the first decision(s) you read are rejections, it will be logical for you to become defensive and rethink all of your earlier work, decisions, List and college choices. You may start to reconsider where you applied and should you apply to another country while you have the time? This second-guessing—in particular for those of you who will only receive deferrals or rejections from Earlies—while natural, must be managed by you and gently pushed aside. This is not the time for second-guessing when you've gone through this process as thoroughly and precisely as you have been guided throughout this book. Recognize this when and if it hits and walk away from it.

STUDENT ADVICE

"I would have never known at the time of my ED rejection—not a fun day, by the way—that it was a blessing in disguise. I ended up at the best possible university for me. I really know this for a fact now! But at the time I could not have seen it. It's a horrible experience but I'm actually glad I went through it now. I know that's not great advice but I hope it helps to hear that there are many of us who go through this rejection and we come out on top!"

—*Heidi, Switzerland*

WORDS OF WISDOM: MERIT AWARDS WITH ACCEPTANCE LETTERS

Many parents ask at this stage if there are scholarships that can come with an acceptance. If you have been fortunate enough to be selected for a merit award—something that you now know is determined on a case-by-case basis by the institution and most often not requiring an application, unless you've applied for a specific scholarship—that award will be granted to you at the time of acceptance or just a few days later, depending on the institution. This is not in your control. If you are one of the lucky ones to receive a scholarship merit award, congratulations. These are difficult to come by and a true testament of how much the institution wants you with them. In "Early" cases this may be a way for the institution to really try to get you to choose them over another acceptance.

Side note: If you are considering deferring an acceptance for a year and have received merit aid, that aid may very well not be "deferred" with you. Discuss this with your institution and know that it might be a one-time offer for enrolling that year only. As always, it's on a case-by-case basis.

PARENT ADVICE

"We would be lying if we said we were not disappointed when Claire's ED application was rejected. We knew it was a 'reach school' and told ourselves that it will be wonderful if she got accepted but it will not be the end of the world if she wasn't; but even so, rejection is not easy. We gave ourselves time 'to mourn' on the rejection but did not dwell on it for long. We then wasted no time in moving forward to focus on the next steps and her List."

—*Zurah, Philippines*

Milestone 2: Reviewing Your Active "To-do's"

These will look strangely familiar to you and please review each to make sure you're doing what you need to at this stage.

1. Confirm you have received portal links from your universities:

   Please make sure you are logging in to each portal that the university sends to you *as soon as you receive it* and check the status of your application. We went through the importance of this in the last chapter. Connect with your Admissions contact if there is a glaring concern or discrepancy. This is your responsibility. If you did not receive the portal link within a week of applying, contact Admissions.

2. Check in with your Guidance Counselor:

   Again? You can be the judge of this by running through the following questions and determining if you need to make an appointment, swing by or send a concise email to your counselor:

   - Remind them where you've applied and, in the case of having applied for a scholarship, let them know/remind them which university this was for.

   - Review your Common Application/other applications before you meet with your school counselor to see if there are any missing documents on their part or from recommenders. Be proactive and alert your counselor to this if it's the case.

   - Ask your counselor if there is anything in your file that needs your attention from their perspective.

   - Of course, also thank your counselor very much for their help during the process and wish them a lovely holiday!

3. Thank your recommenders formally:

   By now, this should come naturally without you even thinking about it. I still remind my students at this stage of this very important step.

Why do I need to send a thank you?

- Writing recommendations takes a lot of time. It's personalized, thoughtful and strategic when done right. Your recommenders surely didn't just have yours to write.

- While your application is truly a reflection of your own work, you got there with your recommender's help.

- The recommendation section of the US application is critically important. The review of these recommendations is taken very seriously by your Admissions officers. That puts a lot of responsibility on the recommender and a lot of weight on what they've taken the time to write.

- Because writing a proper thank you note will never, ever be taken for granted. Let this be a life skill.

  Go ahead and write those today. Of course a handwritten note is preferred but an email will do the trick as well.

4. Retake any standardized tests and send official scores:

  Several of you will be taking your very last standardized test this month. You recall my advice from last month on this topic, Chapter 10. In addition:

- Make sure you are clear in your understanding of how these scores may work for you and for which colleges.

- Do any scores need to be rushed and if so to whom? Will the receiving institution accept "rushed" reports? Give your Admissions officer at said college a head's up.

- Check and see if your IELTS/TOEFL needs to be retaken and for which institutions and when.

- Sending appropriate scores: As you know, this is your responsibility. Don't wait on sending the scores officially once you know what you have to send and certainly make sure you know how you'll use—or not—your December scores if relevant.

IMPORTANT!

For some of you, you have stated that you will not self-report test scores on your main application when asked, most likely because those colleges you were applying to when you checked that criteria on their websites either do not take test scores or give you the option not to submit. Let's say you take the ACT or SAT in December to give it a final shot and you do very well; you want the universities to see these scores. If this is the case, get in touch with your Admissions contact to let them know about your situation. Be upfront and let them know that you'd like to share these results and include them in your application. They will guide you on what to do. Remember that honesty is always the best policy and being open and upfront is your best strategy.

Milestone 3: No Stopping Now

Regardless of the decision(s) that came in for Early applications—and even if you did not enter into the Early process—your final senior year grades and scores are not in, and have yet to be reviewed by any institution, even the one that accepted you ED. What this means is that *every grade you get moving forward still counts towards your university applications and will be reviewed by your colleges.* As a father put it to me this year when his son was accepted ED to his top university with a 16,000 USD merit aid award spanning four potential years, "It's ours to lose now."

WORDS OF WISDOM

When I worked in Admissions for a US university, the university had accepted a student—the year prior—from a very reputable international school based, of course, on his predicted IB grades. Whether it was Early or Regular doesn't matter and I really don't recall how the student had applied. After IB scores came out in July and were sent by the school counselor to our university, we realized that his predicted grade was several points higher than his actual scores. We rescinded the offer in July. The student had, of course, no alternative college to attend that year. This was not the college's fault.

The following recruiting season in October I went to visit the student's high school. They were very keen to meet with me and rather worried—worried for their own reputation with our institution. This was because we now had this international school on our radar—not positively—as the predicted grade they confirmed was so off-base from the actual result of one of their students, we were now evaluating any application that now came from that high school with more concern and precaution. High schools are under a lot of pressure all-around to try to match predicted to actual results, and good high schools do this well, knowing the system and knowing how to teach with excellent teachers.

The bottom line is that all final grades will be reviewed by every institution that accepts you. The institution has every right to rescind an offer when it feels the student did not match their standards up and through his senior year. This does not happen often.

With your "rite of passage" for most of you having been experienced this chapter, you are that much wiser and experienced. Yet, regardless of the decision(s) that came in, now is your time to work your hardest in your classes, with your friendships, and with your teachers. You don't have college applications as an excuse anymore to not go that extra mile for your teachers and classes. You do have a bit more freedom, I think, and you may want to take advantage of it based on what you've learned up until now going through this process.

WORDS OF WISDOM: IF REJECTION IS THE FIRST DECISION YOU RECEIVE

There is no science behind the process of application. This is the month when parents who think they are experts can get in the way. One of my students, Tamasa, did not get into her ED school. She was deferred. This was her first notification from a college and it didn't feel good. She knew her chances and we discussed what could be holes in her application throughout the process. She also understood that there's no science to applying but a deferral was still disappointing.

The next day, her mother called me and said, "I know what it was. Tamasa didn't have the strong alumni contact."

"What are you talking about?" I asked.

"I was at a parents' coffee this morning and we were all talking about Early notifications. Several mothers confirmed for me that at this university if the candidate does not have an alumni contact somehow tied to her application, it's a no-go. We should have known this before and . . ."

I cut her off. I told her this was not true. She replied that these were parents who "knew".

I said, "María, you may think you know but none of you really knows. That's why you've hired me to help Tamasa." I told her to put away her doubts about the process and to stop trying to "figure it out", as hard as it was to swallow and bear.

Be careful of these other parents who think they are experts and are free in giving their advice. Like I tell my students who start to get involved in similar peer discussions, just walk away. Smile and walk away.

The Enlightened Insider: Deferred from my safety?!

Recently we've been seeing some universities very popular with very high-achieving students who use them as their "safety" school, actually end up deferring an unprecedented number of these applicants from their Early Action round to the Regular Decision pool. This is most likely due to yield—that the institution saw clearly what the strategy of those applicants was, to use this university as a safety school—and in very rare cases the applicant would actually accept that school back, something that improves a university's yield. By the end of January all of the students who were accepted ED elsewhere and thus would have lowered the institution's yield were now out of the pile. In fact, there were many more cases of a student with a less strong profile getting into some of these universities Early Action than the strong applicants who used the school as their potential "safety". It seems rather complex but no one said this process isn't.

CHAPTER 12

Anticipating, Deciding, and Arriving

January to 1 May

J anuary to May seems like a long period but the reality is that it goes by more quickly than you'd like and will be a mix of emotions, work, excitement and thrill. For students and parents alike, try to really soak up every stage as you'll never go through this phase in your life again. It's worth recognizing and stopping for a moment to appreciate from time to time.

For most, *January* is a month where school starts back up. For Southern Hemisphere school students, you've graduated and these next few months will be working, interning, volunteering or doing whatever you planned for. For the rest of you in the Northern Hemisphere, you might quickly forget what you just went through over the past months and year as you focus on the final months of high school.

February can be a time of anxiety and doubt, in particular, for the parents. Students are engaged in their work, extracurriculars, and social lives as they realize their school year is coming to an end soon, while parents will sometimes connect with me during this month to say, *"I'm realizing that Elena's List had a lot of universities on it with very low acceptance rates. Should we contact the schools again and let them know anything about her?"* No. You've gone through the entire process with a fine-toothed comb. You know why you applied to the universities you applied to and you controlled everything you possibly could. Now, you must just let go.

March and *April* are when decisions start coming in and, for the US, **by 1 May** you must take your decision and accept back that university that you want to attend (if you were not accepted by your ED1 or 2 schools). There's more after that which we will go over in this chapter. These are the milestones we will cover:

Milestone 1: Tracking Your Applications

Milestone 2: EGI for Deferrals

Milestone 3: Regular Application (and ED2) Decisions Coming in; Your Deposit is Due 1 May

Milestone 4: Being Wait-listed

Milestone 5: Staying Engaged in the Classroom

Milestone 6: Saying Thank You to Those Who Helped (and Sharing Your News With Them)

Milestone 7: Pros and Cons Lists (and Deciding Which Offer to Accept Back)

Milestone 8: Double Depositing

Milestone 9: Student Visa Process

Milestone 10: Conscription

Milestone 11: Gap Year

Case Study

Name: Claire

Gender: Female

City: Manila

Nationality: French and Singaporean

Started process: September of her junior year

Program/Rigor: IBDP, Bilingual diploma. HL courses: Biology, History, English Literature; SL courses: Maths, Economics; French self-study

Grades: Predicted 37

Standardized tests to date: ACT three times. Highest composite: 27

Subject Tests: None

TOEFL/IELTS: Not necessary as she was in IB program with 6's in HL English literature, which satisfied all colleges on her List.

Challenges: Making decisions and second-guessing herself. We started very early and yet even by the time all applications had to be in over a year later, it was a struggle to confirm the List and also manage time. As conscientious as Claire is, she struggled with time management *and* with the peer pressure of a very competitive international school. She came from the French system only a couple of years earlier and a different country and had a lot of transition. Likewise, she went through a series of sports injuries in her junior and senior years, setting her back emotionally. Her grades were strong but, compared to her peers, perhaps not the strongest. Lots of "college chatter" going on at her school which often disarmed and disabled her efforts before she could get back on track.

Strengths: Claire figured out by early summer between her junior and senior year what she wanted in a college and, while she would waver throughout her senior year confirming her list, it was comforting to go back to this criteria and confirm it for her. She is a very hard worker, very determined, not competitive with peers. She experienced over the summer what she may want to pursue within a career path—advocating for the poor and social entrepreneurship—which she was able to adroitly discuss in all her applications. She has an incredibly open mind and open heart.

Fit/Factors: Small to medium commitment to undergraduate studies. Community service involvement by majority of student body. Strong History and Political Science departments; strong liberal arts education. Name recognition of the college did not matter so much, although it was difficult at times to step away from this with the high school college chatter going on. Balanced student body, diverse. Did not want a competitive student body. Opportunities to study abroad.

Interests: Community service related to political science. Strong interest in history. Loves sports. Genuinely loves helping others.

Essay topic: Growing from adolescent to young adult through her summer experience of interning at a social entrepreneurship farm in her host country and how this also exposed her to something she believes she wants to dedicate her life to.

Short List: Tufts ED, Boston College, Vassar, University of Rochester, Kalamazoo EA, Goucher EA (applied for Global Scholars Scholarship), Sarah Lawrence, Skidmore, Colgate.

Interviews: Claire managed to secure a few, including one for the Global Scholars program at Goucher.

(continued)

Visits: Did an East Coast US tour visiting some of the more typical colleges.

EGI: With all of her colleges. It did not come easy at first.

Dream school, if any: Tufts. I found her to be excited about it after her visit. However, she changed her mind and was also afraid it was a poor reflection of her to go back on her first choice at the start of senior year. We knew it would be a reach for her—it's a school on so many international students' Lists—and her parents knew as well and yet were supportive of her decision.

Application strategy: While Claire knew what she wanted in her college, changes were made up until the final hour. This was a great case of her own realizations and preferences for colleges changing with time (totally natural!) and her sometimes reluctance but sometimes acceptance at recognizing this. Kalamazoo and Goucher—not added until October of her senior year—turned out to be two that she really felt she could fit in with, without having visited or done extensive EGI.

MILESTONES

Milestone 1: Tracking Your Applications

You've received all of your portal logins for each university and have officially logged in. What are they telling you about your application? Is there anything standing out?

All portals are not created equal, so take your time reviewing and being thorough.

Please remember that we discussed this in Chapters 9 and 11, with an example of what a portal may look like in Chapter 9 showing the student's "missing" information. It is up to you to determine if that information is truly missing or if it's something the system has not caught up with yet.

Missing information or "red flags" that come up in portals at this time may include the following:

- *Sponsor support document*: This shows that you have a financial sponsor who will be responsible for you throughout your university career.

- *Certificate of Financial Resources*: This was covered in Chapter 9.

- *Midterm report grades*: Sometimes these are truly missing and sometimes it's that they have not come out yet from your school and thus have not been sent. Check in with your school first and Guidance Counselor.

- *Passport photo*: Self-explanatory.

- *First marking period grades*: If this is missing and you are a current student, you need to make a call to your school counselor and to the university Admissions office right away. They should have been submitted with your application at the time of submission. Sometimes this will show up with my students who are in a gap year as this does not pertain to them. Know your situation and be proactive.

You should be referring to your application status regularly and certainly being proactive about any red flags or missing items/pending items for any application.

Milestone 2: EGI for Deferrals

I mentioned in December's chapter your strategy for EGI related to any deferral you may have received from an Early application. Now is your time to put that into action. A few things to consider as you write to your Admissions contact where you have been deferred:

1. What is it that you will share with Admissions that will be new—in addition to what you have already shared with them in your entire application? Does it support your application?

    Don't: Tell them about a new club you joined (e.g., the French club) when you focused your application on the sciences and your interest in studying theoretical physics. It doesn't fit and it's just an irrelevant "add-on" that could actually hurt your application.

    Do: Tell them about a new club you started or additional research you've taken on in your Physics class that supports what you discussed as your passion and interest in your application and *why* you are sharing this with them.

    Don't: Provide them with another list of things you are doing. Again, this is just filler with no substance. It's insincere and will hurt your application.

    Do: Explain what you've done to improve your grades in specific classes and the outcome of that so far. Be specific.

2. If you have done something substantial and relevant over the December break that would support your overall application, you may want to mention this. You may also want to ask your Admissions contact if she would welcome another letter of recommendation from the person who supervised you during such an activity over the December break.

3. *Please don't overdo this step.* One contact is enough, perhaps two at most and if absolutely necessary. You should be doing this by the last week of January to get the information in before they start to make decisions, but also to have allowed enough time to pass to show that you have done something substantive and relevant to speak about.

Milestone 3: Regular Application (and ED2) Decisions Coming In; Your Deposit is Due 1 May

You'll start to receive your news sometime throughout March and April depending on the institution. I have the same advice for you that I had when you were opening your Early notifications from December's chapter and I'll briefly reiterate them here:

1. Determine where you want to be and with whom you want to be when you open your notification letters.

2. Be kind to yourself and to others during this long and sometimes drawn out period. Not everyone is receiving good news.

3. Read the decision letters thoroughly. Please don't stop at "Congratulations!" Not all decision letters are created equal and often there are points that need to be addressed.

4. Please remember if you applied ED2 and are accepted what your obligations are and how to carry through with them. Please see Chapter 11, Milestone 1 for guidance.

Most importantly, remember that, unless you have submitted an ED application, you will have until 1 May to make your decision and make your deposit. Read the instructions carefully. I tell families never to wait until the last minute to make this decision because the deposit from your foreign bank may arrive on 2 May due to the difference in time zones. Sometimes international transfers can take days, too. Be prepared to have your decision made at least two weeks ahead of the 1 May deadline and your deposit sent off by then as well. Schools will not accept a late deposit. It is your responsibility to take into consideration the further "complications" of making your deposit from abroad!

WORDS OF WISDOM: NOTE ON LIKELY LETTERS

Starting a few years ago, some selective institutions began sending out cryptic letters to their RD candidates indicating that they very much wanted to accept them. These letters that were sent in February were called "likely letters". There is an internal agreement among the Ivy League institutions that decisions will not be sent out before end of March so that none can get a leg up on students who are accepted and they want to accept back. What some have done is send a "likely letter" before the 31 March deadline to students who the institution feels will be accepted to other highly selective universities. A likely letter may tell you in so many words that pending your continued academic success and progress you will "likely" be admitted to said institution. Will a likely ever turn into a reject? Only if the student racks up disciplinary action or some other grave issue; but for the most part, a likely letter is a pretty sure bet on a future acceptance letter from said college.

Milestone 4: Being Wait-listed

Your notification letter doesn't congratulate you but it also doesn't go into some long and wordy way of telling you they did not accept you. Instead, you're on a wait-list.

There's a lot to say and not much to say on this topic. I'll give you what counts:

1. While there are some potential action steps to take on a college that wait-listed you (see below), I would encourage you to move beyond this college and think about the ones that have accepted you.

2. Wait-lists are managed by colleges based on a priority system. They are going to see how many students accept them back by 1 May. This is the "yield" we discussed in previous chapters. Based on those numbers, transfer applicants, students declining their original acceptance, colleges will go through the summer taking students off the wait-list to accept them based on their own internal ranking of their wait-listed candidates and how many slots they have left to offer to the incoming freshman class. Some colleges never even resort to their wait-list in a season. You must not have your heart set on this.

3. If you're keen to see how that wait-list will turn out (or not), *you must absolutely, one hundred percent deposit at another institution by the 1 May deadline* (two weeks prior by our timeline as I've stated earlier). If you do not do this, you are not assuring yourself a space at any institution and statistically speaking will have a very high chance of being without a college to attend come August. That deposit, in the case where you are accepted by the wait-listing institution sometime in June or July or even August, will be forfeited by you if you choose to attend the school that took you off your wait-list. The bottom *line is to choose and deposit on one institution by 1 May.*

4. In the case where you are very keen on your wait-listing institution and want to give it every last effort, I encourage you to refer back to my advice on being deferred, both in this chapter and in December's chapter. You'll want to follow similar advice for being wait-listed.

5. Wait-listing stats on a college can be found and these are stats I direct my students to give them an idea of what we are looking at here at this stage in the process. The stats can be found for many universities on the college's own website or by searching for it. Some institutions do not publish this data overtly. This data gives perspective to a last minute hold-out. Psychologically, I believe it's not fair to you to plan for a wait-listed institution when all the cards are already on the table, when you've done your due diligence for months and even years, and have your acceptances from institutions that truly do want you.

Go ahead and follow through with your wait-listed school(s) but you should also move on and focus on the schools that have accepted you.

Milestone 5: Staying Engaged in the Classroom

The universities who want you are watching you. Keep working.

Milestone 6: Saying Thank You to Those Who Helped (and Sharing Your News With Them)

This step is critical and it should come as no surprise to you. Parents are also included in this Milestone. Now is the *time to sit down together and draw up a list of all of those people who have helped you throughout this process and say thanks.*

Writing notecards is preferred. Sending emails will be just as graciously accepted by the recipient. And, when you do send out these notes—to your school counselor, to teachers, to recommenders, to friends of friends, to your neighbor, to your independent counselor—share the outcomes with them. They'll be very interested to know and hear all of it. They worked so hard to help you get to where you are now and you owe it to them to share in the excitement.

Milestone 7: Pros and Cons Lists—(and Deciding Which Offer to Accept Back)

For so long you felt that Admissions was controlling the process and now you have the final say.

I'd like you to take some time—this will take a few days to a week *but start by early April and finish by mid-April*—to fill out Worksheet 12.1.

Note that if you are obligated to serve conscription for your country, please do this as soon as you have all the notifications received to begin the discussion with Admissions. See Milestone 10 below.

A few points on how to do this effectively:

1. Have your university notes beside you as well as your interview and campus visit notes for each institution.

2. Remind yourself of what you need and want in your university. What factors are most important?

3. Engage those self-control techniques you used when you were working on applications for this final true exercise in the process. You owe it to yourself and to your

family to take this seriously. That means turning off your mobile and doing this in a place where you can think clearly.

4. Draw up the list first individually. I would ask the parents as well to do this exercise in Worksheet 12.2 without sharing it with your child first. Then, I would ask you, the student, to share your responses and what you wrote first with your parents. Discuss as a family. I'd like the student to always begin at this stage, so that they are reflecting first and foremost on what they feel are the pros and cons and are not influenced by what the parents say first.

5. Then it's time to discuss as a family. *You should come to your conclusion by mid-April and be ready to deposit by then.*

Milestone 8: Double Depositing

If this option is ever brought up by a student or by their family, I would explain why they should never do this.

Many families are not aware—until it comes in the acceptance letter clearly stated by the accepting institution—that *you are not permitted to deposit to more than one institution.* It is not legal or ethical to do so. You must make your decision on one institution and that's it. It is tough but you know each institution well enough by now and have made your pros and cons lists. You must be able to decide.

Some families have asked me if the colleges would be able to find out that they have double deposited. This is how I explain the situation to them:

1. The counselor may only send a final transcript to one school. That is the school that you deposit with.

2. If you "get around this" somehow, it would be a felony in some instances.

3. Ethically this is wrong. You're teaching your child that unethical behavior is the road to choose. He will have a hard life if he lives by this "value".

4. The schools will find out because you will not end up attending one of them. That school will try its best to find out where the student did attend. Finding out is not difficult as it's easy to contact the student's high school, and the school would most likely call the receiving school to let them know what one of their incoming students has done. It's possible that school would rescind its offer to that student knowing of their unethical behavior.

5. Such a student will have a difficult time finding any institution to attend that year. If the student goes through this whole process again the following year, it will be under a black mark. The school counselor will not want to go to bat for him/her and may

mention this in his/her recommendation letter. The universities will question the "gap year" and teachers may refuse to write further recommendations.

Milestone 9: Student Visa Process

This can vary greatly depending on the country in which you reside and the passport you hold and how the US Embassy "works". Your university, once having received your deposit and welcomed you to their incoming class, will leave it to you to figure out how it works in your country to obtain the necessary I-20 US student visa. *You do not want to wait until the last minute to do this or plan to travel around this time, which will be somewhere around June/July.*

A few important points:

1. Look out for the initial visa documents from your university. Often, they are sent via FedEx or DHL. If you do not receive them by late June, call your Admissions office. I often have students at this stage thinking about so many other things that they are not focused on this.

2. Please refer to the US Embassy's webpage in your country of residence for their procedure in obtaining your student visa. They, of course, can change any step at any time and so their information will be the most updated. Every country's US Embassy will have a unique procedure for doing this on a case-by-case basis.

3. Give this time and be patient. Usually students receive the visa in time. Don't bet on it happening in a week and certainly don't think that just because you have the documents from your university that means you have the visa. You must go through this process. It is not a one-step process.

Milestone 10: Conscription

Many of my students must do conscription in their country, whether they are a permanent resident or a citizen. They know who they are and what is expected of them. Any university familiar with international Admissions will be aware of the conscription requirements of certain countries.

Speaking to those of you who have applied to university while still in high school and plan to defer for your conscription, you have by now either discussed your conscription requirement with your Admissions contact during the Admissions process prior to your being accepted, or it is still something you need to discuss. Let me address both situations:

1. If you've been discussing this with your Admissions contact throughout the admissions process, the contact will be well aware that you will need to defer the amount required by your country when you deposit. Even so, I would ask you to email them

just prior to sending in your deposit and confirm in writing what you are doing. Confirm with your Admissions contact the stipulations of your conscription, that you would be deferring for X number of years, and will be depositing for matriculation in the fall of XXXX year.

2. If you have not yet discussed this with your Admissions contact, gather all of your acceptances and complete Worksheet 12.1 as soon as possible. This should be done as soon as you can so that you can begin discussions with your Admissions officer(s) by early April.

   If students decided not to discuss this openly with Admissions during the Admissions process, I ask them to, at this stage, get answers in writing about the college's understanding of the conscription period so that they can move forward without any questions before depositing. Here's what I advise:

   a. Determine your school of choice.

   b. Write an email to your Admissions contact explaining that you are prepared to deposit and wanted to confirm with them your conscription requirements mandated by your country as a citizen/PR. Explain to her what this means in terms of your enrollment—that you would be deferring enrollment until XXXX year.

   c. Let your Admissions contact know that you would like their confirmation to move forward to deposit and that you are thrilled to be a student at said university in XXXX year.

Get confirmation in writing. As I said above, this is the surest way for you and your family to feel confident about moving ahead and that your space will be held for you post-conscription.

This topic can be very unnerving for students and families as there is often that gray area and very seldom does a university publish on their website their policies for conscription, since it is not a requirement in the US. I will say that I have never had or have never heard of a case of a student's acceptance being turned into a rejection due to his requirement to serve his country for conscription. I hope this continues to be the case.

Milestone 11: Gap Year

This is the advice for students who wish to plan for a gap year:

1. Once you have completed Worksheet 12.1 from Milestone 7 and know which university you are accepting, email your Admissions contact directly to indicate how thrilled you are to be depositing shortly and that you would like to request a year's deferral to be able to take a gap year.

2. I advise my students to give a reason for taking a gap year in this email. There is no need to write an essay but you should be specific on what you are going to do and why, and ask if they need anything more for you to consider your request. Saying "consider your request" shows the Admissions staff that you are not assuming anything, and that you are taking their response as a privilege, not a right.

3. Get a response in writing: A "go-ahead" to deposit now (before 1 May) and the confirmation of when you would matriculate (the year).

4. It is your responsibility to stay in touch with your university throughout the year and make sure that at this point next year you are going through the appropriate processes (visa, orientation sign-up, etc.) to make a smooth transition to university.

IMPORTANT!

In general, public institutions do not allow for one-year deferrals for a gap year unless they explicitly say so. That said, I have had students who have applied to, been accepted to, and then asked for a gap year to a US state school and it has been approved on a case-by-case basis.

Now that you have accepted your place at university, you've finished the process. It's a privilege to have been able to assist you through this important and fantastic journey and I wish you all the success in the world in this next stage of your life!

Worksheet 12.1: Pros and Cons of My Accepting Universities (Student)

University	Specifics of Acceptance (e.g. scholarship)	Location	How it fits my needs/wants	How it does not/ may not fit my needs/wants	Why I applied	Questions I have for the institution	My ranking

Worksheet 12.2: Pros and Cons of My Child's Accepting Universities (Parents)

University	Specifics of Acceptance (e.g. scholarship)	Location	How I believe it fits my child	My concerns	Questions I have about the institution for my child	Questions I have for the institution	My ranking

The Beginning of the Rest of Your Life

July, August and Moving In

STUDENT ADVICE

"Summer between high school graduation and college is a time that I still refer to as paradise. It was the first time in a very long time where I had nothing to worry about. I was done with high school, I knew what college I was going to, I didn't have to be writing essays or studying for an exam. Until mid-August, when college started to become more real, I felt nothing but excitement, happiness and relief. Then in August when I started to pack and buy things for college, that is when I started to feel more nervous and anxious. It was my first time living in the US and the first time living apart from my family. I had great friends at home and counting down the days until I had to say goodbye to them became hard.

During this phase of confusion, the main change I felt was that I was growing up. I feared whether I was able to do well in college, I barely knew anyone who was going to the same college as me, and I was going to be the only Japanese in our year.

By the time I landed in LAX and made my way to college, I felt more confident. Before orientation I realized I only needed to be myself. I realized that I didn't have to blend into the American culture, but embrace who I am and friends who decided to stick with me are still my closest friends now.

(continued)

The advice I will give all of you who are in this phase of in-between high school and college will be to enjoy it. You deserve an amazing summer with friends and family and you should celebrate what you have accomplished. Everyone in your freshman class is also equally nervous and equally excited. If you are worried that you won't have anyone to talk to, start talking to them before school even starts. This will not only allow you to make new friends in advance but can help you figure out what to bring, what to expect, and boost your confidence level."

—*Mei, Claremont McKenna College*

What an accomplishment to have arrived at this point. The following Milestones will be very helpful to you as you embark on this next phase of your life:

 Milestone 1: Thanking Others

 Milestone 2: Choosing Courses

 **Milestone 3:** Roommate Questionnaire

 Milestone 4: Orientation

 Milestone 5: Arrival on Campus and Departing Parents. . .

A good resource is *The Thinking Student's Guide to College* by Andrew Roberts.

MILESTONES

Milestone 1: Thanking Others

After going through this entire guide, I don't have to tell you that this is an opportune time to consider all of the people in your life over the past couple of years and if you've given those people the proper thanks you feel they warrant and deserve. Whether it's a handwritten note, a letter, an email, a phone call or taking the person out for tea, give your thanks appropriately. This will take some time to do—and should.

Milestone 2: Choosing Courses

This Milestone will depend on your university, how and when it requires its incoming students to register for classes. Anytime a student of mine is asked to do this before arriving on campus, I guide them back to their university's very specific instructions on this.

In most cases, there will be required courses you must take and can choose from. Some will be full and you may not get your first choice, so you should do this as soon as you receive the opportunity to and not delay. Once the door is open, it's open, but that also means it can close quickly.

Milestone 3: Roommate Questionnaire

Every university has a different approach to matching its incoming students to one another. The idea is not to give you an-almost-identical "you" to live with your first year, but instead to try to find compatibility measures so that you and your roommate or roommates will live respectfully together. Will you be your roommate's best friend? Perhaps. Perhaps not. Will it take some adjusting to live with your assigned roommate? Usually. Should you request to live with your high school friend who is also attending the same university? Absolutely not. My advice is to try not to control this Milestone too much as most of it is out of your control beyond what you supply your university with within the parameters of what they ask. Once you do get introduced to your new roomies, have fun setting up some Skype calls and asking about them, what they're excited about, what they are nervous about. You'll talk about who is bringing what to the dorm and get to know one another before you meet "in real life" on move-in day.

I have yet to have a student who switched their roommate assigned to them the first year. I have students who chose not to live with that same roommate after first year, but very seldom do I hear of terrible roommate situations. Of course they exist—we are all human beings and there's always the possibility that we won't get along with one another, in particular someone we have to live with—but in most of the cases it not only works out, but also turns out that this roommate you get assigned to for first year plays a huge part throughout your four-year university experience.

Milestone 4: Orientation

Make sure you've signed up for both the International Student Orientation and the "regular" Orientation, if both are offered at your university. Even if some of the agenda items may seem "lame" to you, sign up and attend. It's here where you'll meet your first friends. Don't miss this. You'll want to be a part of it socially, and certainly at the academic and administrative level, you'll receive instructions on things you simply don't want to miss. (e.g., academic advisors, course overloads, campus safety, club activities, etc.)

You'll be signing up for these orientations before arriving on campus.

LD students: Please make sure you're registering with the Office of Disability Services prior to or as soon as you land on campus—this will depend on your university—and assess and then organize the support you'll need before classes begin.

Milestone 5: Arrival on Campus and Departing Parents...

I'm going to leave you with the best advice—not my own but that of parents and students who have been through it. I owe this guide to them and think it's appropriate to sign off by sharing their thoughts with you...

STUDENT ADVICE

"While it may seem like everyone around you is rushing to hang out and meet new people, take the time you need to settle in, say your goodbyes, and make room for alone time. The beginning of college is fun, but full of chaos and hectic irregularity. Although it may feel more comfortable during the early days to stick with a small group, be open to meeting a variety of people and branch out wherever and whenever you can. You will likely not meet your best friends on your first few days on campus, so get to know different people. You never know who you may encounter later down the line in your classes, extracurriculars—even in your dorms! Don't close yourself off to new experiences and opportunities, but at the same time, don't try to do it all on no sleep."

—*Veena, Yale University*

PARENT ADVICE

"After all that rejoicing, reality struck and I was not looking forward to my daughter's departure. I turned into an overprotective and selfish mum who wanted her daughter all to herself. It caused unnecessary friction between us. Would I have done it differently? Definitely. I should have given her the freedom of doing what she enjoyed the most before leaving home. She deserved it after all that very hard work. I want to believe that I have brought her up well; she would have known how to prioritize her time without me nagging at her all the time."

—*Zurah, Philippines*

PARENT ADVICE

"On the day we left KL for the flight to NY for the start of this next stage in Matthew's life, I sailed out of my house into the taxi with my husband and 16-year-old college bound son…and I LEFT MY LUGGAGE AT HOME. No, this Chinese mother didn't cry when she arrived at the airport and realized she had left her luggage at home. She laughed! And guess what. We lost our Emirates seats as we were late checking in. But we enjoyed another Asian meal and chatted together in the airport lounge…boarded the next flight out to NY. We arrived at the University of Rochester with plenty of love and Matthew checked in wonderfully. I never dreamt that sending our son to college would leave me with such ease in my heart. Forgetting my luggage was a profound incident. It is a great metaphor—a Chinese mother no longer tied to fear and/or baggage of self-doubt or doubt about my son's passage and beginning college. I had felt so proud of Matthew when he was awarded a full scholarship and a research grant as the Renaissance Scholar. In the last phase of the process, it was important for Matthew to know we'd continue to champion him and his vision, celebrate the journey so far and the continuing journey ahead. I would not have done anything differently, because I don't see events as milestones or destinations, but experiences."

—*Caroline, Malaysia*

PARENT ADVICE

"I always tell myself that we have given our children wings, now is the time that they learn how to fly. It's all easier said than done. I was really shocked when I arrived at the city where Claire's college is. We did not visit this college during our college tour. I am a city girl and would not have survived for more than a month there. I was very sad for her and she sensed it. It wasn't about me and I should not have voiced my discomfort about the city that she will be living in for the next four years. She told me that the city is not of any importance to her. She was so confident that she will be very happy in the college meeting new and like-minded people.

Before leaving her, we told ourselves that we are allowed to cry our hearts out but when the time came, yes, we hugged and cried, but it wasn't as bad as I thought it will be. I guess we both knew that she is happy where she is and that everything will be alright. Time has passed and I receive texts and calls from her every day. I am relieved to say that she is still very happy, feels she belongs and waxes lyrical about her school. Knowing that your child who is thousands of miles away from you, is happy and contented, is the best gift that any parent could ever have asked for."

—*Zurah, Manila*

PARENT ADVICE

"I was very emotional the month before sending Michelle off. It was the feeling that life as we knew it would be different henceforth. I tried really hard to make our last month together as happy and memorable as possible. I had to bite my tongue many times to keep from scolding and nagging Michelle. I tried to use her 'bad behavior moments' as opportunities to remind her to self-check and reflect on her actions and see if she could have done better. Of course I am far from perfect and there were many times I simply lost my temper! My aim was to create the idea in Michelle's mind that home is a place of security, happiness and comfort, so that when she left for college she would always feel that she would want to come back to us for anything, be it for rest or for help. As a parent I felt it was most valuable to create as many opportunities for discussions on as wide a range of issues as you think they might encounter and help plant some seeds of wisdom in them, and hopefully if they should ever be caught in any of those scenarios you discussed, they would be able to handle them well."

—*Serene, Indonesia*

STUDENT ADVICE

"I kept worrying my mom and dad would lose it, so I tried very hard to be solid and cool, but I was very nervous before leaving in August—really nervous. I think I would say to anyone who gets a bit anxious to not ignore the services offered on a US campus as I should, in retrospect, have gone to some counseling in the beginning just to ease the anxiety and my nervousness. I'm super happy now, but there's an adjustment period and it can be a little much!"

—Laurent, Lewis & Clark

PARENT ADVICE

"Don't skip international student orientation. It's a great opportunity to move in early before the hoards of freshmen descend on campus and get acquainted with other students who've lived abroad (not to mention getting the first pick of the beds in the dorm room!). Go to all of the parent events and be a risk taker—talk to other parents and share your thoughts. You will feel better knowing they are experiencing similar feelings and you aren't alone. Then, once your child has settled in, don't hang about—don't be the last parents to leave. It does not get easier by dragging it out. Universities often have a clear end to their parent orientation program—when the university basically said, "Thanks. We have your kids and will take good care of them. Please go now.""

—Sterling, Singapore

OUTCOMES OF CHAPTER CASE STUDIES

Chapter 2: Shefali

Result: Accepted ED: Cornell, College of Engineering

Long List:

Cornell College of Engineering	Texas A&M
WPI	University of Rochester
Bucknell	Purdue University
Georgia Tech	Stanford University
Harvey Mudd	Texas A&M
Rice University	University of Houston
State University of NY at Buffalo	University of Michigan

Johns Hopkins University	Boston University
UC, San Diego	Washington University
Duke University	MIT
University of Washington	Cal-Poly
Case Western University	Union College
Northwestern University	

Chapter 3: Mei

Result: Accepted ED: Claremont McKenna College

Long List:

Tufts University	Barnard/Columbia
Wellesley College	Swarthmore
Pomona	Williams
Reed	Skidmore
Rice	Brown University
Vassar	Wesleyan
UC Berkeley	UNC-Chapel Hill
UC Santa Barbara	Whittier
UC San Diego	Claremont McKenna
UCLA	Stanford
Connecticut College	Boston College
Pepperdine	Dartmouth
Chapman	Haverford
Middlebury College	

Chapter 4: Maya

Results:

Accepted: UCSD, UCLA, Boston University, Tufts, Northwestern

Wait-listed: Barnard

Rejected: UC Berkeley, Cornell, Columbia, UPenn

Attending: Tufts

Long List:

Boston University	Columbia
Boston College	UPenn
UC Berkeley	Cornell
UC San Diego	University of Rochester
UCLA	Bowdoin
Tufts	Bates
Northwestern	Stanford
Barnard	

Chapter 5: Michelle

Results: Accepted EA: Berklee; did not turn in her other two applications as she was notified mid-December just before the other two were due.

Long List:

VCU	Chapman
University of Rochester and Eastman Conservatory	Cal Lutheran
	SUNY Purchase
Oberlin	Pace
Berklee	Marymount
Lawrence	UC Riverside
Hartt School, University of Hartford	CalArts
USC	San Diego State University
University of Maryland	Manhattan School of Music
Belmont University	New School for Jazz and Contemporary Music
DePaul	
Loyola Marymount	Manhattanville College

Chapter 6: Sacha

Results:

Deferred EA to Regular round: Babson

Accepted EA: Northeastern

Accepted RD: Bentley

Rejected: Boston University, NYU, Tufts

Wait-listed: Boston College, Babson

Attending: Kings College, London

(Yes, this happens! Sacha was totally undecided until the day before her deposit was due and chose Kings in the end and the UK, something we had not expected at all.)

Long List:

Boston College	Barnard College
Boston University	Fordham University
Babson College	University of Rochester
Bentley University	Middlebury College
Georgetown University	Claremont McKenna
American University	Tufts University
George Washington University	Johns Hopkins University
NYU	

Chapter 7: Sara

Results: Accepted ED: Barnard. Immediately withdrew EA application to University of Chicago.

Long List:

NYU	Vassar
BU	UC Berkeley
GW University	Barnard
Northwestern	Smith
American University	Wellesley
Tufts University	UC Santa Barbara
Emory University	UCLA
Pomona	UC San Diego
Reed	Emerson College
Rice	Connecticut College

Pepperdine	Williams
Chapman	Skidmore
Amherst	Brown
Middlebury	Columbia
Swarthmore	UVA
Cornell	Wesleyan
University of Michigan	Washington University (St. Louis)
University of Chicago	UNC-Chapel Hill

Chapter 8: Xavier

Results:

Denied ED: Bowdoin

Accepted: Lewis & Clark EA, Willamette, Goucher, Kalamazoo, Elon, Lawrence

Rejected: Reed, Colby, Connecticut College, Bates

Attending: Lewis & Clark

Long List:

Pitzer	Boston College
Elon	Connecticut College
Lawrence	Haverford
Oberlin	Kenyon
Carleton	Middlebury
Washington University (St. Louis)	Goucher
Colorado College	Skidmore
Whitman	Reed
Bates	Grinell
Bowdoin	Colby
Macalester	Bennington
University of Rochester	Lewis & Clark
Dickinson	Willamette
Tufts	Pomona

Chapter 9: Lori

Results:

ED Deferred to RD: Wellesley

Accepted EA: Northeastern

Denied RD: Wellesley, Barnard, Tufts

Accepted: Smith, Mt. Holyoke, Bennington

Attending: Smith

Long List:

Chapman University	Scripps
Quest	Marlboro College
Bennington College	Kalamazoo College
Smith College	Kenyon
Queen Mary	Reed
Mt. Holyoke	Lewis & Clark
Durham	Wellesley
Queens University	Barnard
NEU	Bard
McGill	Goucher
Vassar	Emerson
Sarah Lawrence College	SUNY Purchase
Hampshire College	

Chapter 10: Veena

Results:

SCEA Deferred to RD: Yale

Accepted RD: Northwestern, Boston College, Tufts, Stanford, UPenn (with "likely letter" sent before notification) and. . .Yale

Rejected: Brown, Georgetown

Attending: Yale

Long List:

Yale	Tufts
Stanford	Amherst
Boston College	Williams
Georgetown	Duke
University of Pennsylvania	Brown
Princeton	Middlebury
Boston University	University of Chicago
Northwestern	

Chapter 11: Matthew

Results:

Accepted EA: Boston College; invited for Presidential Scholar's weekend

Accepted: Carleton, Carnegie Mellon, Johns Hopkins, Swarthmore, UCLA, UC Santa Barbara, UC Berkeley, University of Rochester

Rejected: Brown, Caltech, Chicago, Columbia, Harvard, MIT, Princeton, Stanford

Attending: University of Rochester, Renaissance Scholar

Long List:

Boston College	UC Berkeley
Boston University	UCLA
Tufts	UC Santa Barbara
Harvard	USC
Middlebury	Johns Hopkins
Bowdoin	U Chicago
Bates	Northwestern
Williams	Carnegie Mellon
Amherst	Columbia
Brown	MIT
Caltech	Princeton

University of Rochester	Haverford
Stanford	Carleton
Swarthmore	Macalester

Chapter 12: Claire

Results:

Rejected ED: Tufts

Accepted EA: Kalamazoo; with 20K$/year scholarship; Goucher with 13K$/year scholarship

Accepted: Sarah Lawrence, Bates

Rejected: Boston College

Attending: Bates

Long List:

Tufts	Colby College
Wellesley	Middlebury
University of Rochester	Connecticut College
Pitzer	Vassar
Scripps	Wesleyan
Goucher	Skidmore
Sarah Lawrence	Kenyon
Smith	Oberlin
Holyoke	Chapman
Oberlin	Whittier
Kalamazoo	Occidental
Kenyon	Carleton
Boston College	Barnard
Bowdoin College	Bryn Mawr
Bates College	Haverford

THE WRITING HANDBOOK

Please use this Writing Handbook by following the Milestones that refer to it and when you are told to use it. This Handbook should not be used on its own and is designed to be used alongside its corresponding chapters and Milestones from within the guide itself.

WRITING WORKSHOP 1

Part 1: Why Write?

The point of writing in university applications is simple: to give Admissions an idea of who you are as an individual. Your grades, test scores, activities, first-place finish in the regional games, and even your summer volunteering may be the same as several other applicants. Your writing is simply what sets you apart.

Many of you will use one of the portals to apply to the majority of your universities, namely the Common Application or, in other cases, the Universal College Application, the Coalition Application or university-specific applications. These allow students to apply to many, if not all, of their universities under one portal or umbrella, saving you some time from inputting similar information (i.e., personal data, activities, family data, etc.) for multiple university applications. These portals, along with university-specific applications, will have essay prompts that will be required of every applicant. Many state schools and some private schools—such as the University of Texas system, MIT, the University of California system—will not work with any outside portal and will have their own applications whereby you will submit a separate application through the university website/portal to these schools if you are applying.

In addition to these essay prompts, the Common Application allows students to choose one from a choice of seven, whereby that one essay you write will be sent to every university you apply to who asks for it. You may also be required to submit university-specific "supplements". These can range from anything from additional essays to short-answer questions to video requests.

For university-specific questions, you must respond with writing that is specific to that university. You certainly won't tell them something you love that pertains to another school or that is not specific to them in order to try to get in to their school. You'll be detailed and precise in your responses specifically for that school. This is critical. And, we'll get to the university-specific supplements in this Handbook.

Top 10 "don'ts" for writing:

1. Don't strive for perfection.

2. Don't make things up.

3. Don't use fluffy language or words you've never used before.

4. Don't talk about being a third culture kid. (It's the natural go-to for many international applicants and tends not to be a stand-out.)

5. Don't be boring.

6. Don't let your parents tell you what to write about. (The most important?)

7. Don't be clichéd.

8. Don't write what you think they want to read. They won't want to read that.

9. Don't get too many opinions on your writing. One or two are sufficient.

10. Don't let anyone else write your essay for you.

Top 10 "do's" for writing:

1. Be yourself.

2. Start your writing with something that will draw the reader in.

3. Sometimes the seemingly most banal topics make the best essays. Think simple.

4. Tell a story and make sure it's your own story.

5. Create visualizations for the reader. This doesn't have to be eloquent or fancy; again, sometimes simple is the most powerful.

6. Be honest.

7. Be self-introspective.

8. Use humility.

9. Show something.

10. Answer the question.

What you should know about writing before you begin:

1. Admissions can read—literally and figuratively—right through a rushed essay. I don't ask you in this guide to start writing in May and June to torture you; it is done for a reason. A well-thought-out written piece (and you'll have more than one) can be identified easily against the one that was done in two days. You can guess whose application will get tossed aside.

2. Admissions places a very high emphasis on the writing portions of an application. In some cases, the writing will be what makes or breaks an application.

3. You heard from a friend that a classmate has hired someone to write their essay for them. These essays are some of the easiest ones to identify by Admissions and will not only get your application tossed, it could get a call to your school by the university to alert them to the issue. In some cases, if the university reading this "doctored" essay happens to know where else you applied they may make some phone calls and alert their colleagues at other institutions to your egregious "error". Good luck with getting any acceptances and your name will carry a stigma moving forward. This is not a strategic or ethical move.

4. Writing is personal. It should be written by you and from your perspective. Share something. Show who you are. Answer the question. Be creative. Be interesting. Be yourself.

Part 2: How Do You Write?

I often get students telling me they don't know how to write. This is nonsense. Everyone knows how to write. We all write differently and we all struggle with words from time to time. But, don't tell me you don't know how to write. You do. You just have to put effort and a bit of confidence into this and know that what you need you already have. It's you that the application needs; now you need to get it down on paper.

Of course I cannot tell you how to write since that's like telling someone how to cook noodles. We all have different styles and that's what makes writing so personal—just like cooking noodles—and what makes us stand out as individuals. Imagine how boring this world would be with restaurant after restaurant offering the exact same noodles! But, like a good cookbook or cooking show, I do have some advice for you as you begin—advice that will allow you and encourage you to add your own style and buzz, and I'd like you to refer back to this when writing becomes difficult and challenging.

1. Be professional by setting up a day and time when you'll start writing. This should be a formal session to write. You won't just start writing randomly on the couch. You'll need to set this up in your calendar and be prepared. Your mind needs that clarity and your writing will reflect it.

2. Make sure you choose a place to write in that is comfortable and free of distractions. This means you should have your mobile and the connection to the Internet turned off.

3. Tell your friends and family not to bother you during this time that you set aside.

4. What will you write with? With paper and pen or on a laptop? Set it up beforehand.

5. Take each prompt/question at a time. Give yourself time to answer each. Although you may have been sitting there for 10 minutes without any ideas and think you've given it a shot, it takes more than that. Give yourself at least 45 minutes to think for ideas to come, to jot them down on paper/on your laptop. After that, you will need more time to write and flesh out those ideas.

6. All of us write differently. Some of you will need to just scribble words to get started. Some of you will draw mind maps. Some will start from the beginning and go until the end. Just follow your thoughts. There's no right way to go about writing.

7. Don't ask for a lot of feedback, in particular in the beginning. If you have one person who knows you and will give you thoughtful advice, ask them. Sometimes this is a

teacher or counselor. While our parents and friends are lovely, I do not think they are necessarily the best judges of your writing. Sometimes I have parents who think their child needs to sound different from how they actually come across. That only hurts the student as their essay comes out sounding like their parents, which will not result in a favorable response from Admissions. (This requires restraint from many of you, Parents! Please do your best as your input here can really do more harm than good.)

8. Don't leave too much time in between the first writing session and the next to work on a single draft. You will lose your train of thought and lose the entire feel of what you were starting with if you don't discipline yourself. At university, this will always be expected of you when you do any writing.

WORDS OF WISDOM: THE PRE-COOKED ESSAY

In early August, I was just finishing up an evening call with a student when I received an email from another student of mine, Diana, who owed me the first draft of the Common Application prompt she had previously chosen and we had discussed. Strangely, she said she had two versions; one I would recognize and the other, she said, was something she also wrote and perhaps that would be a replacement to the former.

The first attachment was the essay on the theme we had been fleshing out for a couple of months now; it was not profound but instead wholly genuine, thoughtful and true to this student. It read just like an 18-year-old might write; it was flawed but honest and was almost ready to go. Why, I thought, would Diana draw up a second essay after all of the tooth-pulling it took to get through this first one?

The second one started like this: "One must be ready for the finish before it even starts. . ." and continued with similar platitudes throughout the first paragraph. It was forced, fake, and, it was indeed, pre-cooked. Here was an essay written by someone other than the person who was supposed to write it.

I didn't need to read more than the first two sentences to know that this essay was one not written by an 18-year-old. Any Admissions staff would see this right away too. If for some reason they did not, all they would have to do is compare the diction and writing in the essay to the applicant's English grades, standardized testing scores and perhaps ask her school counselor for a writing sample if any doubt remained. The student's application would have been tossed immediately and it might have had even more far-reaching consequences.

After discussing this in great depth with Diana and her family, it was resolved and Diana reverted back to her original essay, flawed and less-than-perfect as it was, and she got into 8 out of 10 universities she applied to.

WRITING WORKSHOP 2

Part 1: Talking About Yourself

Let's get the juices flowing by going back to some of the self-assessment you did in the earlier chapters. There are two parts to this section and I'll ask you to do both of them in one sitting.

Please answer the following directly in this book:

IMPORTANT!

Go back to the Do's and Don'ts listed earlier in Part 1: Why Write? even when answering these questions. You should not answer these questions with an assumption of what you think the reader would like to know. Instead I would like you to answer these free of that thought. Remember, the most thoughtful (and therefore most successful) essays are true to the writer!

---

1. What have you thought about writing about?

   _____

   _____

   _____

   _____

2. What could you write about?

   _____

   _____

   _____

   _____

3. Consider what you might want to tell the reader. What is unique about you that you might want to write an essay about?

   _____

   _____

   _____

   _____

4. Consider your greatest accomplishment *as well as* the things you enjoy doing that are not organized, not structured, that will not fall on your "activities" list. It's these things that can be the most interesting and can make a memorable and beautiful essay.

_____

_____

_____

_____

5. Refer back to Worksheet 1.1: Thought Questions. Is there anything you wrote in those answers that might be something you'd like to expound on in an essay?

_____

_____

_____

_____

6. Personality Traits. How would you describe yourself in words? Choose five words that describe you and write them down below. You'll be surprised—this may take longer than you expect!

_____

_____

_____

_____

7. What activities or thoughts do you think distinguish you from your peers? Explain.

_____

_____

_____

_____

8. Are you an animal activist, a quiet thinker, a chocolate freak, an aquarium-keeper, a photographer, a giver, a person who loves to tell stories? Or what special talent do you have? What do you know or do that others might not even suspect that you know or do?

_____

_____

_____

_____

9. How would your friends describe you? Your parents or guardians?

_____

_____

_____

_____

10. Describe the biggest challenge you have faced yet and what you learnt from it and/or how you faced it and overcame it.

_____

_____

_____

_____

11. Do you have a hero? How is she/he heroic?

_____

_____

_____

_____

12. What activity, topic, language or country do you wish you knew more about?

_____

_____

_____

_____

13. What fears do you or have you had and how have you managed them?

_____

_____

_____

_____

14. Who has influenced you in your life? What qualities do you admire in this person?

_____

_____

_____

_____

15. How is happiness important to you? What do you need to be happy in your life?

_____

_____

_____

_____

16. What do you believe the purpose of life is? What is your philosophy on life?

_____

_____

_____

_____

17. How have you grown, in your own opinion, through the course of secondary school?

_____

_____

_____

_____

18. If you were given the time and resources to develop one particular skill, talent or area of expertise, what would it be?

_____

_____

_____

_____

19. What is the summer or break activity you most enjoy? Talk about this.

_____

_____

_____

_____

20. Tell me something that would surprise me about you.

_____

_____

_____

_____

21. How have you contributed to your community either at school or outside of school in a way that was not required or "forced" upon you to do?

_____

_____

_____

_____

22. What is the best advice you have ever received? How has it influenced you?

_____

_____

_____

_____

23. Describe the personal experience that has given you the greatest satisfaction.

_____

_____

_____

_____

24. What is your favorite place or way to relax? Talk about this.

_____

_____

_____

_____

25. Tell me about a failure in your life.

_____

_____

_____

_____

26. Go back to your answers above from Question 3. Would you consider using any of those answers as a theme to your essay? Which ones? Circle those.

Part 2: Starting Is the Hardest Part

Before we get started writing the actual essays, I'd like to share with you the opening passages of three essays written by former students of mine. Please read each and answer the very simple yet relevant questions following them.

Introduction 1   *A light green bookcase occupies a place of pride in my room and houses my trea-sure trove of 300 Amar Chitra Kathas, comic books of Indian mythology, fables and heroes. These stories are my mother's way of keeping me entertained and close to my roots, despite never living in India, my home country. They have become my gateway to understanding Indian history and culture. My favourite is 'The Mahabharata', the ancient Indian epic that features a great battle between good and evil. Its central themes of karma and selfless action have influenced me throughout my childhood. Arjuna, one of the main heroes, personifies values that are dear to me and which I seek to emulate in my life: adaptability, curiosity and humility.*

Introduction 2   *Trust. It may seem like a simple word, but to me it is one of the more complex predicaments. I have often asked myself questions: Why do I not trust easily? Does this make it harder for me to communicate? Will I ever be able overcome not trusting easily? Trust is perhaps the most important part of my relationships with others. I came to understand this in my childhood when my friend had told a secret of mine to an acquaintance. I wasn't furious that my secret of how I wasn't fascinated by Barbie dolls was known to more than one person, clearly you now know it; however, I think the fact that she could divulge it with no feeling of allegiance to me hurt. No doubt she felt remorse as I later found out but that didn't change the fact that I was now hesitant to tell her anything personal.*

Introduction 3   *The phone rang. A hand reached to pick it up, take it to their ear, and put it back down. I braced myself for impact, and heard the shout of "One thousand two hundred and four!" before the transmitter even hit the receiver. The phone call came every hour, with a higher number being called each time. I wanted it to stop, but more than anything, I wanted the number to follow a different verb—"survived", maybe, or "found a home"—anything but "dead". Unfortunately, it was what I heard on an hourly basis during my newsroom internship in Istanbul.*

Answer the following questions:

1. Which introduction stands out the most to you? Why?

     _____

2. Which one sounds most genuine to you? Why?

     _____

3. Do you think there's a right or wrong answer to Questions 1 and 2?

_____

The answer to Question 3 is "of course not". There is no key to get the answers to 1 or 2. It is very subjective. You cannot control how the passages are viewed but what you can control is what each of these writers did.

What have you noticed about these introductions? Have you noticed that not one is too polished? That they sound like they are written by someone in your age bracket? They are honest, draw the reader in from the start, and are very personal. Your essay does not need to be a literary masterpiece; it should, however, be true to you, and that means reflecting who you are. Remember our "do's" to writing back in Writing Workshop 1, Part 1. It would be a good time to review those vis-à-vis the introductions you just read.

IMPORTANT!

I do not advise my students to look at sample essays on the Internet, save for the example I will give you below. You'll lose your own train of thought, unique ideas and personal style if you do. The idea is to create an original, thoughtful and honest essay that is about you and written in your words, in your tone, with your own unique style. Why would you ever want that to come from somewhere else? That said, the one resource I refer my students to at the start are the essays that The New York Times publishes annually around June of each year of essays that "worked" from students who applied to university for that year's matriculation. Why do I make this exception? I believe the essays here follow precisely the advice that I give to you and I also think it can help at the start of the process for students to get a "feel" for what a university essay might read like. But once the students have read them, I ask them not to read them again. Remember, the strength of your application will be directly tied to the unique, very personal, authentic voice you share through your essays. Like DNA, everyone's is unique.

WRITING WORKSHOP 3

There are three sections to Writing Workshop 3 and they are divided up by possible essays that you will have to write.

- The Common Application/Main College Essay
- Supplement Essays
- Other Questions and Video

Each section will give points and questions to help guide you to writing and developing this part of your application.

Part 1: The Common Application Essay/Main College Essay

The Common Application gives students the option to choose one essay prompt out of seven about which they are to write an essay that will be seen by every university to which they apply. Note: Some universities can elect not to review this essay; you may still be given the option of including it in your application to them. Refer to each university's admissions policy to know what will be reviewed.

Applicants this year are given the choice to elect one of the following prompts from the Common Application. Please read them and the "explanation" for what the prompt is asking you to do:

IMPORTANT!

Whether you use the Common Application or any other portal or university-specific application, you will see that many of the essay prompt themes overlap from application to application. It is critical that you read this and go through this step regardless of which application portal you are using.

1. "Some students have a background, identity, interest, or talent that is so meaningful they believe their application would be incomplete without it. If this sounds like you, then please share your story."

   This is a very open-ended prompt and students can almost take this wherever they like. The translation of this prompt? Basically, what do you want to share with the Admissions staff about yourself that you feel is important they know (and may not be gleaned from other parts of your application)?

2. "The lessons we take from obstacles we encounter can be fundamental to later success. Recount a time when you faced a challenge, setback, or failure. How did it affect you, and what did you learn from the experience?"

    They are not asking about a time you failed a test. Or when you got injured and could not finish out the season. This is about real—tragic or humorous—failures, challenges or setbacks. Did you train all season slated to be the number one sprinter, only to go on to finish last? Please remember that in US culture, failure is valued when it teaches us a lesson, prompting us to go on further and make changes to our life.

3. "Reflect on a time when you questioned or challenged a belief or idea. What prompted your thinking? What was the outcome?"

    Did you stand up for a friend risking alienation from peers or challenge someone for what you felt were racist comments? If you're going to choose to write about something deep and profound, make sure you don't come across as self-righteous or offensive. Make a clear and strong argument for your position.

4. "Describe a problem you've solved or a problem you'd like to solve. It can be an intellectual challenge, a research query, an ethical dilemma—anything that is of personal importance, no matter the scale. Explain its significance to you and what steps you took or could be taken to identify a solution."

    There is a lot of leeway in this question; they're not just talking to scientists or engineers. In fact, this could be most profound when it's not taken so literally.

5. "Discuss an accomplishment, event, or realization that sparked a period of personal growth and a new understanding of yourself or others."

    Avoid the obvious. I would suggest avoiding religious ceremonies and formalities; they'll come across as clichéd, boring or typical. Take this a bit further than its literal prompting and take note of the words "realization" and "new understanding". Perhaps a book you read marked this for you, perhaps starting to give your younger sibling advice or perhaps something even less or more profound marked this transition for you. There's no wrong answer here.

6. "Describe a topic, idea, or concept you find so engaging that it makes you lose all track of time. Why does it captivate you? What or who do you turn to when you want to learn more?"

    Don't try to be too smart here; the more you are you, the more genuine and powerful the essay will be. This is precisely what they are asking for and expecting to see if you choose this prompt: the real you. A great opportunity.

7. "Share an essay on any topic of your choice. It can be one you've already written, one that responds to a different prompt, or one of your own design."

    A risk for the lazy student and an opportunity for the creative one. I would make sending an already-written essay your last resort. For the free-thinker and creative student, go for it. You have carte blanche here.

There are no wrong answers to any of these prompts; however, there are better and more thoughtful answers than others. By stepping out of that literal "translation" of the essay prompt, you can give yourself the opportunity to be more creative, to develop a more powerful and thoughtful response that may be something no one has ever written about before. Think about making an impression with what you write.

IMPORTANT!

Don't be too literal on what these questions have asked of you. If you have come up with a theme from Workshops 1 and 2 that you would really like to focus on, fit it into one of these prompts. I always tell my students to give themselves flexibility and a bit of writer's freedom to take a question a bit further or beyond what it might literally be asking you.

Please answer these questions for *each* of the prompts in order to help you gauge which might be best to write about. *Keep in mind that these prompts can change from year to year or from application to application but the general questioning and themes are all parallel. Answering the questions related to the prompts above, which may be different, for instance, to the University of California prompts, are really helping you to answer those University of California essays as well. I go through the same process with my students who are applying on five different portals—the themes are always consistent and their ideas come out of doing this exercise:*

1. What is the theme of the question?

    Prompt 1:   Prompt 5:

    Prompt 2:   Prompt 6:

    Prompt 3:   Prompt 7:

    Prompt 4:

2. What ideas pop up after you consider this question? (Jot them down without the need for using full sentences or correct syntax.) Start to brainstorm.

Prompt 1:   Prompt 5:

Prompt 2:   Prompt 6:

Prompt 3:   Prompt 7:

Prompt 4:

3. Could you potentially choose this prompt to write about? Why and how?

Prompt 1:   Prompt 5:

Prompt 2:   Prompt 6:

Prompt 3:   Prompt 7:

Prompt 4:

4. What would you want to impart to the reader if you were to expound upon this prompt? What examples might you use or stories might you tell that could support this theme?

Prompt 1:   Prompt 5:

Prompt 2:   Prompt 6:

Prompt 3:   Prompt 7:

Prompt 4:

After going through the exercise above, you should have a clearer idea of which prompt/theme you would choose.

Now, please write down which prompt/theme you will choose to write about.

★ ★ ★ ★ ★

Now that you have chosen your prompt and the theme about which you will write, using the answers to the four questions above, begin to brainstorm the content for your essay and the *reasoning* behind that content. For each "reason" you should also give an example or recount an incident or anecdote.

I will share an example with you from Pakhi, one of my students, and how she started to brainstorm and *reason* her main college essay. Pakhi chose to take a bit of leeway with the first prompt to share with Admissions why trust—and trusting others—is so critical to her being and how she forms relationships with others. Here are her "content", "reasoning" and "anecdotal evidence" for developing her essay:

Content	Reason for including it in essay	Anecdote
Element of trust	To show the type of person I am—how much I value trust beyond anything else in relationships	Barbie story
Introspective/thinker	I am strong on philosophy and thinking and want the reader to see this	Growing up in Africa; pondering thoughts out loud thoughtfully
Trust and challenges/ strengths that brings to relationships	To show that I am still understanding how to manage my feelings of trust—but that I believe it builds very strong relationships	Explaining why I don't believe this leads to superficial relationships; blue bracelet to my friend
Open-minded	To show that while cautious I take risks and always learn from those	Moving from Africa to Singapore and now to university

Now fill in your own chart with the content, reasoning and anecdotes that you may use in your essay:

Content	Reason for including it in essay	Anecdote

Pakhi's final essay included some of the results of her brainstorming. Take a look at how it turned out:

Trust. It may seem like a simple word, but to me it is one of the more complex predicaments. I have often asked myself questions: Why do I not trust easily? Does this make it harder for me to communicate? Will I ever be able overcome not trusting easily?

Trust is perhaps the most important part of my relationships with others. I came to understand this in my childhood when my friend had told a secret of mine to an acquaintance. I wasn't furious that my secret of how I wasn't fascinated by Barbie dolls was known to more than one person, clearly you now know it; however, I think the fact that she could divulge it with no feeling of allegiance to me hurt. No doubt she felt remorse as I later found out but that didn't change the fact that I was now hesitant to tell her anything personal.

Over the years I have found that the saying "think before you speak", although cliché, can be modified to fit trust—"think before you trust". As a result the word "caution" seems apt to my definition of trust. Of course, this experience wasn't the sole one in determining my perception of trust. Looking back I think that living in Africa for eight years during my foundation years, until I was eight, heavily contributed to my notion of trust. Living in Africa wasn't easy as many would expect and yet gave me experiences that define who I am now. Constant coups led to a rather unsafe environment, something I see increasing in many countries today. As a result caution became a part of my life pretty early on. I hold trust to be dependent on circumstances. And circumstances such as not being able to use public transport required caution to be a core aspect, therefore caution has been a prominent part of my life, and how I see things, especially trust. And is the reason why it takes time for me to build relationships in which I trust completely.

Despite people often telling me that inserting caution into trust allows for more superficial relationships, I disagree. It allows me to take relationships to a deeper level because I trust the other person completely. I am willing to support them in any situation and help in whatever way I can, even if it means giving up something of my own, like giving away my favorite blue beaded bracelet to a friend who broke hers. If it means that I have to stand against someone I don't even know, I'll do it. So when people ask me if doing something like this negatively affects me, I say perhaps it does but it is diminished in comparison to the feeling that I stood up for my friend in her time of need.

When I think about the future, the feeling of the unknown rises. I don't know what it holds and yes that scares me, but at the same time I want to know how new experiences will change my perception of trust. Perhaps I may start to trust more easily, or maybe I will trust even fewer people. Whatever it may be I want to be open to it so that I have the courage to embrace whatever may come.

Coming to the present I relish that I have this clarity about trust and what it means to me. I acknowledge that caution is a part of my perception of trust and when friends ask me why, the simple answer is I wouldn't want to change any experiences that have ultimately made me who I am, because I accept myself the way I am. I am grateful for my stay in Africa because it has taught me to take risks by trusting people in a calculated manner. I am grateful for moving to Singapore where I have been able to use that skill in a safe environment. And in this moment, without mention of the future, trusting with caution is one value I hold onto strongly.

Please go ahead now and write your first draft of your main college essay, referring back to your notes and the guidance in this Writing Handbook.

Part 2: Supplement Essays and Questions

These come in the form of an essay or question, some give guidance (for example, word limits or key words that you should be picking up on) and some are very basic, giving the applicant more flexibility to answer but also less to indicate what the intention of the question is.

If you're asked for any supplement essay or question, you should know that these are going to be examined, read and re-read with a fine-toothed comb by Admissions. This is where Admissions wants to see if you're a fit, and if you're able to articulate and really show them—not just tell them—that they are a fit for you. It takes extra work for any Admissions staff to read longer applications, so they expect the same from you on your end. Here's where you get the chance to speak directly to this particular university and where the Admissions officer will expect you to be speaking specifically to and about them and their institution.

Here's the most typical writing supplement question: *Why us?*

Just about every one of my students will roll his/her eyes at these questions as they can seem open-ended and thoughtless. However, there's a right way to answer them. There is also a way to make the work that goes into answering them more interesting and thus the reading of them—on the part of the Admissions officer—even more so. Here's an example from Kalamazoo's most recent application:

In 500 words or fewer, please explain how Kalamazoo College's approach to education will help you explore your ideas and interests both inside and outside of the classroom.

Basically: Why Kalamazoo?

The key with this type of question is specificity. You want *to show*—whether it's through citing specific professors and their research, certain clubs unique to Kalamazoo, their focus on international education, and how that's different from other institutions and fits you or their curriculum and program in Literature—that you have done your very specific research into this institution and *connect it to why* it's a fit for you—and *very specifically so.*

The golden rule to a successful supplement is that none of it can be copied and pasted for any other institution asking the same question.

Here's another type of question that could pop up in the supplements:

> *We know that colleges ask a lot of hard questions on their applications. This one is not so hard and we promise, there is no hidden agenda – just have fun! We have all heard the saying "laughter is the best medicine". Recount a time when something really made you laugh.* (Smith College, 2016)

When they say there is no hidden agenda, there isn't. They expect a perfectly spelled response that is thoughtful, honest, smart, perhaps quirky, and perhaps risky. Keep the institution in mind as you write your answers. You should know about them, their culture and their student profiles by now.

IMPORTANT!

I'd like to remind you: Perfect spelling and syntax are non-negotiable. I have a zero tolerance policy—as do most Admissions officers of any solid academic institution—for misspellings and grammatical errors, including poor syntax. How old are you? How many systems are in place for spell-checking and grammatical accuracy? There are no excuses. This is the one case where perfection is expected.

Let's look at another type of question, this one from Lewis & Clark College:

> *Lewis & Clark College is a private college with a public conscience and a global reach. We celebrate our strengths in collaborative scholarship, international engagement, environmental understanding and entrepreneurial thinking. As we evaluate applications, we look for students who understand what we offer and are eager to contribute to our*

community. In one paragraph, please tell us why you are interested in attending Lewis & Clark and how you will impact our campus.

This is another version of "why us?" but giving the student a bit more guidance. There are four key elements there, one of which you do need to address in this response—collaborative scholarship, international engagement, environmental understanding or entrepreneurial thinking—with key words such as "contribute" and "community". You'd be wise to evaluate this question appropriately and give clear examples of how you would be an active member of such a community.

Some key points to remember about writing supplements and questions:

- These supplement questions and their answers are incredibly important to the college. You must show them that you've done your research, know them, understand why they are a fit for you, and connect who they are to who you are with specific details. When you show your holiday photos to a friend of yours, you expect them to look with interest and ask questions and be engaged. This is how the college feels. They are the ones showing you their photos. You need to show you're engaged by engaging with them as well.

- Do your research: Draw on specifics from that particular university and connect those specifics to your story—what is important to you that you've been showing throughout your application that can be connected to the answer to this question?

- Show your fit. This should be done through your answer and tying it to the rest of your application and the college—its programs, culture, values, and so on. You're creating a full story about yourself and this is the time to get specific. "Here's what you, university X, will get from me as a student and here is what I will be involved in, create, contribute to and champion at your institution." Obviously this needs to connect to the whole of your application.

- Use the rule about cutting and pasting. If you can cut and paste your answer for another college, it's not specific enough and won't pass the test.

Part 3: Other Questions and Video

Once Mei (Chapter 3) turned in her application to Claremont McKenna she received—a few weeks later—an invitation to submit a video of less than three minutes. By now she had gotten the hang of what US Admissions officers were looking for: authenticity, humility, honesty and being yourself. I knew that Mei—whatever she was going to say—would make an impact on whoever was going to watch her video. So, it was a no-brainer that she should take the opportunity to submit, and she did.

The use of videos in the application process is becoming more and more common. If you're given the opportunity to create a video of yourself, there are some important points to take into consideration:

- Script out what you will say. Answer the question in your script and get to the point. This will be your guide, but not your crutch.

- Practice several times but not too many times. Once you have a good idea of what you want to say, start recording.

- When you record the video, don't read from said script. In fact, don't strive for perfection. This was one thing I suggested to Mei when she recorded actually correcting herself in the video itself. I told her to keep it in there; it was more natural and real. She laughed at her own tiny mistake in the video and it made it more genuine. (She kept it in there.)

- Watch your background when you're recording. It should be neutral. Don't have your background of the mansion your family lives in or of the slum that you're volunteering in. Use good judgment.

- Watch the rules from writing and apply those—use humility, don't use slang, be yourself, tell a story, answer the question—to your video.

REFERENCES

Antonoff, Steven (2008). *The College Finder: Choose the School That's Right for You!* (3rd edn). Wintergreen Orchard House.

Fiske, Edward B. (2016). *The Fiske Guide to Colleges 2017* (33rd edn). Sourcebooks.

Hedberg Maps (2006). *US College and University Reference Map: Over 1400 top colleges in the US and Canada* (3rd edn).

Lauenstein, Ray and Galehouse, Dave (2004). *The Making of a Student Athlete*. Advisor Press.

Loveland, Elaina (2010). *Creative Colleges: A Guide for Student Actors, Artists, Dancers, Musicians and Writers* (3rd edn). Supercollege.

Pope, Loren (2012). *Colleges That Change Lives: 40 Schools That Will Change the Way You Think About Colleges* (4th edn). Penguin Books.

Princeton Review (2016). *The K&W Guide to Colleges for Students with Learning Differences, 13th Edition: 353 Schools with Programs or Services for Students with ADHD, ASD, or Learning Disabilities.*

Roberts, Andrew (2010). *The Thinking Student's Guide to College: 75 Tips for Getting a Better Education*. Chicago: University Of Chicago Press.

Selingo, Jeffrey J. (2016). *There Is Life After College: What Parents and Students Should Know About Navigating School to Prepare for the Jobs of Tomorrow*. New York: William Morrow.

Steinberg, Jacques (2002). *The Gatekeepers: Inside the Admissions Process of a Premier College*. Penguin Books.

filter reading 37
final writing 219–21
financial resources 205–7, 210
first choice universities 182–3
First Marking Period Grades 205, 241
fit
  admissions based on 20, 31–2, 37, 39
  defining 178
  factors and 99
  process of 1–2
  self-assessment 24
  Short List 54–5, 111
  strategy 60
  supplements 186, 285
  unique for each college 179
foreign language courses 27
full-pay candidates 34–5, 70
fundraising 206

gap years 49, 141, 205, 247–8
genuine interest *see* Efforts of Genuine Interest;
    interests
GPA grading 27
grade reports 114
grades
  admissions assessment 25, 26–7
  decision to submit 181
  different high school 189
  First Marking Period 205, 241
  interviews and 30
  Long List development 73
  Midterm Report 240
  putting effort into 49, 234
  upward trajectory 27
grammar 200, 284
Guidance Counselor 189, 193, 199–200,
    217–18, 232
  see also counselors
guidance offices 166
guides 57, 76

high school
  attending more than one 189
  awards 118
  courses taken 26–7, 66, 181–2, 189
  grades 26, 73
  limiting applications 179–80
  momentum change 83
  Northern Hemisphere calendar 237
  penultimate year 7–8, 97
  pressure on 234
  rankings 74
holistic process, admissions 25, 29, 203
homeschooling 224, 225
honors 29

IB (International Baccalaureate) 87
Ideas and Opportunities Survey 68, 80–1
IELTS tests 64–6, 112, 118, 141, 169, 216, 233
"in-range" schools 59, 60, 70, 111, 180
intellectual curiosity 36
interests 50, 68
  see also Efforts of Genuine Interest
internal deadlines 215–16
International Baccalaureate (IB) 87
Internet sample essays 276
internships 68, 91
interviews
  campus visits 116, 117, 144–9
  conducting 170–1
  contact/schedule/questions 160
  CV creation 12
  early application 194
  finishing/final requests 219
  master schedules 149
  mock interviews 112–14, 125–35
  opportunity to be interviewed 29–30
  possibilities 91
  post-campus visits 149
  requesting 93, 95, 112, 170–2
  Worksheet 158–9

Regular Decision (RD) applications 204,
  213–14, 227–8, 229
rejections 229–31, 235
relationship-building 89, 93
reminders
  recommenders 191–3
  submission dates 220
  testing plans 63
removing universities from List 88
research
  Long List 55–6, 60–1, 69, 76, 87–9
  mock interviewer 113
  questions 93
  supplements 285
Research Pages 77–81
residential stays 116–17
Resources 1, 52, 57, 87, 220
  see also guides
Restricted Early Action (REA) schools 185
rigor 25, 26–7, 181–2
rolling admissions policy 196
roommate questionnaire 253
"rounding out" Lists 179

safety schools 235
sample essays 276
SAT test 28, 62–4, 118, 169–70, 211
SCEA (Single-Choice-Early-Action)
  institutions 185
scholarships 33–4, 70, 88, 171, 231, 234
scores
  Long List 73
  "rushing" 169
  sending 233
  submitting/reporting 202–3
  testing plans 63
  see also test scores
Scripps College 146–7
self-assessment 1–2, 24–5, 40–5, 83, 270–4
self-evaluation 19–20

self-reflection 55
self-reporting 202–3, 233
Short List
  accomplishing 55
  campus visits 115–16
  case studies 58
  components 111
  confirming 143–4, 167–8
  drafting 107
  ED applications 183
  EGI review 173
  fit and 54
  from Long List 69, 110–12
  internal deadlines 215
  mock interviews 129
  re-confirming 178–80
  recommender confirmations 165
  registrations 165
  requirement confirmations 180–2
  supplement essays 174
  testing plans 118
  Worksheet 122–4
showcasing talents 29
signing the agreement 9–11
Single-Choice-Early-Action (SCEA)
  institutions 185
social media 66–7, 94, 107, 220
sources for essays 87
Southern Hemisphere calendar 8, 161,
  196, 237
special talents 29
specificity, questions 284
spelling 94, 200, 284
Sponsor Support Documentation
  207, 240
stakeholder's commitment 10
standardized testing 62–5, 118, 152–3
  not required 218
  preparing for 168–70
  retaking 211, 216–17, 233

Notes